La Dolce Vegan!

VEGAN LIVIN' MADE EASY

La Dolce Vegan!

VEGAN LIVIN' MADE EASY

SARAH KRAMER

ARSENAL PULP PRESS

VANCOUVER

ARSENAL PULP PRESS
200 - 341 Water Street
Vancouver, B.C.
Canada V6B 1B8
arsenalpulp.com

The publisher gratefully acknowledges the support of the Government of Canada through the Book Publishing Industry Development Program for its publishing activities.

Book and cover design by Lisa Eng-Lodge
Production assistance by Judy Yeung
Edited by Nicole Marteinsson and Brian Lam
Cover photo by Charlotte Kinzie
Cover food styling by Sarah Kramer
Interior photos by Gerry Kramer and Sarah Kramer
Cover author photo by Charlotte Kinzie

Printed and bound in Canada

Library and Archives Canada Cataloguing in Publication:
Kramer, Sarah, 1968-
    La dolce vegan! : vegan livin' made easy / Sarah Kramer.

Includes index.
ISBN 1-55152-187-3

    1. Vegan cookery. I. Title.

TX837.K73 2005   641.5'636   C2005-903687-7

ISBN-13 978-1-55152-187-9

CONTENTS

ACKNOWLEDGMENTS

"It's not heavy . . . it's just awkward."

I may be the only author listed on the cover, but a book like this does not get written without the loving support and generous input of many.

First and foremost, I have to thank my husband, Gerry. He is such a loving, supportive person and I would not be able to do what I do without him. You are the love of my life, Gerry Kramer! I am so lucky to have such a partner/lover/best friend/cheerleader like you in my corner. This book is for you, buddy. It's all because of you. I love you. You are AMAZING!

Fergus. You're cute. You're a puppy. I'm a puppy. Thank you for keeping my bum warm as I wrote this book and for always making me laugh when I'm down in the dumps . . . oh yeah, and for making me go for walks. You're the best dog in the world. Woof.

Thank you to my family. You know who you are – stop denying it. Oh yeah. And I love you.

Okay, mushy stuff aside. I also need to thank YOU! That's right. YOU – the person who bought this book. You, who have supported and stuck by *GoVegan.net* and me since its inception in 1997. It has not gone unnoticed. I am thrilled to be a part of your life and I am touched and inspired every single day by your love and support.

I need to thank those in the veggie community whose support never wavers. Josh and Michelle at *Herbivore Magazine (HerbivoreMagazine.com)* for being the best friends I never-ever see; Erica and Sara at MooShoes *(MooShoes.com)* for keeping my feet warm; Claire at Coquette Faux Furriers *(CoquetteFauxFurriers.com)* for helping me to stay glamorous; the Murdock family; and the one and only Dave Shishkoff for watching my bandwidth.

And a HUGE thank you to *FoodFightGrocery.com, VeganEssentials.com, Nunweiler Flour Co. (NunweilerFlour.com)*, Ener-G Foods *(Ener-g.com), EstrellaSoap.com*, Pacific Natural Foods *(PacificFoods.com)*, ViaVegan *(ViaVegan.com)*, and OTSU *(VeganMart.com)* for generously donating products. Your support of me and the book means the world to me – my husband and his belly thank you.

A HUGE thank you to all my little munchkins at the *GoVegan.net* forum. You guys are so good at not feeding the bears; you should so be proud of yourselves for creating such a wonderful environment to chit-chat in. You are so much fun to hang out with and I really appreciate each and every one of you. You guys rock!

Thank you to the entire team at Arsenal Pulp Press, especially Brian Lam. I can't thank you enough for all the hard work you do. Having your input and support means more than I can say. Thanks also to Nicole Marteinsson for the wonderful copyediting job, and Lisa Eng-Lodge and Judy Yeung for designing not only this book but my first two as well.

Donna Wong-Juliani – your sage advice over the years has been priceless. Thank you.

A big shout out to Julie Robinson in Alpharetta, Georgia, for coming up with *La Dolce Vegan* as the title. Yay, Julie!

A HUGE thank you to Shirley Wolff, a.k.a. Wolffie, for donating some of the best vegan recipes I've ever had the pleasure of testing. Also, thank you for keeping me company via the Internet on those lonely days when I never thought I'd get through this book alone. You are a sweetheart. Thank you, Shirley!

Thank you to my Wednesday Night Girls: Claire for being so bootyliscious, Hayley for always making me laugh, and Sarah M for all the chopped walnut suggestions. Thank you for all your insight, laughter, brainstorming ideas, and junk food binges. You ladies make "Girls Night" my favorite night of the week. Jennifer Stacy – I don't know what I would do without your no-bullshit way of looking at life. You are my voice of reason and I treasure you. Shoshana Sperling – I'm madly in love with you and I don't care who knows! You inspire me to be creative and not to be afraid to express myself.

Thank you to all the ladies in the Wild Cherry Scooter Club! You girls rock. Thanks to the boys in the Royal Crowns. You ain't so tough, but you sure are cute! Thanks to Frontline Films *(FrontlineFilms.net)* for helping me get over my fear of zombies. Thanks to Romalotti *(LaymanBooks.com)*. Thanks to Cheryl for helping keep Fergus so fancy. Thanks to everyone at Tattoo Zoo *(TattooZoo.net)*. Oh, by the way . . . Danica . . . you're fired.

Thanks to Wendy, Tracy, and Emma for totally getting my Go-Go's obsession. Thanks to Jane Wiedlin, Kathy Valentine, Belinda Carlisle, Gina Schock, and Charlotte Caffey for writing the soundtrack of my life. Thanks to Ad Rock – you know you love me. Don't fight it.

Thanks to: Teresa, Graham, and Maury, for loving me from afar; Paula, for helping me clear out the cobwebs in my brain; Gail, for always knowing where I'm hurting, and rubbing it away; and Charlotte, for taking such pretty pictures of me. And let's not forget my lawyer Ron: thanks for all your help.

Writing books can be a lonely, solitary job, so thank you to CBC Radio for keeping me company during my time in the kitchen, especially the shows "GO" with Brent Bambury and "Definitely Not the Opera" with Sook-Yin Lee. You made Saturday my favorite day to work.

Thank you to anyone else I forgot to list by name. You know I love you. Don't be like that. And for those of you who live out of town – why do you live so far away? I wish you lived closer . . . I miss you so much – so write me already! Thank you all for your support. You know who you are and you know I love you.

Lastly, thanks to Tanya Barnard, who in 1996 came to me with an idea to write a cookbook as a homemade gift project that we could give our friends and family for X-mas. That little snowflake of an idea rolled into a giant snowball called *How It All Vegan* and the rest is history.

It's a new veginning, my friends. Let's see where it takes us! Enjoy the book!

xoxo
SARAH

"Nothing worth having comes without some kind of fight. You gotta kick at the darkness till it bleeds daylight." – Bruce Cockburn

Introduction

Well, here we are. Again. Book number three. Are you ready for it?

I GET REALLY EXCITED BY ORDINARY THINGS

The scent of fresh basil. The crunch of an empty sun-bleached clamshell as my foot runs across it on the beach. The deep, soft sigh of my dog as he's about to fall asleep. The smell of my kitchen when I'm baking bread. For me, all these tiny moments add up to a life worth living: a life I never thought I could have and a life that I never knew existed.

It has taken me years to understand that my life is happening now – right in front of me. *So pay attention, damn it!* I no longer look anxiously at the horizon for what's coming next or look behind me with regret at the things I could have done differently. Now, I stand with my feet planted firmly where I'm at today. Today is happening right now, and it's an opportunity to shine.

Each book I write reflects my needs and my life at the time. With *How It All Vegan!*, it was all about how to make my life as a new vegan easy. I was really missing conventional recipes, so the book was chock full of comfort food. *The Garden of Vegan* was an extension of the first book, but with a more grown-up, contemporary flair. It was when I was finally comfortable in my veganism and wanted to eat some good food.

La Dolce Vegan comes at a time when I find myself multi-tasking to the nth degree. I'm busy running a tattoo shop, maintaining the *GoVegan.net* website, testing and creating recipes, taking photos, making sure my dog and my husband get enough exercise. I always seem to be working on eight million projects all at once. So lately I've been looking for ways to live a simpler life.

Sometimes I want to spend a little extra time in the kitchen, making something fancy for guests or for a romantic evening at home with the husband. I love to peruse the shelves in Chinatown or the health food stores looking for interesting and unusual ingredients. I enjoy working in the kitchen perfecting new dishes.

But most of the time, I don't want to spend hours planning my next meal. I don't have a lot of free time to muck about in the kitchen and I suspect you don't either. I want to walk in the door, bang some pots together, and eat so I can get to work on the rest of my life.

CHANGE IS GOOD, RIGHT? RIGHT?

I'm not good with change. In fact, it freaks me out, and that makes me laugh at myself because change happens every second of the day. You'd think I would have the hang of it by now.

So if something changes, it rocks my world. I get all panicky and think I can't handle it; I stress, bitch, moan, and feel like everything is too complicated. But now, if the last few years have taught me anything, I try to take a deep breath and repeat my new mantra: "Change is good. Change is good."

When Tanya Barnard, my co-author on *How it all Vegan!* and the *Garden of Vegan*, decided to leave our partnership to pursue a career in nursing, I had to have a really long talk with myself about whether I wanted to continue or not. Who was I without my sidekick? Did I still have things to say? Did I still have more recipes inside of me? Was turning a sequel into a trilogy something I was prepared to do on my own? I had a bit of an identity crisis.

So I took a deep breath, and I reminded myself that change is good. I've learned that with every change, a new opportunity presents itself. As soon as I let go of my fear and panic . . . in walked the readers.

I AM THE GIRL OF 100 LISTS

I am about to get my period and it's like I'm on a giant roller coaster of emotions. You know the PMS drill: happy one second, murderous the next.

I'm having a great day. I'm happy as a clam as I drive my dog back from the doggie hairdresser. But somewhere on the drive home, I start thinking about the new book and start unnecessarily stressing myself out and feeling down, shitty, and frazzled – ready to scream and cry and laugh and freak out. Like I said . . . PMS.

I get home and figure out what to make for dinner, then go pick my husband Gerry up from work. As we swing by the grocery store on the way home, he's being his usual fun loving self, but today it was *really* getting on my nerves.

I say to him, "I'm sensitive today. **Please just give me some extra love!**"

At the grocery store, we get the usual stuff, and as I'm snuggling Gerry while we wait at the check-out counter, I feel like I'm on the verge of tears and laughing at the same time because my pre-period has me feeling insane.

Then suddenly someone taps me on the shoulders and asks, "Excuse me, are you the girl who wrote *The Garden of Vegan*?"

"Why, yes. Yes I am," I say as I try and hide my enormous cold sore with my shoulder/scarf/hand (none of it is working so I give up and pretend it's not there).

"Oh my God," he says. "My girlfriend and I love your book. Your books. We think they're brilliant. You're brilliant. I can't believe I'm meeting you."

I'm like, "Aww, thanks. That's so cool. It's nice to meet you." Yadda yadda yadda.

Then I pay for my groceries, say goodbye to the nice man, and walk out to the car with a big grin on my face.

Gerry takes my hand. "There's your extra love," he says.

Then I bawl.

Like a baby.

The universe is so good to me sometimes. I need to learn how to pay better attention.

INSPIRATION IS EVERYWHERE

Writing cookbooks takes a lot of time. I don't think people realize how time-consuming it is: recipe testing, tweaking, testing again. Walking the dog. Shopping for ingredients, writing blurbs, and making sure there are no typos. More recipe testing, eating, and doing the dishes. My God – the dishes!

By the time I was finished with *The Garden of Vegan*, I was convinced I would never go into the kitchen again. I was sooo tired of food and recipes consuming the better part of my day. I stopped caring about fancy meals and wanted recipes that I didn't have to think about. I wanted to look in my cupboard and say, "I have potatoes. What can I make with potatoes?" then find a recipe that would take 30 minutes or less to prepare and then eat.

For the new book, I started working on recipes that were simple: minimal ingredients with maximum taste. One of the biggest complaints received about the first two books was that the portions were too large; many of you are only cooking for one, sometimes two people. Almost all of the recipes in *La Dolce Vegan* make 2 large servings or 4 small servings. You can chow down until you have to undo your pants to make room, or save some for lunch the next day. And all the recipes double easily . . . so voilà! Instant dinner party.

There are a few fancy entrées here that take more than 30 minutes to prepare; these are marked with a little clock beside them so you know they'll take a little more time. But don't let that clock freak you out – the recipes are still easy to make. The rest of the recipes can be made lickety-split. There are also a few recipes that make larger portions, so be sure to invite some friends over when you make those.

Besides the fun of recipe creating, testing, and tweaking, my biggest joy with this third book has been testing reader-submitted recipes. They've come from all over the world and it has been so much fun testing them all.

Writing books is a lonely, solitary job, especially without a co-author to work with. Most of my time is spent alone in the kitchen or on the computer. Thank goodness for the Internet or I'd go mad. *GoVegan.net* has a wonderful community of people who kept me company as I wrote this book. Some of my favorite submissions came from Shirley a.k.a. Wolffie, who lives down in Davie, Florida. She provided me with some of the best recipes I've ever had the pleasure of testing. So if you're looking for a new recipe to start with, start with one of Wolffie's.

As the recipes rolled in and I started to test them, I became quite friendly with a few of the readers. There were the people who have been around since day one, like Dilip, Random Hag, Auntie Bonnie, Shoshana, Josh, and Jennifer. And then there were some new friends: Wolffie, Debbie, and Danielle, to name a few. Every day I would check my inbox to find words of encouragement, recipes, and even more encouragement.

It's been such a joy to write this third book because of all your input. Thank you.

K . I . S . S .

Knights In Satan's Service? No. Keep It Simple, Stupid!

I try to keep things simple. The less stress I have in my life, the better I feel.

It's all about choice. You can't stop a wave from crashing down on you, but what you *can* do is choose to let it wash over you. Instead of exhausting yourself by fighting back the wave, try going with the flow. Enjoy the ride, because with more experiences comes new wisdom, new confidence, and a really wonderful life.

I don't think I'm the only one who gets overwhelmed. I get heaps of emails via *GoVegan.net* from people who are panicked by the thought of how difficult it might be to go vegan. Most are daunted by the thought of to read every single ingredient on every single package of food, or stressed about the hunt for obscure ingredients and the high cost of vegan specialty items. They all seem to want vegan recipes that are EASY to make with easy-to-find ingredients.

My goal with *How it all Vegan!, The Garden of Vegan*, and now *La Dolce Vegan* is to make veganism fun, accessible, and easy. But most importantly – to make it taste good.

So. Here it is. My new baby. Love it. Hug it. Get it dirty.

I love you guys.

xoxo
SARAH

MY LIFE

YOU CAN ALWAYS MAKE ANOTHER CHOICE

Sometimes it seems like our choices don't affect the world around us, but each of us can make a difference. Every single decision we make either propels us forward or holds us back. But whatever happens, we can always make another choice.

As I started to prepare my thoughts for writing a third cookbook, I spent some time looking through my *GoVegan.net* scrapbook. I merrily looked at the original version of *How It All Vegan!*, which you may not know, started as a small, 50-page homemade zine. It was printed out on my laser printer and bound by hand in my living room. I laughed as I looked through all the rejection letters we received for *How It All Vegan!* and then got a little shiver as I looked at the first contract we signed with Arsenal Pulp Press. As I re-read some of the fan mail, I got a little misty-eyed, and I realized that I've been doing this for close to 10 years.

How did this happen? How did this suddenly become my life's passion? That is what the books and *GoVegan.net* have become – a passion. I'm not rolling in mountains of green dough from writing these books; more like rolling around in vegan dough. Literally. Baking my ass off so you guys can have some fun and easy vegan recipes to make.

There comes a time when you reach certain milestones in your life when it is beneficial to stop and reflect. Like when you turn 13 and you leave childhood behind and start your life as a teen. Or the day you turn 30 and realize with glee that you're no longer considered a girl but can now walk around as a woman! Hear me roar! Or when you get your first kiss, your first tattoo, or the day you feel the warm sun on your skin and you realize that after a long dreary winter it finally feels like spring. It's those small moments in your life when you stop and actually pay attention to what's happening around you. I think it's healthy to stop and take stock in where you're headed in life; reassess the choices that you've made thus far and determine if things you were doing 10 years ago, or even 10 minutes ago, are still the things you want to be doing now.

I didn't watch scary movies. In 1979, I went to see *The Amityville Horror* in the theater and I peed my pants, I was so scared. I was 11; to pee your pants at that age was almost as horrifying as the movie. On the walk home, with my hoodie wrapped around my waist to cover my pants, I vowed never to watch another scary movie.

Well, it hit me the other day – I'm a grown-up, damn it! I know the difference between real and fake. I know that movies are fake. So I decided that the vow I made as a young person was not what I wanted to do now, so my husband and I have been watching scary movies like crazy. And it's actually been kind of fun.

So what about veganism, then?

I was raised a vegetarian since birth, so I didn't choose it as my own path to walk down. It was all I knew. As a curious teenager, I "experimented" with meat in high school, but decided that meat wasn't something I felt comfortable eating. As I matured into a young adult, I decided that using any animal products – whether it be food, clothing or products tested on animals – was something I was uncomfortable with. I made a clear choice to be vegan. And here I sit now – a woman in my mid-thirties – writing another cookbook and wanting to reflect back for a moment and reassess the choices I made as a young adult and see if veganism is still the lifestyle I want to live today.

I stopped reading literature about animal cruelty years ago. I don't watch videos about meat production and animal testing anymore. I can't. They make me feel sick and for good reason. The way we harvest, conduct tests on, and destroy animals and the planet, with no thought of the consequences, is disheartening and always makes me feel quite hopeless. Sometimes I felt as though I was the only one who could see how horrifying it all was, and that the choices I made were only a drop in a bucket. But if these last 10 years have shown me anything, it's that I'm not the only one who feels the way I do. What a journey I've been on. I've been able to travel to places I never thought I'd go. I've been able to meet and feel the support and love from terrific, enthusiastic fans. I've been able to try incredible vegan food and restaurants in cities I've only seen in movies. Best of all, I feel like I have a worldwide family. Everyone I've met through having written these books (either in person or via *GoVegan.net*) is like a long-lost family member. What a joy it's been to share these last 10 years with all of you.

THROUGH THE DARKEST DAYS

Through the years, I've had many friends who fall to the dark side and give up their veganism for various reasons. One friend gave up because she became sick and was convinced it was because of her vegan diet. But I watched how she ate and if you eat nothing but cake, potato chips, and cookies, and never touch fresh veggies, my friend – of course, you're going to get sick. I had another friend who wanted to lose weight and try the Atkins diet. Wow. Like that diet makes any sense. I had another friend justify her new leather boots to me by saying, "At least they're using the entire cow. I'm recycling."

Uh-huh.

What I have a hard time wrapping my brain around is how you can have all this information about animals suffering horrendous cruelties for the sake of fashion and food, and one day be horrified about animal genocide and complacent the next? As my friend Josh, at *HerbivoreMagazine.com*, always says, "Once the curtain is pulled back, how can you not remain a committed vegan?"

I've always believed that it's not my job to be the Vegan Police. This is MY vegan journey, not anyone else's, and it's up to individuals to decide for themselves. While I may feel disappointed when my friends fall off the wagon, what I really wonder is, where did their lack of enthusiasm come from? What was the moment when they decided that their principles didn't mean more than that Meat Lovers pizza they've been missing?

Where does that "burn out" come from? How does an enthusiastic, compassionate person become apathetic? Is it really about missing cheese? Or is there something missing in your life? What is it that's making you disconnect?

I understand how having this rigid list of rules can be exhausting: reading labels, bringing your own food to family dinners so you'll have something to eat, having to spend extra money on vegan-specific items. I get all that, but it's not *so* difficult that it can squash your spirit, is it? Frustrating, maybe. But difficult? Life in general can be complex at times. A life worth living takes a lot of work. It takes a lot of work to be a doctor, a parent, to keep your room clean, to go to work every day when your job is mundane. It takes a lot of work to teach your dog not to pee on the rug. Life is work.

I think if you find yourself becoming bogged down by the path you're taking, then make another choice. I'm not saying give up on your veganism, but take stock. Look at your choices. Identify the aspects of your life that are dragging you down or making you feel uninterested, and get rid of them. Concentrate on what inspires you, what gives you joy.

If you find yourself waning, then try re-visiting those things that gave you inspiration in the first place. Read Herbivore magazine. Watch *Meet Your Meat*. Go to a Howard Lyman lecture. Find where you lost your passion and fire it up again. On the flip-side, if reading animal rights literature has you sobbing into your sheets every night, maybe you've read enough. Maybe it's time to channel your energy in a different way.

And I'm not talking about being perfect. There is no such thing. But what you can strive for is excellence. Do what you can, and if you make a mistake or fall of the wagon – who cares? Each day is a new opportunity to be the best vegan you can be. It's impossible to be 100 percent vegan. But what you can do is try your best.

By allowing yourself some slack from the guilt of not being perfect, veganism suddenly and simply becomes part of your lifestyle rather then a list of rigid rules to follow. My advice is simply to try your best and not worry about being perfect. It's important not to dwell on what you're not doing, but rather focus your energy on what you're doing well.

The other day my husband and I were eating some fries; he grabbed a tiny, crunchy one from the bottom of the pile and suddenly realized he had eaten a piece of fried shrimp. Does that mean he's lost all his vegan points? No. Shit happens and you move on to your next adventure and try to be the best vegan you can be.

And yes. We got the fries for *free*.

I'm not making a difference.

If you feel like you're a revolution of one and your choices are not making a difference, remember that every day and every action makes a statement to the powers that be. While it takes an army of many to change the world's problems, that army is made up of individuals.

One of the best ways to make a statement is to remember that your money is one of your most powerful weapons, and where you spend it speaks volumes. Support locally-owned businesses, and buy local organic fruits and veggies and products whenever possible. Power to the little people – people! Spend your money on companies that are trying to make a difference, rather than on those that test on animals.

Your money is powerful; at times it can be louder than your voice. Remember that.

It's too expensive to be vegan.

You can save your money by not spending it on vegan junk food like "faux meats" and packaged vegan food. Making your own food is the cheapest and best way to save money, and by doing that, you can splurge on organic products (or the occasional tub of vegan ice cream.)

I'm on a fixed income and my parents help me out by giving me food that's not vegan. I can't afford not to eat it.

I guess that makes you a Free-gan. Look – do what you can, until you can do better. Don't beat yourself up.

I don't like tofu.

That's just silly. That's like saying you don't like cake flour.

Eating new foods is about opening your mind and expanding your horizons. Example: I went to a party and brought a really tasty, sweet fruit dip made from tofu. I put it on the table and my "non-vegan" friends went to town. They loved it. But when I told them it was simply made from tofu and maple syrup with a little cinnamon, you could hear a pin drop. One girl actually covered her mouth and shrieked in horror. "I just ate tofu?" I laughed. I mean, two seconds before she was gobbling it up and loving it. Now suddenly she hates it?

It's about letting go of your preconceived notions about what vegan food can be.

I miss macaroni and cheese.

Go to pg 125. You have no excuses anymore.

I miss cheese.

I hear ya. While there are countless cheese alternatives out there, I have yet to try one that is superb, but a sacrifice isn't a sacrifice without a little suffering. Just ask the cow whose milk the cheese is made from.

It's too much work to read labels all the time.

I hear ya, sista, but lump it. It's just something you have to do, like brushing your teeth and looking both ways before you cross the street.

I want to try (insert new diet fad plan here).

Diets are for suckers. Lifestyle change is the new diet.

Whether you choose being vegan for ethical reasons, or if you want to get more whole grains into your diet, any reason that brings you to a place where you are thinking about what you're putting into your body is a good thing.

We saturate ourselves regularly with poison (junk food, pop, white sugar, white flour) so when we make a step towards a better lifestyle, whether it be veganism or simply cutting out the white sugar, it's win-win all around.

I'm not healthy being vegan.

You alone are responsible for your health, and being vegan isn't the magic key to good health and nutrition. It's a great start, but you can also eat a lot of vegan cake and make yourself sick.

I also don't believe that everyone can be vegan, but vegan or not, it's your responsibility to arm yourself with knowledge. Learn what it means to have a healthy balanced meal. I highly recommend the book *Becoming Vegan* by Vesanto Melina and Brenda Davis; chock full of nutritional information, you cannot read this book and walk away not knowing your stuff.

Knowledge is power. Food is fuel. If you can learn what makes your body healthy, and arm yourself with the power to make it strong – there will be no stopping you.

My friends say I'm not vegan enough.

It's human nature to compare yourself to other people. My advice on this is to pay attention to your own life. It doesn't matter what other people think as long as you're happy with the boundaries and lines that you draw. It's your life, so make up your own rules and enjoy yourself.

I can't find good vegan shoes/belts/bags.

Have you been to *MooShoes.com* or *VeganMart.com* lately? Cuz they have vegan shoes aplenty.

I hate having to defend myself. I'm tired of being smacked down by other people.

If your veganism has you isolated and alone in a sea of meat eaters, and you're feeling beat down by fighting with other people about your beliefs – relax. You can still have conversations with those who have a different viewpoints. Maybe they'll even share a salad with you when you start talking about the meat that's rotting in their colon.

You can agree to disagree – it doesn't always have to be a fight or a tug-of-war. It can simply be a conversation.

My partner/lover/family isn't supportive.

Have you told them you don't like it when they badger you? Have you told them you need them to be supportive of your choices? Have you asked them to stop ragging on you about your lifestyle choice?

You don't get what you want unless you ask for it. If they can't do what you need to feel comfortable, then what kind of a relationship is that? Now you have a whole kettle of tofu to talk about, don't ya? Time to call a therapist.

I'm too lazy to be vegan.

Good luck with that.

WHEN YOU ARE CLEAR ON WHO YOU ARE AND WHAT YOU STAND FOR ...

Nothing is difficult. It's just your life.

For some, being vegan means arming themselves with facts and figures. For some, it means knowing everything there is to know about protein, calcium, and iron. Some are vegan for health reasons, some for compassionate reasons.

For me, it's all these reasons and more. For me, veganism is about thinking outside of your own needs, seeing a world beyond yourself and opening your heart up to compassion, empathy, and understanding.

I am confident in my choices. This is a lifestyle choice that I made for myself – not so I'd be cool, or fit in. It's a compassionate lifestyle choice that I made to feel comfortable being myself.

I will not apologize for my opinions. I will not be a shrinking violet in the face of adversity. I will do everything I can to be the best vegan I can be. Every day is a new opportunity to make a difference. Whether it is a small or large contribution, it all adds up.

My desire with *How It All Vegan!, The Garden of Vegan,* and now *La Dolce Vegan!* has been to make veganism fun, accessible, tasty – and effortless. I hope these books help make your vegan life a little easier.

I really believe that small changes can have a huge impact. Even one drop in a bucket will make that bucket wet. Imagine what it would be like if it rained.

"The only thing I'll ever need is the truth. The truth and what it means to me. The only source of strength I'll ever need." – TRIAL

Kitchen
Wisdom

Over the years, I've gleaned many little kitchen tricks to make cooking easier. Take some time to sit down and read all these tips before you head back into the kitchen. You might find some of them handy!

TIME MANAGEMENT

CLEAN AS YOU COOK
While your dish is cooking away on the stove or in the oven: wipe down the counters, and wash utensils and other cookware used while preparing your recipe.

DO IT NOW . . . NOT LATER
Wipe up spills as they happen, so you don't end up with a sticky or hard-to-clean mess. If you have a spill that's hardened, leave a damp cloth over it and let sit for 15-30 minutes before wiping.

TAKE NOTES
Have a notepad handy and keep a running grocery list so when you hit the stores, you're not racking your brain for what it was you needed for dinner.

MAKE SURE YOU HAVE WHAT YOU NEED
Read your recipe all the way through and check to see you have all your ingredients BEFORE you start cooking. There is nothing worse then the pained look on your husband's face when you send him off to the store for that one crucial ingredient.

HOSTESS WITH THE MOSTESS
When having friends over for dinner, write out a menu and make a schedule. Prepare in advance as many dishes and ingredients as possible so you don't have to scramble at the last minute trying to get everything all done.

CLEANING

MOTHER THANKS YOU
There are all sorts of eco-friendly cleansers on the market now and Momma Nature thanks you for spending the extra bucks so she can breathe easier. But if you don't have access to them where you live, don't fret. There are easy ways to keep your kitchen and house sparkling clean without hurting your Momma.

ALL-PURPOSE ALL THE TIME
All-purpose cleaner can be easily made by combining 2 tablespoons of baking soda, ½ cup ammonia, ¼ cup vinegar, and 8 cups warm water. And while you're at it – can you also sweep the front walk?

CINDERWELLA CINDERWELLA

It's time to mop. You hate it. I hate it. But it has to be done. ½ cup vinegar and 8 cups of hot water will have us doing the polka on a clean floor in no time.

BURNED YOUR BOTTOM?

If you have a bad burn on the bottom of your pan: fill the pan with 2 inches of water and add 1 tablespoon of baking soda. Bring to a boil, then cover with a lid for 5 minutes. Remove from heat and let stand for 30 minutes before scrubbing. Or . . .

Scrape as much of the burn off as you can, cover with water and add ½ cup of salt. Bring to a boil and continue boiling for 20 minutes. Remove pan from heat and let stand for 30 minutes before scrubbing.

STOP SCOURING AT ME

½ cup baking soda, ½ cup borax, and 1½ cups of hot water will scour away even the most sourpuss of messes.

STOP LOOKING AT YOURSELF

. . . and start cleaning those mirrors. ½ cup of vinegar and 8 cups of water makes your reflection say, ahhh. I'm so pretty. And streak-free.

EMERGENCIES

THE ROOF IS ON FIRE

Baking soda will help to put out an electrical fire, so keep a box near your stove.

BETTER THAN SALT IN YOUR EYE

Toss salt on a grease fire. Never use water.

BETTER SAFE THAN SORRY

Inexpensive fire extinguishers can be purchased at your local hardware store. Pick one specific day every year (like New Year's Day or your birthday) to check or change your fire extinguisher and the batteries in your fire alarm.

YOU STINK

To remove garlic smell from your fingers, rub them with lemon juice and salt, then rinse and wash with soap. Voilà!

FRESH VS. DRIED

If you're in a pinch and don't have the fresh herbs that you need for your recipe: 1 tablespoon of fresh herbs is approximately equivalent to 1 teaspoon of dried.

PASTA TIPS

RINSE . . . LATHER . . . REPEAT
Only rinse pasta after draining when you are going to use it in a cold dish, or when you are not going be serving it immediately. Rinse under cold water to stop the cooking process and drain well. If you rinse it when you're serving it as a hot dish, the noodles will become slippery and your sauce won't stick.

SALT VS. OIL
Always salt your pasta water before cooking. It will enhance the pasta's flavor and you won't have to salt your dish later when it's served. Adding oil to pasta cooking water is unnecessary as it will make your pasta slippery and your sauce won't stick.

AL DENTE
Pasta is ready when it's "al dente." It should be cooked completely through, yet firm enough to offer some resistance to your bite.

PAS-TUH YIELDS
1 cup or 8 oz of dry pasta = approximately 4 cups of cooked.

RICE TIPS

NO PEEKING
Set your timer; don't lift the lid to check on its progress. If you do, you'll let out steam and slow down the cooking process.

NO STIRRING
Don't stir your rice; just let it be.

RICE YIELDS-ISH
1 cup white rice + 1½ liquid = approximately 3 cups cooked
1 cup brown rice + 2 cups liquid = approximately 3 cups cooked

ARE YOU DONE YET?
Check to see if your rice is done by tasting some; it should be firm, but tender. If it's too firm, then add ¼ cup of water and let it cook until water is absorbed. If the rice is done but there's still water, remove the lid, fluff the rice, and keep cooking until water is absorbed.

TOFU TIPS

I HATE THE TASTE OF TOFU
That's ridiculous. Tofu on its own is bland but has the ability to take on the flavor of whatever ingredients it's cooked with. I think what you're really saying is that you're afraid of trying new things. Get over it.

WHICH ONE GOES WITH WHICH
Tofu comes in various states of firmness: soft, medium, firm, and extra firm, as well as silken (which is very smooth and soft). These different states of firmness are for different kinds of recipes. For example, a soft or silken tofu is perfect for puddings, smoothies or as an egg replacer in baking. A medium tofu is good for recipes where you don't mind if the tofu keeps its shape, like chili or tofu scrambler. Firm or extra-firm tofu is perfect for cubing and using in recipes like a stir-fry or shish-ka-bobs.

DRAINING
Drain your tofu by placing it in a colander over the sink or a plate. Soft or silken tofu generally doesn't need to be drained.

WHAT DO I DO WITH LEFTOVERS?
You can easily store leftover tofu in the refrigerator, but for no longer than a week. Tofu should be stored in a container filled with water. The tofu should be below the surface of the water, and the water should be changed daily. You can freeze it for up to three months, but that will change the texture (see below).

CHANGE THE TEXTURE
If you want your tofu to have a chewier texture, then drain it well, store in an air-tight container (no water), and place in the freezer. Thaw by running under cold water.

VEGETABLE TIPS

REMOVE GREENS
If you buy veggies with the greens attached (e.g., carrots, beets), remove the greens when you get home, as they leech moisture.

WASH UP!
Always wash your vegetables with a vegetable soap. It doesn't matter if you bought it sealed in cellophane or if it's organic; you don't know where it's been. So wash it.

ARE YOU LIMP?
If veggies like carrots or celery are limp, try soaking them in ice water for an hour and see what happens.

YOU'RE MAKING ME CRY?
To prevent onions from making you cry, cut them in half and sit them in a bowl of cold water for 15 minutes before using. Then chop to your heart's content – tear-free.

BAKING TIPS

OVEN THERMOMETERS
Ovens are notoriously temperamental; for example, my oven is off by about 25°F (4°C). That's a HUGE difference and can make or break your baking! An oven thermometer is a great and inexpensive investment that will make your baking projects easier to deal with.

CLEANER MEASURING CUPS
Before measuring sticky sweeteners like maple syrup or corn syrup, lightly coat the measuring cup or spoon with vegetable oil. The syrup will easily slip out and you won't have as much of a sticky mess to clean up.

ARE YOU DONE YET?
Check your cookies at their minimum baking time. If they're not ready, check again in 5 minutes.

PREHEAT
Unless otherwise stated, always preheat your oven 10-15 minutes before beginning to bake.

OVER THE HILL
Baking powder has an expiry date and if it's old, it can mess up your baking. Check the bottom of your baking powder before buying, and buy in small quantities to make sure it's always fresh. Once opened, baking powder is good for about 6 months. Write the date of opening on the canister so you know when to get a new supply.

WHATEVER BUBBLES . . . BUBBLES UP
If you're not sure if your baking powder is dead, in a small bowl combine 1 teaspoon of baking powder with ⅓ cup of hot water. If it bubbles vigorously, it's fine to use.

NEVER DIP A WET SPOON
Never dip a wet measuring spoon into your baking powder, because moisture will cause it to deteriorate.

DON'T WAIT TO BAKE
Baking soda and baking powder begin releasing gas the instant they're in contact with liquids, so they should always be added to the dry ingredients before any liquid ingredients are added. Once everything is combined, the batter should be placed in the oven without delay. Have your baking sheets/pans oiled and ready to go and your oven preheated before you start mixing.

YEAST
Yeast comes in packages or by the jar. Make sure it's stored in the refrigerator to avoid spoiling. The only difference between quick-rising yeast and regular dry yeast is that quick-rising will leaven in a ⅓ of the usual rising time.

IT'S ALIVE!
Check the expiry date on your yeast. If you're not sure if it's still working, combine 1 teaspoon of sugar with 2 teaspoons of yeast and add ¼ cup of warm water. If the mixture starts to swell and bubble, it's alive. If there is no activity, toss it out and head to the store. It's done for and time to let it go.

CAKE TIPS

DUSTING SUCKS
For fun, when baking a chocolate cake, instead of using flour to "dust" the pan, try cocoa instead.

SHH! THE CAKE IS SLEEPING
Don't open the oven door during the first 20 minutes of baking time. Always open the oven door gently as sudden movements or temperature change can make the cake fall in the middle.

ARE YOU DONE YET?
Test your cake's readiness by poking the center with a toothpick, wooden skewer, or clean knife. If it comes out clean, the cake is done. If it comes out wet and sticky, let it bake for an additional 5 minutes and check again.

CHILL
Let your cake cool in the pan for 10 minutes before turning it over onto a cooling rack. This will keep it from falling apart during the transfer.

TOTALLY CHILL
Your cake should be completely cooled before you frost it.

YOU'RE ALWAYS IN SUCH A HURRY
To quickly cool a cake before frosting, pop it into the freezer for 10-15 minutes while you make your frosting. Remember that this will change the temperature in the freezer drastically, so make sure you're ready for that.

MAKE ME PRETTY, BUT DON'T MAKE A MESS
It's easiest to ice a cake when it sits directly on its serving plate, so to prevent a mess, place strips of wax paper or parchment paper under the edges of the cake, so that they hang over the edge of the plate. Frost the cake, then quickly pull out the paper, leaving your serving plate nice and clean.

STICKY-ICKY-ICKY
Prevent your freshly baked cake from sticking to your serving platter by dusting the plate with icing sugar.

PIE TIPS

KEEP IT COOL
Keep everything cool while you're making a pie crust and you'll have a much easier time making your dough. Use cool water, keep your margarine cool, and even throw your rolling pin and flour into the refrigerator before you start making your crust.

GET THE RIGHT FLOUR
Pastry flour or all-purpose flour work best when making a crust.

MIDDLE OF THE ROAD
Always move your oven rack to the center of the oven before you preheat and bake your pie.

DON'T GET SOGGY
Don't pour your pie filling into your pie shell until right before you're ready to bake. Otherwise, you'll end up with a soggy crust.

OOPS. I SPILLED
If the juice from a fruit pie overflows while you're baking, sprinkle some salt onto the spill. It will burn to a crisp, making it easier to remove once the oven has cooled.

MISCELLANEOUS COOKING TIPS

TOO SALTY

If your soup is too salty, add some raw cut potatoes to your cooking. Remove them before serving as they will have absorbed a lot of the salt. Or add 1 teaspoon each of apple cider vinegar and sugar to your salty soup and that will remedy the problem.

SAME SIZE PANCAKES

Keep your pancakes all the same size by using a lightly oiled measuring cup. Use ⅓ cup for medium-sized or ½ cup for bigger pancakes.

DON'T BE AFRAID

Try new things. If it doesn't work, try something else. The more you experiment, the easier cooking gets. Trust me!

45 THINGS TO DO WITH SALT

There is an old English belief that says that "every grain of salt spilled represents future tears." Wow, like we don't have enough things to worry about.

1. Rubbing salt in your wound is only an expression. Don't do it.

2. Enhance the flavor of your food – duh.

3. Use as an abrasive. Toss some salt onto a stubborn kitchen counter stain and scrub with a damp dishcloth.

4. In the winter, de-ice the sidewalk when it freezes by tossing some salt on top of it. Wait 20 minutes and shovel your walk with ease.

5. Sprinkle salt in areas where you have ants and watch them flee.

6. Put a few grains of rice in your salt shaker to keep your salt from sticking together.

7. If you've burned your food, scrape as much of the burn off as you can, cover with water, and add ½ cup of salt. Bring to a boil and continue boiling for 20 minutes. Remove pan from heat and let stand for 30 minutes before scrubbing.

8. Add a pinch of salt to fresh-cut flowers to help them last a little longer.

9. To remove the smell of garlic from your fingers, rub them with lemon juice and salt, then rinse and wash with soap.

10. Fresh piercing? Use a simple saline (salt) solution of ½ cup warm water + 1 teaspoon of sea salt to soak your piercing in. It will speed up the healing process.

11. Too many bubbles while you're doing the dishes? Sprinkle them with a pinch of salt and watch them disappear.

12. Run out of toothpaste? Use equal parts of salt and baking soda (with a drop of peppermint extract if you like) instead. Dip your wet toothbrush in and brush away!

13. If wine is spilled on a tablecloth or rug, blot up as much as possible and immediately cover with a generous amount of salt, then leave until dried. Vacuum up salt and rinse with cold water. The stain will (cross your fingers) be gone.

14. A mixture of lemon juice and salt will remove mildew.

15. Wet a bee sting immediately with water and cover it with salt.

16. If your dish boils over onto the oven floor, sprinkle salt on top to stop smoke and odor. Once oven is cool, wipe spill away.

17. Always salt your pasta water before cooking. It will enhance the pasta's flavor and you won't have to salt your dish when it's served. Adding oil to pasta cooking water is unnecessary as it will make your pasta slippery and your sauce won't stick.

18. Remove stains from old teacups by rubbing with salt and a bit of water.

19. Salt enhances sweetness, so add a pinch when making sweets like kettle corn or hot chocolate.

20. A mixture of lemon juice and salt will remove rust stains.

21. Remove odor from a cutting board by pouring a generous amount of salt directly on the board. Rub lightly with a damp cloth. Wash in warm, soapy water.

22. If the juice from a fruit pie overflows while you're baking, sprinkle some salt onto the spill. It will burn to a crisp, making it easy to remove once the oven has cooled.

23. For a sore throat, gargle with ½ cup of warm water and ¼ teaspoon of salt.

24. Stuffed up nose? Snort a solution of ¼ cup warm water and ½ teaspoon of salt and then blow!

25. Draw the bitterness out of chopped eggplant by salting. Let stand a few minutes and then rinse before cooking.

26. Salt can be used as a skin softener. Throw ½ cup Epsom salt or sea salt into your bath water and you'll be smooth as a baby's bum when you get out.

27. For a crispier skin on your baked potato, slather with olive oil and salt before baking.

28. Make scented bath salts with a mixture of 1 cup Epsom salt, 1 cup baking soda, and 3-4 drops of your favorite essential oil.

29. Sore feet? Soak them in a salt bath: 12 cups warm water, 2 tablespoons of salt, and 2 tablespoons of baking soda.

30. Fill a nail hole with a mixture of 1 tablespoon of salt, 1 tablespoon of corn starch, and 2 teaspoons of water to make a thick paste. Fill hole. Let dry and sand if necessary.

31. Wash dirty green vegetables such as spinach in a sink of mildly salted water to make them easier to clean.

32. When adding flour to a recipe for thickening, stir flour with a pinch of salt to prevent lumps.

33. A greasy pan will wash easier if you rub a little salt on it first. Wipe with a paper towel and then wash pan in hot soapy water.

34. Toss salt on a grease fire. Never use water.

35. Stinky thermos? Add salt and a little hot water. Cap, shake, and rinse. No more smell.

36. Remove blood stains by soaking item in cold salt water, then wash in warm, soapy water and hope CSI doesn't knock on your door.

37. Sooth aching muscles in a hot bath with some Epsom salts.

38. Make your skin glow by rubbing it with equal parts olive oil and salt. (Please do this while standing in your bathtub.)

39. Back in the day, Roman soldiers were paid in salt. So take a satchel of salt down to the store and see if it will buy you groceries.

40. Pour salt into a vase to hold dried or artificial flowers in place.

41. Salting water does not make it boil faster, but it does make it boil hotter, so your cooking time can be reduced.

42. Soak older, wrinkled apples in mildly salted water to revive them.

43. Keep sliced potatoes, apples or pears from browning by placing them in a bowl of mildly salted cold water.

44. Salt can repel fleas, so dunk your dog in the ocean before you head home from your walk or give him a bath in some salt water.

45. If you spill salt, throw a pinch over your shoulder to hit the devil in the eye.

Breakfasts

Breakfast is a big deal at our house. Monday and Tuesday are my husband's days off, so Monday is really our Saturday and Tuesday is our Sunday – are you still with me? We usually lay around in bed, until Gerry's "I need coffee" headache starts to get on my nerves, then we get up and make breakfast. Which by that time is really lunch, or how you say with your big fancy words . . . brunch?

FREEDOM FRENCH TOAST

The best tip I have for this recipe is to use stale bread. Alternatively, leave some bread out overnight or lightly toast it before using and cook on a nice hot oiled grill. Serve with Organic Maple syrup and a cup of hot coffee. Yum!

¾ cup soft *or* **silken tofu**
2 tbsp maple syrup
¾ tsp ground cinnamon
½ tsp vanilla extract
¼ tsp salt
¼ cup apple juice *or* **water**
1 tbsp oil
4 - 6 large slices bread, stale

In a blender or food processor, blend the tofu, maple syrup, cinnamon, vanilla, salt, apple juice, and oil until smooth. In a large shallow bowl, pour batter; dip bread slices into batter and coat both sides. Fry bread in a hot non-stick pan or a lightly oiled frying pan and cover. Let sit on medium heat until underside is golden and crusty. Flip toast over and cook other side until golden brown. Repeat process until bread is gone. Makes 2 large or 4 small servings.

APPLE PIE PANCAKES

These are a favorite in the Kramer house. I use spelt flour, but you can use whatever you have on hand.

- ¾ **cup flour**
- ¼ **cup rolled oat flakes**
- ½ **tsp ground cinnamon**
- 2 **tsp baking powder**
- ¼ **tsp salt**
- 1 **cup "milk"**
- ¼ **cup raisins**
- ½ **large apple, diced**

In a medium bowl, stir together the flour, oat flakes, cinnamon, baking powder, and salt. Add the "milk," raisins, and apples and stir together gently until "just mixed." Portion batter onto a hot non-stick pan or a lightly oiled frying pan and cover. Let sit on medium heat until the center starts to bubble and become sturdy. Flip pancake over and cook other side until golden brown. Repeat process until batter is gone. Makes 2 large or 4 small pancakes.

RASPBERRY WALNUT PANCAKES

Raspberries are high in Vitamin C and an excellent source of fiber. They are like little nuggets of love.

- 1 **cup flour**
- ½ **tsp baking powder**
- ½ **tsp baking soda**
- 1 **tbsp sugar**
- 1¼ **cup "milk"**
- 1 **tbsp oil**
- ½ **cup raspberries**
- ¼ **cup walnuts, finely chopped**

In a medium bowl, stir together the flour, baking powder, baking soda, and sugar. Add the "milk" and oil and stir together gently until "just mixed." Stir in the raspberries and walnuts until well blended. Portion batter onto a hot non-stick pan or a lightly oiled frying pan and cover. Let sit on medium heat until the center starts to bubble and become sturdy. Flip pancake over and cook other side until golden brown. Repeat process until batter is gone. Makes 2 large or 4 small pancakes.

BANANA PECAN PANCAKES

Bananas are one of our best sources of potassium, but because they contain so many natural sugars, they tend to brown quickly . . . so keep an eye on your pancakes. You don't want them to burn.

> **1 cup flour**
> **1 tsp baking powder**
> **¼ tsp salt**
> **⅛ tsp ground cinnamon**
> **1 cup "milk"**
> **1 banana**
> **1 tsp vanilla**
> **½ cup whole pecans, chopped**

In a medium bowl, stir together the flour, baking powder, salt, and cinnamon. In a blender or food processor, blend the "milk," bananas, and vanilla until smooth. Pour into flour mixture and add pecans. Stir together gently until "just mixed". Portion batter onto a hot non-stick pan or a lightly oiled frying pan and cover. Let sit on medium heat until the center starts to bubble and become sturdy. Flip pancake over and cook other side until golden brown. Repeat process until batter is gone. Makes 2 large or 4 small pancakes.

COCONUT PIE PANCAKES

If you don't feel like opening a can of coconut milk, you can use "milk," but the nutty, creamy flavor of the coconut in this recipe is really enhanced when you use it.

> **¾ cup flour**
> **2 tsp baking powder**
> **¼ cup shredded coconut, unsweetened**
> **½ tsp ground cardamom**
> **¼ tsp salt**
> **¾ cup "milk"**
> **¼ cup coconut milk**
> **1 banana**

In a medium bowl, stir together the flour, baking powder, coconut, cardamom, and salt. In a blender or food processor, combine the milk(s) and banana and blend until smooth. Pour into flour mixture and stir together gently until "just mixed." Portion batter onto a hot non-stick pan or a lightly oiled frying pan and cover. Let sit on medium heat until the center starts to bubble and become sturdy. Flip pancake over and cook other side until golden brown. Repeat process until batter is gone. Makes 2 large or 4 small pancakes.

DANIYELL'S BANANA PANCAKES

Oh, little Danielle. You're so cute . . . and so are your pancakes.

1½ cups flour
1½ tsp baking powder
⅛ tsp salt
1 cup "milk"
3 tbsp oil
1 banana
3 tbsp sugar

In a medium bowl, stir together the flour, baking powder, and salt. In a blender or food processor, combine the "milk," oil, bananas, and sugar and blend until smooth. Pour into flour mixture and stir together gently until "just mixed." Portion batter onto a hot non-stick pan or a lightly oiled frying pan and cover. Let sit on medium heat until the center starts to bubble and become sturdy. Flip pancake over and cook other side until golden brown. Repeat process until batter is gone. Makes 2 large or 4 small pancakes.

ECONOMY "MAPLE" PANCAKE SYRUP

In Canada, maple syrup comes out of the tap instead of water, but in other areas of the world it can be quite expensive. So if you're broke, but are dying for some yummy syrup for your pancakes, try this as an easy, cheap alternative.

1½ cups water
½ cup sugar
1 tbsp cornstarch
1 tsp maple extract

In a medium saucepan, bring the water, sugar, and cornstarch to a boil. Reduce heat and stir constantly until thickening occurs. Remove from heat and stir in maple extract. Let cool to room temperature before placing in clean container and storing in the fridge. Makes approx. 2 cups.

CINNAMON-WALNUT COFFEE CAKE

Hey Sarah . . . this is really good. I thought you might be able to use it for your breakfast chapter.
– Wolffie, Davie, FL *(Breakfast? How decadent. Yum. How about with a cup of tea and some saucy gossip? This recipe is so sweet and tasty, I had to include it in the desserts chapter as well!)*

Topping:
½ cup sugar
1 tsp ground cinnamon
2 tbsp vegan margarine
¾ cup walnuts, chopped

Cake:
1½ cups flour
½ cup sugar
1 tsp baking powder
½ tsp baking soda
½ tsp salt
¾ cup Faux Sour Cream (pg 293)
⅓ cup oil
½ cup "milk"
1 tsp vanilla extract

Preheat oven to 350°F (175°C). Lightly oil an 8x8-inch baking pan and set aside. In a small bowl, stir together topping ingredients, and set aside. In a medium bowl, whisk together flour, sugar, baking powder, baking soda, and salt. Stir in the "sour cream," oil, "milk," and vanilla. Pour evenly into baking pan then sprinkle topping evenly over the top. Bake for 30-35 minutes. Makes 1 cake.

BLACK BEANS ON TOAST

This recipe can be made in less than 15 minutes and gives you a nice healthy dose of protein to jump-start your day.

1 19-oz (540-ml) can black beans, drained and rinsed
½ tsp ground cumin
½ tsp salt
¼ tsp ground black pepper
¼ tsp garlic powder

¼ cup salsa (pg 63)
¼ cup vegetable stock
4 slices bread, toasted
½ cup vegan "cheese," finely grated (optional)

In a medium pot, combine the black beans, cumin, salt, pepper, garlic, salsa, and stock; bring to a boil. Reduce heat and simmer for 8-10 minutes. Mash beans with back of spoon or potato masher and serve over toast garnished with grated "cheese." Makes 2 large or 4 small servings.

EENY MEENY CHILI BEANY ON TOAST

Another great recipe from Wolffie that's not only fast, easy, and a source of protein, but will fill your belly till Money Mart opens and you can cash that check your Gramma sent you. Great for breakfast, lunch, or dinner . . . serve over toast or a bun, topped with any of your favorite fixins: tomatoes, chopped lettuce, avocado, pickles – the works! *This recipe also appears in the entrées chapter.*

1 14-oz (398-ml) can beans (e.g. pinto, kidney, black) INCLUDING liquid
1 3.8-oz (114-ml) can chopped green chilies, including liquid
¼ cup ketchup
1½ tsp chili powder
1 - 2 tsp sugar
½ tsp onion powder
⅛ tsp garlic powder
¼ tsp salt
⅛ tsp crushed red pepper flakes
1 tsp tamari
4 slices bread, toasted

In a medium pot, stir together the beans, chilies, ketchup, chili powder, sugar, onion powder, garlic powder, salt, red pepper flakes, and tamari. Bring to a boil, then reduce heat. Simmer, uncovered, for 10-15 minutes. Serve over toast with fixins of your choice. Makes 1 large or 2 small servings.

WOLFFIE'S BLT BRUNCH CASSEROLE

A fantastic brunch casserole that you can throw together, go have a shower, cut your toenails, and then return to the kitchen and serve.

Casserole:
4 slices bread, toasted
¼ cup vegan "mayonnaise" (pg 293)
1 lb medium/firm tofu, crumbled *or* **mashed**
¼ tsp turmeric
½ tsp onion powder
¼ tsp salt
¼ tsp ground black pepper
2 tbsp vegan margarine

Layers:
⅓ cup imitation "bacon" bits
1 large tomato, thinly sliced
3 green onions, chopped
2 cups lettuce, chopped

"Cheese" sauce:
½ cup nutritional yeast flakes
2 tbsp flour
½ tsp salt
1 cup water
2 tsp oil
1½ tsp Dijon mustard
1½ tsp tamari

Preheat oven to 325°F (165°C). Lightly oil an 8x8-inch baking dish. Spread "mayonnaise" evenly on toast. Cut toast into 1-inch cubes and place in the bottom of the baking dish, mayonnaise side up; set aside. In large saucepan, scramble the tofu, turmeric, onion powder, salt, and pepper in margarine until tofu is browned. Set aside. To prepare the cheese sauce: in a small saucepan, whisk together all the sauce ingredients. Bring to a boil, then reduce heat. Simmer for 2-4 minutes, stirring constantly. To arrange the casserole: pour half of the "cheese" sauce over the bread cubes. Layer with half the "bacon" bits. Add all of the tofu mixture on top. Next, layer tomato slices, remaining cheese sauce, remaining "bacon" bits, and green onions. Bake uncovered for 15 minutes. Serve over chopped lettuce. Makes 2 large or 4 small servings.

SLEEPY SUNDAY MORNING SCRAMBLE

What? NO! Is it really time to get up already? Serve with a side of toast or English muffins and a giant cup of coffee.

1 small onion, chopped
2 tbsp olive oil
1 pound medium/firm tofu, crumbled
2 garlic cloves, minced
2 tbsp nutritional yeast flakes
1 tbsp tamari
2 tsp Dijon mustard
½ tsp turmeric
1 tsp sage
¼ tsp basil
¼ tsp salt
¼ tsp ground black pepper
1 medium tomato, chopped

In a large saucepan on medium-high heat, sauté the onions in oil until translucent. In a medium bowl, stir together the crumbled tofu, garlic, nutritional yeast, tamari, mustard, turmeric, sage, basil, salt, and pepper until well mixed. Add tofu mixture to onions and scramble until tofu is browned and all the liquid has evaporated. Toss with tomatoes and serve immediately. Makes 2 large or 4 small servings.

SALSA SCRAMBLE

Serve with tortillas or toast. Everybody salsa!

> ¼ **cup red onion, chopped**
> **1 tbsp oil**
> **1 lb medium/firm tofu, crumbled**
> ½ **cup salsa (pg 63)**
> ¼ **cup fresh cilantro, chopped**
> ½ **tsp turmeric**
> ½ **cup vegan "cheese," finely grated**
> **1 avocado, pitted and sliced**

In a medium saucepan on medium-high heat, sauté the onions in oil until translucent. In a medium bowl, stir together the crumbled tofu, salsa, cilantro, and turmeric until well mixed. Add tofu mixture to onions and scramble until tofu is browned and all the liquid has evaporated. Toss with the "cheese" and avocado and serve immediately. Makes 2 large or 4 small servings.

CAJUN TOMATO POTATOES

This recipe goes great with a tofu scramble (pg 44) and a cup of green tea. The smaller you cut the potato, the faster it will cook. Potato. Tomato. Potato. Tomato. Let's call the whole thing off!

> **1 small onion, chopped**
> **2 tbsp olive oil**
> **1 large potato, cubed**
> **2 tsp tamari**
> ½ **tsp Cajun spice (pg 303)**
> ¼ **tsp ground black pepper**
> **4 - 6 cherry tomatoes, halved**
> **1 green onion, finely chopped**

In a large saucepan on medium heat, sauté the onions in oil until translucent. Add the potatoes, tamari, Cajun spice, and pepper; cover with lid and sauté until potatoes are cooked, stirring often to avoid sticking. Toss with tomatoes and green onions and serve immediately.

VEGAN "SAUSAGE" HASH

If you can't find any vegan "sausage" where you live, you can chop up a veggie or tempeh burger.

1 cup vegan "sausage," chopped
1 small onion, chopped
2 tbsp vegan margarine
1 medium potato, grated
2 tbsp "milk"
¼ tsp salt
¼ tsp ground black pepper

In a large saucepan on medium heat, sauté the "sausages" and onions in margarine until onions are translucent. Stir in the potatoes, "milk," salt, and pepper and fry until potatoes start to brown. Stir and continue frying until done. Makes 2 large or 4 small servings.

MONDAY MORNING MUESLI

Most mueslis sold at supermarkets contain milk powder, so here's a recipe for those of us who think that cows' milk is for baby cows. Serve with vegan "milk" or "yogurt" and throw in some fresh fruit if you're feeling fruity. For a sweeter muesli, add a little stevia powder or sugar.

3 cups rolled oat flakes
½ cup wheat germ
½ cup sesame seeds
½ cup sunflower seeds
¼ cup pumpkin seeds
½ cup nuts (your choice), roughly chopped
1 cup dried fruit (your choice)

In a large bowl, stir together all the ingredients and store in an airtight container. Makes approx. 6 cups.

TOASTED OIL-FREE GRANOLA

Oil-free? Why not?

2 cups rolled oat flakes
2 cups quick oats
½ cup walnuts, roughly chopped
½ cup sesame seeds
1 tsp ground cinnamon
½ tsp salt
½ cup water
¼ cup maple syrup
1 tsp vanilla extract
1 cup dried fruit (your choice)

Preheat oven to 250°F (120°C). In large bowl, combine the oat flakes, oats, walnuts, sesame seeds, cinnamon, and salt. Add the water, maple syrup, and vanilla extract and stir until well mixed. On two 9x13-inch baking pans, spread out even amounts of the mixture on both pans and bake for 1 hour, stirring every 15 minutes. Let cool and stir in dried fruit. Store in an airtight container. Makes approx. 6 cups.

APPLE CINNAMON GRANOLA

Apples and cinnamon – oh my!

4 cups rolled oat flakes
½ cup shredded coconut, unsweetened
1 cup pecans, roughly chopped
½ cup sesame seeds
2 tsp ground cinnamon
¾ tsp salt
½ cup maple syrup
⅓ cup oil
½ tsp vanilla extract
1 cup dehydrated apple, finely chopped

Preheat oven to 350°F (175°C). In large bowl, combine the oat flakes, coconut, pecans, sesame seeds, cinnamon, and salt. Add the maple syrup, oil, and vanilla and stir together until well mixed. On two 9x13-inch baking pans, spread out even amounts of the mixture on both pans and bake for 20-25 minutes, stirring every 10 minutes. Let granola cool before stirring in dried apples. Store in an airtight container. Makes approx. 8 cups.

CRANBERRY ALMOND PECAN GRANOLA

How many vegetarians does it take to screw in a light bulb? I don't know, but where do you get your protein? Bwwaa ha ha ha!

4 cups rolled oat flakes
⅔ cup almonds, slivered
⅔ cup shredded coconut, unsweetened
⅔ cup pecans
1 cup sugar

2 tsp ground cinnamon
1 tsp ground allspice
⅔ cup cranberry *or* **apple juice**
¼ cup oil
1½ cups dried cranberries

Preheat oven to 325°F (165°C). In large bowl, combine the oat flakes, almonds, coconut, pecans, sugar, cinnamon, and allspice. Add the cranberry juice and oil, and stir together until well mixed. On two 9x13-inch baking pans, spread out even amounts of the mixture on both pans and bake for 20-25 minutes, stirring every 10 minutes. Let granola cool before stirring in dried cranberries. Store in an airtight container. Makes approx. 8 cups.

SIMPLE CRUNCHY GRANOLA

Mix this with that. Throw it in the oven. Voilà – you have breakfast for the next week . . . could anything be simpler?

4 cups rolled oat flakes
½ cup shredded coconut, unsweetened
1 cup wheat germ
1 cup walnuts, roughly chopped
1 cup sunflower seeds
½ cup sesame seeds
1 tbsp ground cinnamon
¾ cup maple syrup
½ cup oil

Preheat oven to 325°F (165°C). In large bowl, combine the oat flakes, coconut, wheat germ, walnuts, sunflower seeds, sesame seeds, and cinnamon. Add the maple syrup and oil and stir together until well mixed. On two 9x13-inch baking pans, spread out even amounts of the mixture on both pans and bake for 25-30 minutes, stirring every 10 minutes. Let cool and store in an airtight container. Makes approx. 8 cups.

BAKED APORRIDGY

I'm sorry but I have no regrets. This might take longer than regular porridge, but it's worth the wait. Go fold my laundry or something until it's ready.

1 cup rolled oat flakes
1¾ cup water
½ cup "milk"
3 tbsp maple syrup
2 tbsp ground flax seeds (pg 296)
2 tsp molasses
½ tsp salt
¼ tsp ground nutmeg
¼ tsp ground cinnamon
¼ tsp ground ginger
¼ cup raisins
¼ cup walnuts, chopped

Preheat oven to 350°F (175°C). In a lightly oiled 8x8-inch baking pan, stir all ingredients together and bake for 40-45 minutes. Serve immediately.

BREAKFAST COUSCOUS

Couscous can be found in most grocery stores or Middle Eastern markets. Couscous is granular semolina (wheat) and is a great quick alternative grain to rice when you're super strapped for time. Breakfast, lunch, or dinner, I'm coo-coo for couscous!

¾ cup "milk" *or* **water**
¼ cup juice (e.g. apple, cranberry, orange)
½ cup couscous
1 banana, sliced
¼ tsp ground cinnamon

In a small pot on high heat, bring the "milk" and juice to a boil. Reduce heat and stir in couscous, bananas, and cinnamon; cover with lid and simmer for 2-3 minutes. Turn off heat and let sit for an additional 2 minutes. Serve immediately. Makes 1 large or 2 small servings.

UBER QUICK BREAKFAST OATS

This recipe is so simple, I feel ridiculous putting it down on to paper for you, but it's a nummy way to eat oats when you're in a hurry.

> **¾ - 1 cup rolled oat flakes**
> **"milk"**
> **¼ cup dehydrated** *or* **fresh fruit (your choice)**
> **maple syrup (optional)**

Place oat flakes into cereal bowl. Cover with desired amount of "milk" and some dried fruit. Drizzle a little maple syrup on top and eat. Makes 1 serving.

QUICK BREAKFAST QUINOA

Quinoa is an über nutritious grain that is not only high in protein, but is a complete protein all on its own. Don't forget to rinse it thoroughly before cooking.

> **1½ cups "milk"**
> **½ cup quinoa**
> **¼ cup raisins**
> **½ cup fresh fruit (your choice)**

In a medium saucepan on high heat, bring the "milk" to a boil. Reduce heat and add the quinoa and raisins. Cover and simmer for 15 minutes or until the quinoa is cooked. With a blender or food processor, blend the quinoa till smooth. Stir in the fresh fruit and serve immediately. Makes 2 servings.

APPLE-WALNUT PUDDING

This is terrific for either breakfast or dessert! – Wolffie, Davie, FL *(I like to serve this with a little almond milk poured over top. I agree with Wolffie: breakfast or dessert . . . this recipe sure is a terrific dish. It also appears in the desserts chapter.)*

Filling:
½ **cup flour**
⅓ **cup sugar**
¾ **tsp baking powder**
¼ **tsp salt**
¼ **tsp ground cinnamon**
⅛ **tsp ground cloves**
¼ **cup "milk"**
½ **tsp vanilla extract**
2 **medium Granny Smith apples, cubed**
¼ **cup walnuts, finely chopped**

Topping:
⅓ **cup water**
¼ **cup sugar**
2 **tbsp maple syrup**
2 **tbsp vegan margarine**

Preheat oven to 375°F (190°C). In a medium bowl, whisk together the flour, sugar, baking powder, salt, cinnamon, and cloves. Stir in the "milk," vanilla, apples, and walnuts until well mixed. Spread into an 8x8 inch baking dish. Set aside. In a small saucepan, bring the water, sugar, maple syrup, and margarine to a boil. Reduce heat once margarine has melted. Pour over the batter in the baking dish. DO NOT STIR. Bake for 40-45 minutes. Makes 2 large or 4 small servings.

BREAKFAST BROWN RICE PUDDING

This is a great way to use leftover rice and can be served for breaky or dessert garnished with fresh fruit. Feeling nutty? Add coconut milk instead of "milk" and garnish with toasted sesame seeds. *This recipe also appears in the desserts chapter.*

1 cup cooked brown rice	**1 tbsp maple syrup**
1 cup "milk"	**½ tsp vanilla extract**
2 tbsp raisins	**⅛ tsp ground cinnamon**

In a medium saucepan, combine all ingredients and bring to a boil. Reduce heat and simmer for 15-20 minutes. Serve hot or cold. Makes 1 large or 2 small servings.

BREAKFAST BANANA SMOOTHIE

I always keep bananas in the freezer for when I want to make a quick smoothie. To freeze, peel and roughly chop them, then place them in a bag or container before storing. It will make your life mucho easier.

2 cups "milk"
3 tbsp tahini
1 banana, frozen
1 tbsp flax oil
1 tbsp maple syrup

In a blender or food processor, blend all ingredients until smooth. If you like a thinner shake, add a little more "milk." Makes 1 large or 2 small servings.

ANYTHING GOES FRUIT 'N' NUT SMOOTHIE

I know that I'm bound to answer when you propose, anything goes!

3 tbsp nut butter (your choice)
1 cup "milk"
1 banana, frozen
1 cup frozen fruit (your choice)
1 tbsp maple syrup
1 tbsp flax oil

In a blender or food processor, blend all ingredients until smooth. If you like a thinner shake, add a little more "milk." Makes 1 large or 2 small servings.

ON THE RUN BREAKFAST SMOOTHIE

Hurry! You're going to miss your bus!

> **2 tbsp ground flax seeds (pg 296)**
> **1 cup juice (your choice)**
> **½ cup "milk"**
> **1 banana, frozen**
> **½ cup frozen fruit (your choice)**
> **1 tbsp tahini**

In a blender or food processor, blend all ingredients until smooth. If you like a thinner shake, add a little more "milk." Makes 1 large or 2 small servings.

BANANA DATE SMOOTHIE

Mmm, mmm, mmm – a smoothie with a chewy treat at the bottom!

> **¼ cup cashews**
> **8 dates, pitted**
> **¼ cup soft tofu**
> **1 cup "milk"**
> **1 banana, frozen**
> **2 tbsp maple syrup**
> **1 tbsp flax oil**

In a blender or food processor, puree the cashews, dates, and tofu until smooth. Add the remaining ingredients and blend until smooth. If you like a thinner shake, add a little more "milk." Makes 1 large or 2 small servings.

Appies & Snacks

APPIES & SNACKS

When is an appetizer a snack and a snack an appetizer? Appetizers are generally served as a first course before the main meal. Snacks are generally for between-meal noshing or when you're having tea with friends or watching a movie. But then sometimes an appie can be eaten as a snack, and a snack can be eaten as an appie. I'm so confused . . . and that's why they're both here in one chapter!

APPIES

NANA'S PESTO PIN-WHEEL ROLLS

Sarah, here's a submission for the new book. This is a veganized version of my grandma's awesome pesto rolls and they work great as an appetizer. I love your books, by the way! (Duh...) – Naomi, Brooklyn, NY *(Think cinnamon buns, only with pesto. Mmm. Yummy! Make sure you have a rolling pin and that you thaw out your dough at least 2 hours before you get need it. Or to make things even easier, buy tubes of ready-to-use puff pastry or crescent roll dough. Either way, you're going to be hard-pressed not to eat these all before your guests arrive.)*

> **½ cup pesto (pg 177)**
> **vegan puff pastry dough, thawed**

Preheat oven to 370°F (185°C). Roll out dough to a large rectangle approximately the size of a cookie sheet. Spread a thin layer of pesto evenly over dough. Roll up dough, and cut into rolls about ½ inch thick. Place cut side down onto a baking sheet and bake for 10-12 minutes or until golden brown. Makes approx. 8-10 crescent rolls.

SHOOK 'N' COOK BREADING

There is nothing in the world better than something that is breaded and fried. How about pickles? Tofu? Bananas? How about a chocolate bar? This wicked breading recipe makes anything taste good. Elvis would be proud.

1 cup cornflake-type cereal
½ cup flour
2 tsp salt
½ tsp ground black pepper
½ tsp paprika
½ tsp sugar
½ tsp garlic powder
½ tsp onion powder
¼ tsp Cajun spice (pg 303)

In a food processor, blend all ingredients until coarse. Store in airtight container. Makes approx. 1½ cups.

SHOOK 'N' COOK PICKLES

If you don't want to shake your pickle, you can always just roll it around on a shallow plate. We are talking about the same thing . . . right?

¼ cup maple syrup
1 tbsp Dijon mustard
½ cup Shook 'N' Cook breading (pg 56)
4 - 6 medium pickles

In a shallow dish, stir together the maple syrup and Dijon mustard. Set aside. In a medium bag, portion out ½ cup of breading mixture. Slice pickles in half, lengthwise. Dip each pickle slice in Dijon sauce and then place in bag with breading mixture. Shake until well coated. In a medium saucepan on medium heat, sauté the pickles in oil until browned. Makes 8-12 pickle portions.

SHOOK 'N' COOK ZUCCHINI

You can choose to dunk your zucchini in any type of salad dressing. Personally, I think the Caesar Salad Dressing works the best.

> ¼ **cup Caesar salad dressing (pg 93)**
> ½ **cup Shook 'N' Cook breading (pg 56)**
> **1 medium zucchini**

In a shallow dish, portion out the salad dressing. Set aside. In a medium bag, portion out ½ cup of breading mixture. Slice zucchinis into bite-sized wedges. Dip each zucchini slice in dressing and then place in bag with breading mixture. Shake until well coated. In a medium saucepan on medium heat, sauté the zucchini in oil until browned. Makes 8-12 zucchini sticks.

SHOOK 'N' COOK TOFU

Tofu, BBQ sauce, and a frying pan. If this isn't heaven . . . then where am I?

> ¼ **cup BBQ sauce**
> **1 tsp Cajun Spice (pg 303)**
> ½ **cup Shook 'N' Cook breading (pg 56)**
> ½ **lb firm tofu**

In a shallow dish, stir together the BBQ sauce and Cajun spice. Set aside. In a medium bag, portion out ½ cup of breading mixture. Slice tofu into bite-sized wedges. Dip each tofu slice in sauce and then place in bag with breading mixture. Shake until well coated. In a medium saucepan on medium heat, sauté the tofu in oil until browned. Makes 6-8 tofu slices.

MELISSA'S STUFFED MUSHROOMS

Hey Sarah, I just joined the *GoVegan.net* forum and saw your post yesterday that you were coming out with a new book! I was whipping up something for a snack/dinner tonight, and I thought of you, since what I made was so fast and easy. I would be really honored if it makes the cut for the book! – Melissa, via the Internet

16 - 20 button mushrooms
2 garlic cloves
¼ cup shallots, roughly chopped
1 small carrot, roughly chopped
1 slice of bread, roughly chopped
1 tbsp fresh parsley
½ tsp dried rosemary
¼ tsp salt
¼ tsp ground black pepper
¼ tsp nutritional yeast flakes
3 tbsp vegan margarine

Preheat oven to 350°F (175°C). Remove mushroom stems and set aside. Place mushroom caps in 8x8-inch baking dish set aside. In a food processor, blend the mushroom stems, garlic, shallots, carrots, bread, parsley, rosemary, salt, pepper, and nutritional yeast until coarse. In a large saucepan on medium-high heat, sauté the blended stuffing in margarine for 2-3 minutes. Remove from heat and allow to cool a little before spooning equal amounts of stuffing into mushroom caps. Bake for 15 minutes. Makes 16-20 mushroom caps.

STUFFED CHERRY TOMATOES WITH OLIVADA

For something different, you can also stuff the cherry tomatoes with the Fish-Friendly Tapenade on pg 63 or Edamame Hummus on pg 62.

10 - 15 cherry tomatoes
½ cup Kalamata olives
1 garlic clove, minced
2½ tbsp oil (e.g. flax, hemp, olive)
⅛ tsp ground black pepper
2 tsp fresh parsley, minced

Cut each tomato in half, lengthwise. Using a small spoon, remove seeds and juice from each tomato half. Set tomato halves aside. In a food processor, blend together the olives, garlic, oil, and pepper. Stuff each tomato half with olivada mixture and garnish top with parsley. Makes 20-30 tomatoes.

WOLFFIE'S MAGNIFICENT BAKED BEAN CHIP DIP

I was scared to test this recipe because of the baked beans . . . thank goodness I trust Wolffie's recipes, cuz they are all so yummy. This dip is so terrific. I like to serve this with a big bowl of fresh corn tortilla chips. The dip won't last long, so don't worry about being rude – double dip if you have to. My gut can't handle the raw onion, so I omit it from this recipe . . . it's just as good, and it makes my tummy happy.

1 14-oz (398-ml) can vegan baked beans in tomato sauce, drained but not rinsed
¼ small onion, chopped
1 tsp nutritional yeast flakes
½ tsp chili powder
¼ tsp garlic powder
¼ tsp salt
⅛ tsp cumin
⅛ tsp cayenne pepper
1½ tsp red wine vinegar
1 tsp tamari
¼ teaspoon liquid smoke
1 tbsp imitation "bacon" bits (optional)

In a food processor, combine all ingredients and blend until smooth. Makes approx. 1½ cups.

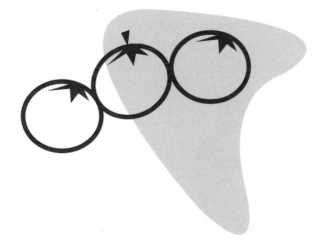

MUSHROOM PÂTÉ

Conventional pâté is meat-based but veggie pâté is guilt-free and can be served with slices of pita, crackers, or bread. And it even makes a great sandwich filler.

1 cup vegetable stock
1 red onion, chopped
2 garlic cloves, roughly chopped
1 cup button mushrooms, roughly chopped
1 cup shitake mushrooms, roughly chopped
1 tsp ground sage
1 tsp dried rosemary
1 tsp ground nutmeg
½ tsp ground thyme
1 tsp salt
½ tsp ground black pepper
1 cup walnuts, toasted (pg 295)
1 tbsp tamari
2 tsp balsamic vinegar
1 tbsp ground flax seeds (pg 296)
1 slice of bread, roughly chopped

In a large saucepan on medium-high heat, bring the stock to a boil. Add the onions, garlic, mushrooms, sage, rosemary, nutmeg, thyme, salt, and pepper and simmer for 8-10 minutes or until liquid has been absorbed and evaporated. In a food processor, combine mushroom mixture with walnuts, tamari, balsamic vinegar, ground flax seeds, and bread and blend until smooth. Press evenly into an 8-inch loaf pan (or fancy serving dish with a 2-inch lip) and refrigerate for at least 2 hours before serving. Makes 1 loaf.

OH BABY ONION DIP

Oh baby . . . hurry up and kiss me before you smell my breath.

> **1 large onion, finely chopped**
> **1 garlic clove, minced**
> **1 tbsp olive oil**
> **¾ cup vegan "sour cream" (pg 293)**
> **⅛ cup fresh parsley, finely chopped**
> **¼ tsp salt**
> **⅛ tsp ground black pepper**

In a large saucepan on medium heat, sauté the onions and garlic in the oil until onions are translucent. In a small bowl, stir together the onions, "sour cream," parsley, salt, and pepper. Refrigerate for at least 1 hour before serving. Makes approx. 1½ cups.

GILLIAN'S LENTIL DIP

My sister is making me do this . . . this is our favorite summer dip recipe. – Gillian, Toronto, ON *(Serve this delicious dip with flatbread or crackers and try not to eat it all before the guests arrive.)*

> **1 cup red lentils**
> **1½ cups water**
> **2 tbsp olive oil**
> **3 tbsp oil (e.g. flax, hemp, grapeseed)**
> **¼ cup lemon juice**
> **1 - 2 garlic cloves**
> **1 tsp ground cumin**
> **¼ tsp salt**

In a medium pot, bring water and lentils to a boil. Reduce heat and simmer for 2-3 minutes. Remove from heat, cover, and let stand for 12-15 minutes. In a food processor, blend the lentils, oils, lemon juice, garlic, cumin, and salt until smooth. Makes approx. 2 cups.

EDAMAME HUMMUS

Ahhh. The ever popular vegan hummus . . . with a twist. Behold, the edamame!

¾ cup frozen edamame beans, pre-shucked
2 cups spinach, tightly packed
2 - 3 garlic cloves
½ cup tahini
2 tbsp olive oil
2 tbsp oil (e.g. flax, hemp, grapeseed)
1 tbsp lemon juice
1 tbsp tamari
1 - 2 tsp Asian chili garlic sauce (*or* other hot sauce)
½ tsp salt
¼ tsp ground black pepper

Steam edamame until bright green and thawed. In a food processor, combine the edamame and all other ingredients, and blend until smooth. Makes approx. 2 cups.

ROASTED RED PEPPER HUMMUS

Roasted red bell peppers can be found in the pickle aisle of your local grocery store. This hummus is great when served with pita bread or as a sandwich spread.

1 19-oz (540-ml) can chickpeas (garbanzo beans), drained and rinsed
¼ cup tahini
3 garlic cloves
½ cup roasted red bell peppers, drained
2 tbsp balsamic vinegar
2 tbsp apple cider vinegar
½ tbsp tamari
¼ cup oil (e.g. flax, olive, hemp)
1 tsp dried basil
1 tsp paprika
1 tsp salt
½ tsp dried oregano

In a food processor, combine all ingredients and blend until smooth. Makes approx. 2 cups.

BETTY'S SALSA

Sarah, here is a recipe that my roommate whips up for parties. It's very good served with tortilla chips . . . party on down. – Wolffie, Davie, FL

1 small red onion, roughly chopped
1 4-oz (133-g) can diced green chilies (you decide heat)
¼ cup fresh cilantro leaves
1 tsp celery seed
½ tsp salt
¼ tsp ground black pepper
2 large tomatoes, seeds and juice removed

In a food processor, blend the onions, chilies, cilantro, celery seed, salt, and pepper until smooth. Add the seeded tomatoes and pulse until roughly chopped. Makes approx. 2 cups.

FISH-FRIENDLY TAPENADE

Traditionally, tapenade is a thick paste made from capers, anchovies, olives, seasonings, and sometimes small pieces of tuna . . . but fish are our friends, not food. So try this cruelty-free version spread over some nice crusty bread or crackers and enjoy.

1 cup Kalamata olives, pitted
¼ cup capers, drained
4 - 6 sun-dried tomatoes
¼ cup roasted red bell peppers, drained
1 tbsp oil (e.g. olive, flax, hemp)
¼ tsp salt
¼ tsp ground black pepper

In a food processor, blend together all ingredients and serve. Makes approx. 1 cup.

SNACKS
VESANTO'S CHOCO-CURRANT CRANBERRY SQUARES

Here's a tasty recipe from the *Food Allergy Survival Guide* by V. Melina, J. Stepaniak, and D. Aronson. This book shows how adults and children can be well-nourished despite food sensitivities, and provides recipes that are entirely free of the major allergens: dairy products, eggs, gluten, tree nuts, peanuts, soy, yeast, fish, shellfish, and wheat. It clarifies links between diet and conditions such as arthritis, asthma, Attention Deficit Hyperactivity Disorder (ADHD), candida, depression, dermatitis, digestive disorders, fatigue, and headaches. These squares are an ideal combination of dried fruit, chocolate, and cereal that you can stir together in minutes. Vesanto Melina is one of my all-time favorite people; her books are so helpful and chock full of information. Due to my chocolate intolerance, I made this recipe with ¼ cup of carob and it turned out perfectly. This recipe also appears in the desserts chapter.

> **½ cup maple syrup or rice syrup**
> **¼ cup seed or nut butter (e.g., tahini, almond butter)**
> **2½ squares (2.5-oz) semisweet baking chocolate**
> **⅓ cup dried currants**
> **⅓ cup cranberries**
> **1¼ cups puffed rice-type cereal**
> **1¼ cups flakes-type cereal**

Lightly oil a 4x9-inch loaf pan. Set aside. In a large pot, stir together the syrup, nut butter, and chocolate on medium-low heat until melted; stir often to prevent burning. Once evenly melted and mixed, remove from heat and add the currants, cranberries and cereals; mix together until well coated. With damp hands, press mixture firmly and evenly into loaf pan and refrigerate for at least 30 minutes to set. Makes 8 squares.

FRUIT DIPPING SAUCE

This sauce is great for dipping sliced apples or orange wedges or for pouring over your fruit salad. I promise that if you try it, you'll never be sad, you'll grow taller, be stronger, be smarter and . . . um . . . rich! OK, maybe I'm fibbing a little, but this dip is wicked awesome.

> **1 12-oz (300-g) pkg soft or silken tofu**
> **¼ cup maple syrup**
> **¾ tsp ground cinnamon**

In a food processor, combine all ingredients and blend until smooth. Makes approx. 1½ cups.

DANICA'S POPCORN BALLS

My forbidden popcorn recipe, stolen from my mom. But hey . . . it's still good! And seriously, don't forget to dip your hands in cold water when shaping the balls; it makes all the difference in the world. This recipe is a little messy but keep in mind, messy is good. Just don't get any in your hair. Trust me. – Danica, Victoria, BC *(I like to use an air popper to make my popcorn, but do your popcorn the way you like it best. You may find that the sauce outweighs the amount of popcorn you have, so add more popcorn if it seems too wet. Danica, is the piercer at The TattooZoo.net, and when we're not talking about MAC makeup, boys, psycho ex-friends, and lip-gloss . . . we're talking about food. I loves her. She's my Skull-Sista. Ahh ha, Danica – your recipe is about balls.)*

> **¼ cup popcorn kernels (approx. 8 cups when popped)**
> **½ cup packed sugar**
> **¼ cup vegan margarine**
> **½ cup dark corn syrup**
> **¼ teaspoon salt**
> **¼ - ½ cup extra goodies (e.g. carob chips, hemp seeds, peanuts) (optional)**

Pop popcorn and place in a large bowl and set aside. Lay a sheet of wax paper on a large plate or cookie sheet. Set aside. In a medium saucepan, bring the sugar, margarine, corn syrup, and salt to a boil. Reduce heat and simmer for 2 minutes. Pour sauce over popcorn and stir quickly with a wooden spoon, until well incorporated. Set aside a few minutes and allow to cool enough to be handled. Dip your hands in cold water and roll into balls out of handfuls of popcorn mixture. Press balls tightly together and place on to wax paper. Refrigerate for at least 30 minutes before serving. Makes 20-24 balls.

MARSHMALLOW POPCORN BALLS

Mmm, mmm, marshmallows! For extra "hoo-haa," add a teaspoon of mint extract.

¼ cup popcorn kernels (approx. 8 cups when popped)
6 - 8 (8-oz) vegan marshmallows (pg 290)
2 tbsp vegan margarine
½ cup extra goodies (e.g. carob chips, candy, hemp seeds, peanuts) (optional)

Pop popcorn and place in a large bowl and set aside. Lay a sheet of wax paper on a large plate or cookie sheet. Set aside. In a medium saucepan on medium heat, melt the marshmallows and margarine, stirring constantly. Pour sauce over popcorn, add extra goodies, and stir quickly with a wooden spoon, until well incorporated. Set aside a few minutes and allow to cool enough to be handled. Dip your hands in cold water and roll into balls out of handfuls of popcorn mixture. Press balls tightly together and place on wax paper. Refrigerate for at least 30 minutes before serving. Makes 20-24 balls.

SPICY CORN CHIP POPCORN

This is a great snack for when you're sitting around with your girlfriends watching "America's Next Top Model" and reveling in the fact that you can eat without guilt and that you don't have an eating disorder.

¼ cup popcorn kernels (approx. 8 cups when popped)
4 cups corn chips
2 tbsp vegan margarine
1 tbsp Asian chili garlic sauce (or other hot sauce)
½ tsp celery seed
¼ tsp salt

Pop popcorn and place into a large bowl with the corn chips. Set aside. In a small saucepan, melt the margarine until liquefied. Stir in the chili sauce, celery seed, and salt. Spoon evenly over popcorn, tossing until well incorporated. Makes approx. 12 cups.

CAJUN POPCORN

Oh, wicked corn. Why do you hurt my belly so? I eat you anyway. I have no will power.

¼ cup popcorn kernels (approx. 8 cups when popped)
2 tbsp vegan margarine
½ - 1 tsp Cajun spice (pg 303)
1 tsp lime juice

Pop popcorn and place into a large bowl. Set aside. In a small saucepan, melt the margarine until liquefied. Stir in the Cajun spice and lime juice. Spoon evenly over popcorn, tossing until well incorporated. Makes approx. 8 cups.

BBQ POPCORN

I have this jar of BBQ sauce in my fridge that I don't use very often. One day – one very PMS-y day – I decided to add it to my PMS popcorn and wow! What a treat!

¼ cup popcorn kernels (approx. 8 cups when popped)
1 cup mini pretzels
2 tbsp vegan margarine
1 tbsp BBQ sauce (or other marinade)
¼ tsp garlic powder
¼ tsp salt
¼ tsp ground black pepper

Pop popcorn and place into a large bowl with the pretzels. Set aside. In a small saucepan, melt the margarine until liquefied. Stir in the BBQ sauce, garlic powder, salt, and pepper. Spoon evenly over popcorn, tossing until well incorporated. Makes approx. 9 cups.

HOT NUTS

Hot nuts! Get your hot nuts here!

> **2 tbsp vegan margarine**
> **2 garlic cloves, minced**
> **2 - 3 tsp Asian chili garlic sauce (or hot sauce of your choice)**
> **¼ tsp salt**
> **3 cups assorted raw nuts (e.g. pecans, almonds, walnuts)**

Preheat oven to 250°F (120°C). In a medium saucepan on medium heat, sauté the margarine and garlic together until garlic starts to soften. Turn off heat, stir in chili sauce, salt, and nuts; toss until well coated. Spread evenly on cookie sheet and bake for 1 hour, stirring every 15 minutes. Makes approx. 3 cups.

SPICED NUTS

Roasting brings out nuts natural flavors but unlike raw nuts, roasted nuts will not keep as long, so consume them within a few months of roasting.

> **3 cups assorted raw nuts (e.g. pecans, walnuts, almonds)**
> **2 tbsp olive oil**
> **½ tsp ground cumin**
> **½ tsp cayenne pepper**
> **½ tsp thyme**
> **½ tsp nutmeg**
> **1 tsp salt**
> **½ tsp ground black pepper**

Pre-heat oven to 350°F (175°C).In a medium bowl, toss together all the ingredients. Spread evenly over cookie sheet and bake for 20 minutes, stirring every 10 minutes. Makes approx. 3 cups.

CAROB-COVERED MINI-PRETZELS

You can use chocolate chips instead of carob, but I'm allergic to chocolate (sob), so there you go. If you don't have a double boiler, just place a small pot in a larger pot containing water.

> **½ cup carob chips**
> **1 tbsp "milk"**
> **2 cups mini-pretzels, salted**

Line 2 cookie sheets with wax paper. In a small double boiler, melt the carob chips and "milk" on medium heat, stirring until smooth and creamy. Dip half or all of the pretzel in carob sauce and lay on cookie sheet. Repeat until done. Place cookie sheets into refrigerator and allow carob to set. Makes approx. 70 mini-pretzels.

Salads
& Dressings

SALADS

Salads can stand alone as a meal or complement many main dishes. Unfortunately, when it comes to salads, I'm a creature of habit, and even though I often say, "Today I'm going to make something different," I usually end up making a simple green salad with an oil and vinegar dressing. It's terrible. Thank goodness I have my buddy Shirley, a.k.a. Wolffie, from Davie, Florida, who provided me with several of the great recipes in this chapter. Thanks, Wolffie! You're awesome.

AUNTIE BONNIE'S CHICKPEA SALAD

My Auntie Bonnie needs a chickpea intervention; she has them stockpiled in her kitchen cupboards. Does anyone really need 35 cans of chickpeas "just in case"? But incredibly simple yet fresh and delicious salad is purrrrfection. Just like my Auntie Bonnie.

> **1 19-oz (540-ml) can chickpeas (garbanzo beans), drained and rinsed**
> **¼ small red onion, minced**
> **1 - 2 garlic cloves, minced**
> **1 large tomato, diced**
> **¼ cup fresh parsley, finely chopped**
> **3 tbsp oil (e.g. flax, hemp, olive)**
> **1 tbsp red wine vinegar**
> **1 tsp lemon juice**
> **¼ tsp salt**
> **¼ tsp ground black pepper**

In a large bowl, toss all ingredients together and refrigerate for at least 1 hour before serving. Makes 2 large or 4 small servings.

WOLFFIE'S BLACK BEAN & LENTIL SALAD

I'm not a big fan of "The Bean Salad"; it's usually the one dish at vegan potlucks that I tend to skip over. If you're like me and don't care for the bean salad . . . well, let me blow your mind. I can't urge you enough to try this fantastic recipe from the amazing Wolffie. Her dishes never fail and are a treat to eat. TRUST ME!

Dressing:

¼ **cup olive oil**

¼ **cup oil (e.g. flax, hemp, grapeseed)**

¼ **cup red wine vinegar**

½ **tbsp Dijon mustard**

¾ **tsp ground cumin**

1 garlic clove, minced

¼ **tsp salt**

¼ **tsp black pepper**

1 tsp sugar

Salad:

1 19-oz (540-ml) can black beans, drained and rinsed

1 19-oz (540-ml) can lentils, drained and rinsed

¾ **cups frozen corn niblets, thawed**

1 small red onion, minced

1 small red bell pepper, chopped

¼ **cup fresh cilantro, minced**

To prepare dressing: In a jar or dressing bottle, combine all ingredients. Cap and shake well before using. To prepare salad: In a large bowl, combine salad ingredients and dressing and toss together well. Refrigerate for at least 1 hour before serving. Makes 4-6 servings. Dressing makes approx. ¾ cup.

WOLFFIE'S FIESTA MACARONI BEAN SALAD

This is one of those recipes that I didn't want to cut down to make only two servings, to avoid having half a can of beans left over. It's the perfect recipe to take to a potluck, enjoy for lunch, and serve as leftovers. It's just wicked!

3 cups elbow macaroni pasta, uncooked

Dressing:
¾ cups vegan "mayonnaise" (pg 293)
2 tbsp fresh parsley, minced
1 tbsp red wine vinegar
1 tbsp sugar
1 tsp dried basil
½ tsp celery seed
½ tsp paprika
½ tsp salt
¼ tsp ground black pepper
¼ tsp garlic powder

Salad:
1 large carrot, grated
1 small green bell pepper, chopped
1 small red onion, minced
¼ cup sweet pickle relish
1 19-oz (540-ml) can kidney beans, drained and rinsed

In a large pot of salted water, boil the pasta. While pasta is cooking, prepare the salad ingredients and place into a medium bowl. To prepare dressing: In a jar or dressing bottle, combine all ingredients. Cap and shake well before using. Set aside. To prepare salad: Once pasta is done, drain and rinse pasta under cold water until cooled. Shake off excess water and add to salad bowl. Toss ingredients with dressing and refrigerate for at least 1 hour before serving. Makes 2 large or 4 small servings. Dressing makes approx. 1 cup.

ADAM'S BLACK BEAN & CORN SALAD

Hey Sarah, how's it going? I wanted to give you a recipe that my mom makes that's really simple. You had a more complicated version in one of your other cookbooks . . . but this one is so easy and it rules, so try it out! – Adam, Highland, IN

1 19-oz (540-ml) can black beans, drained and rinsed
1 12-oz (341-ml) can corn niblets, drained
⅓ cup lime juice *or* **juice of one lime**
⅓ cup oil (e.g. olive, flax, hemp)
¼ small red onion, minced
2 - 3 green onions, minced
⅛ cup cilantro, minced
1½ tsp ground cumin
1 large tomato, chopped
¼ tsp salt
¼ tsp ground black pepper

In a large bowl, combine all ingredients and refrigerate for at least 1 hour before serving. Makes 4-6 servings.

, I own your first two cookbooks and I am very excited for the new one to come out! Today, I'm
the Amazing Pasta Salad from *The Garden of Vegan* to take to my in-laws for dinner. They are very
al Oklahoma meat-and-potatoes folks, but they went nuts over the pasta salad and now they ask me
e it every time I visit. Isn't that great? Your cookbooks show it's possible to use no animal products but
able to create a delicious, healthy meal. Thanks for being an inspiration! Here is a quick and easy recipe
d like to share with you. – Sara, Norman, OK

1 19-oz (540-ml) can black beans, drained and rinsed
1 12-oz (341-ml) can corn niblets, drained
1 small red bell pepper, diced
1 small green bell pepper, diced
1 small red onion, diced
1 tsp ground cumin
1 tbsp oil (e.g. olive, flax, hemp)
2 tbsp balsamic vinegar
¼ tsp salt

n a large bowl, combine all ingredients and refrigerate for at least 1 hour before serving. Makes 4-6 servings.

QUINOA BLACK BEAN SALA

Quinoa cooks in about the same amount of time and manner as white basmati rice minutes) and like rice, it needs to be washed and rinsed before cooking. Quinoa is ve when combined with black beans make a perfect protein. Ooh la la.

Dressing:
1 tbsp olive oil
2 tbsp oil (e.g. flax, hemp, grapeseed)
2 tbsp balsamic vinegar
¼ tsp chili powder
¼ tsp salt
¼ tsp ground black pepper

Salad:
¼ cup quinoa, washed and rinsed
1 19-oz (540-ml) can black beans, rinsed
2 green onions, minced
1 large tomato, chopped
1 large celery stalk, chopped
¼ small green bell pepper, chopped
1 small avocado, cubed
¼ cup cilantro, finely chopped
¼ cup frozen corn niblets

In a small pot of water, cook the quinoa accordingly. While quinoa is cooking, in a large bowl, stir together the black beans, onions, tomatoes, celery, green peppers, avocado, and cilantro. Set aside. In a small bowl, stir together the oils, vinegar, chili powder, salt, and pepper. Set aside. Once quinoa is done, remove from heat and stir in the corn. Let sit, covered, for 5 minutes. Remove lid and let quinoa cool. Add quinoa and dressing to salad and toss together well. Refrigerate for at least 1 hour before serving. Makes 2 large or 4 small servings.

BABY SPINACH & APPLE SALAD WITH SWEET RED WINE VINAIGRETTE

"I'm strong to the finich, 'cuz I eats my spinach!" Popeye was right! Raw spinach is an excellent source of Vitamin C and is also rich in iron, calcium, potassium, and Vitamins A and B. Now if we could just get Olive Oyl to eat a little something. . . .

Dressing:
1½ tbsp apple cider vinegar
1½ tbsp red wine vinegar
½ tbsp sweetener (e.g. sugar, maple syrup)
2 tbsp olive oil
2 tbsp oil (e.g. flax, hemp, grapeseed)
⅛ tsp paprika

Salad:
4 cups baby spinach, tightly packed
½ cup raisins
1 large apple, finely sliced
¼ cup pine nuts, toasted (pg 295)

To prepare dressing: In a jar or dressing bottle, combine all ingredients. Cap and shake well. To prepare salad: Separate spinach into bowl(s). Garnish with raisins, apples, and pine nuts. Drizzle with vinaigrette just before serving. Makes 2 large or 4 small servings. Dressing makes approx. ¾ cup.

WOLFFIE'S SPINACH-WALNUT SALAD WITH RASPBERRY VINAIGRETTE

Wolffie's Raspberry vinaigrette is to *die* for. You'll need a mesh strainer, but they're easy to find. You can pick them up at any kitchen store or dollar store for a few bucks.

Dressing:
1 cup unsweetened frozen raspberries
3 tbsp sugar
2 tbsp olive oil
1 tbsp flax oil (*or* **hemp, grapeseed, etc.)**
1 tbsp red wine vinegar
½ tsp tamari

Salad:
4 cups baby spinach, tightly packed
1 small red onion, finely chopped
½ cup walnuts, chopped and toasted (pg 295)

In a medium saucepan, bring raspberries and sugar to a boil, stirring constantly. Boil for 1-2 minutes and remove from heat. Place a fine mesh strainer over a small bowl and strain the raspberry mixture, discarding the seeds. Add the oils, vinegar, and tamari; stir together well and refrigerate before serving. Prepare spinach and place into bowl(s). Garnish with onions and walnuts. Drizzle salad with vinaigrette. Salad makes 2 large or 4 small servings. Dressing makes approx. ½ cup.

BABY SPINACH SALAD WITH STRAWBERRY VINAIGRETTE

This quick and easy salad first appeared in *Herbivore* Magazine *(herbivoremagazine.com)* back in the spring of 2004. It is packed full of iron, vitamins A and C, and even Vitamin K – which is important for maintaining healthy bones.

Dressing:
¼ **cup olive oil**
¼ **cup oil (e.g. flax, hemp, grapeseed)**
⅓ **cup rice vinegar** *or* **apple cider vinegar**
4 - 6 strawberries (depending on size), tops removed
1 tsp Dijon mustard
⅛ **tsp salt**
¼ **tsp ground black pepper**

Salad:
¼ **cup pine nuts, toasted (pg 295)**
8 cups baby spinach leaves, tightly packed
6 - 8 strawberries, tops removed and thinly sliced

To prepare dressing: In a blender or food processor, combine all the ingredients until smooth and creamy. To prepare salad: Separate spinach into bowl(s). Garnish with strawberries and pine nuts. Drizzle with vinaigrette just before serving. Makes 2 large or 4 small servings. Vinaigrette makes approx. 1 cup.

COLD COCONUT CURRIED NOODLE SALAD

This cold noodle salad is perfect for hot summer days. If you want to add a little more weight to this recipe, throw in ¼ lb of firm cubed tofu when you add the basil and tomatoes.

> **dry broad rice noodles, enough for 2 large servings**
> **¼ cup shallots, minced**
> **2 cloves garlic, minced**
> **1 tbsp dark sesame oil**
> **2 tbsp curry paste (you decide the heat)**
> **2 tbsp tamari**
> **½ tsp turmeric**
> **1 tsp salt**
> **1 13.5-oz (400-ml) can coconut milk**
> **½ cup fresh basil, roughly chopped**
> **1 large tomato, chopped**

In a large pot of salted water, boil the rice noodles. While noodles are cooking, in a large saucepan, sauté the shallots and garlic in oil, until shallots are translucent. Add the curry paste, tamari, turmeric, salt, and coconut milk and simmer on medium-high for 6-8 minutes. Remove from heat, stir in basil and tomatoes, and set aside. Drain noodles and rinse under cold water until cooled. Return noodles to pot, add the sauce, and toss together well. Chill well before serving. Makes 2 large or 4 small servings.

NOODLE SALAD WITH SPICY NUT DRESSING

I love to use rice noodles in this chilled salad, but you can use your favorite noodles. I am intolerant of peanuts, so I use almond butter and chopped dry roasted almonds as a garnish, but you can use peanuts if you want an authentic Thai flavor. Sui choy (sometimes called napa cabbage) is available at most grocery stores or Asian markets.

dry rice noodles or noodles of your choice (enough for 2 people)

Dressing:
3 tbsp nut butter
2 tbsp vegetable stock *or* **water**
1½ tbsp rice vinegar
1½ tbsp tamari
½ tbsp dark sesame oil
2 tsp sugar
¼ tsp cayenne pepper
1 inch fresh ginger, finely grated

Salad:
1 small red *or* **yellow bell pepper, finely chopped**
1½ cups sui choy, finely chopped
⅛ cup fresh cilantro, minced
¼ cup toasted nuts (pg 295), your choice, roughly chopped

In a large pot of salted water, boil the pasta. While pasta is cooking, in a small bowl, whisk together the nut butter, stock, rice vinegar, tamari, sesame oil, sugar, cayenne, and ginger. Set aside. Drain pasta, rinse with cold water until cooled, and transfer to a medium bowl. Add the red peppers, sui choy, cilantro, and dressing. Toss together well and garnish with nuts. Serve chilled. Makes 2 large or 4 small servings.

WOLFFIE'S PASTA SALAD

This pasta salad is perfect for any time of the year, but especially in the summer when you can use fresh basil for the dressing or use 1 teaspoon dry basil if you don't have any fresh on hand.

Dressing:

1 tbsp balsamic vinegar
1 tbsp red wine vinegar
¼ cup rice vinegar
2 tbsp maple syrup
2 tbsp water
1 tbsp oil (e.g. flax, olive, hemp)
1 tbsp fresh basil
½ tsp salt
⅛ tsp ground black pepper
2 tbsp vegan "Parmesan cheese" (optional)

Salad:

3 cups corkscrew pasta, uncooked
¼ cup pitted black olives, sliced
2 tbsp pitted green olives, sliced
1 medium tomato, finely chopped
½ small red onion, finely chopped
2 tbsp fresh parsley, minced

In a large pot of salted water, boil the pasta. While pasta is cooking, in a medium bowl, combine remaining salad ingredients. To prepare dressing: In a jar or dressing bottle combine all ingredients. Cap and shake well before using. To prepare salad: Drain noodles and rinse under cold water until cooled. In a large bowl, combine salad ingredients, pasta, and dressing and toss together well. Refrigerate for at least 1 hour before serving. Makes 2 large or 4 small servings. Dressing makes approx. ¾ cup.

COOL CUCUMBER SALAD

A lovely light salad that goes perfectly with the Vegetable Biryani recipe on pg 150.

1 large English cucumber, chopped	1 tbsp lemon juice
1 large tomato, finely chopped	1 tsp maple syrup
1 tsp fresh mint, minced	½ inch fresh ginger, finely grated
¼ cup soy yogurt	½ tsp ground cumin
1 tbsp apple cider vinegar	½ tsp ground coriander
1 tbsp oil (e.g. olive, flax, hemp)	⅛ tsp ground black pepper

In a medium bowl, combine cucumbers, tomatoes, and mint. Set aside. In a jar or dressing bottle, combine the remaining ingredients. Cap and shake well, until smooth. Drizzle dressing over salad just before serving and toss well. Makes 2 large or 4 small servings. Dressing makes approx. ¾ of a cup.

EDAMAME & ASPARAGUS COUSCOUS SALAD

I'm koo-koo for couscous!

1 cup vegetable stock
1 cup couscous
¼ cup shallots, finely chopped
1 small red onion, chopped
1 tbsp olive oil
8 large asparagus spears, ends removed and cut into thirds
2 tbsp balsamic vinegar
1 tsp tamari
1 tsp maple syrup
1 cup edamame beans (pre-shucked)

In a small pot on high heat, bring the stock to a boil. Remove from heat and stir in couscous; cover with lid and let sit for 10 minutes. In a large saucepan on medium-high heat, sauté the shallots and onions in oil until onions become translucent. Add the asparagus and sauté for 4-6 minutes, or until asparagus can be pierced easily with a fork. Turn off heat. Stir in the vinegar, tamari, maple syrup, and edamame and let sit covered for 5 minutes. In a medium bowl, toss the couscous and vegetables together and refrigerate for at least 1 hour before serving. Makes 2 large or 4 small servings.

RED BEAN COLESLAW

Sarah: Here's a great slaw recipe. My omni friends love this. – Wolffie, Davie, FL

Dressing:
¾ cup vegan "mayonnaise" (pg 293)
¼ cup red wine vinegar
1 tbsp sugar
1 tbsp fresh parsley, minced
1 tsp dried oregano
½ tsp salt
¼ tsp ground black pepper

Salad:
3 cups cabbage, finely chopped
1 small red onion, finely chopped
1 large celery stalk, sliced
1 19-oz (540-ml) can kidney beans, drained and rinsed
¼ cup imitation "bacon" bits

To prepare dressing: In a jar or dressing bottle, combine all ingredients. Cap and shake well before using. To prepare salad: In a medium bowl, combine all ingredients, add dressing, toss well, and refrigerate for at least 1 hour before serving. Salad makes 4-6 servings. Dressing makes approx. 1 cup.

FLORIDA SLAW

Here's another knockout salad from Wolffie. Board up your windows cuz a hurricane of cabbage is coming your way!

1 8-oz (227-ml) can pineapple tidbits, drained – reserving liquid

Dressing:
½ cup reserved pineapple juice
1 tbsp cornstarch
3 tbsp sugar
¾ cup "sour cream" (pg 293)
1 tbsp lemon juice
½ tsp salt

Salad:
4 cups cabbage, finely chopped
1 banana, sliced
1 cup mandarin orange segments
1 cup unsweetened coconut
1 cup walnuts, finely chopped
1 cup raisins
1 cup vegan marshmallows (pg 290), finely chopped (optional)

Drain the canned pineapple, reserving the juice for the dressing. Set pineapple aside. To prepare dressing: In a small saucepan, combine the pineapple juice, cornstarch, and sugar. Bring to a boil, reduce heat and simmer, stirring constantly until thickened. Remove from heat and cool completely. When cooled, stir in "sour cream," lemon juice, and salt. Refrigerate until needed. To prepare salad: In a large bowl, toss together the pineapple, cabbage, banana, orange segments, coconut, walnuts, raisins, and dressing. Toss together well. Stir in marshmallows just before serving. Makes 4-6 servings.

CREAMY TROPICAL FRUIT SALAD

Sarah, this is a great fruit salad. I love it . . . but I love anything with mayonnaise in it, so what do I know? Hahaha! – Wolffie, Davie, FL *(It's also perfect for those lazy summer nights when fruit is plentiful, you're wearing a hula skirt, and you can't find your coconut bra!)*

1 8-oz (227-ml) can pineapple tidbits, drained – reserving liquid

Dressing:
¼ cup reserved pineapple juice
2 tbsp vegan margarine
2 tbsp sugar
½ tbsp lemon juice
1 tbsp cornstarch
1 tbsp water
½ cup vegan "mayonnaise" (pg 293)

Salad:
2 large apples, chopped
½ cup green grapes, halved
½ cup red grapes, halved
2 bananas, sliced
1 kiwi fruit, sliced
4 - 6 large strawberries, chopped
½ cup mandarin orange segments
⅓ cup pecans, finely chopped
½ cup vegan marshmallows (pg 290), finely chopped (optional)

Drain the canned pineapple, reserving the juice for the dressing. Set pineapple aside. To prepare dressing: In a small saucepan, combine the pineapple juice, margarine, sugar, lemon juice, cornstarch, and water. Bring to a boil, reduce heat, and simmer, stirring until thickened. Remove from heat and cool completely. When cooled, stir in "mayonnaise." Refrigerate until needed. To prepare salad: In a large bowl, combine the pineapple, apple, grapes, banana, kiwi, strawberries, oranges, pecans, and dressing. Toss together well. Stir in marshmallows just before serving. Makes 4-6 servings.

WOLFFIE'S "PEPPERONI" PASTA SALAD

Yet another fabu recipe from Wolffie. I like to use garlic stuffed green olives in this recipe instead of black olives. Experiment. It's fun . . . and oh yeah – Wolffie rocks!

Dressing:
1 tbsp oil (e.g. flax, hemp, grapeseed)
2 tbsp olive oil
1½ tbsp red wine vinegar
½ tsp salt
½ tsp dried basil
½ tsp dried oregano
⅛ tsp garlic powder

Salad:
2 cups small pasta shells, uncooked
8 - 10 cherry tomatoes, halved
½ cup black olives, sliced
¼ cup vegan "pepperoni," thinly sliced
¼ small green bell pepper, chopped
2 green onions, minced

In a large pot of salted water, boil the pasta. While pasta is cooking, in a large bowl, combine remaining salad ingredients. To prepare dressing: In a jar or dressing bottle, combine all ingredients. Cap and shake well before using. To prepare salad: Drain pasta, rinse under cold water until cooled. Add pasta and dressing to other ingredients and toss together well. Refrigerate for at least 1 hour before serving. Makes 2 large or 4 small servings.

PERFECT PESTO POTATO SALAD

This salad recipe cuts Tyler & Phoebe's Perfect Pesto Sauce (pg 177) recipe in half to make the perfect potato salad. If you want, you can replace the sun-dried tomatoes with cherry tomatoes cut in half. No matter how you cut it . . . it doesn't get any better than this.

Salad:

2 lbs new potatoes, quartered
½ lb green beans, cut into 1-inch pieces
4 - 6 sun-dried tomatoes, finely chopped
2 tbsp balsamic vinegar

Pesto Sauce:

1½ cups fresh basil
¼ cup pine nuts, toasted (pg 295)
2 garlic cloves
¼ tsp salt
¼ tsp ground black pepper
¼ cup oil (e.g. olive, flax, hemp)

In a large pot of salted water, boil the potatoes until they can be pierced easily with a fork. Drain, rinse under cold water; set aside to cool. To prepare pesto sauce: In a food processor or blender, combine the basil, pine nuts, garlic, salt, and pepper. Slowly add the oil while processing, until well mixed. To prepare salad: In a medium bowl, combine the cooled potatoes, green beans, sun-dried tomatoes, vinegar, and pesto sauce. Toss gently and serve chilled. Makes 4 servings. Pesto makes approx. ½ cup.

VEGAN GERMAN POTATO SALAD

You may already have your own favorite potato salad, but I've had a hard time finding a vegan German potato salad I like. Here's mine. – Greg, Seattle, WA

1½ lb potatoes, cubed
3 - 4 slices vegan "bacon," chopped
1 small onion, minced
1 large celery stalk, chopped
1 tbsp olive oil
1 tbsp flour

2 tsp sugar
½ tsp salt
⅛ tsp ground black pepper
½ cup water
2 tbsp vinegar

In a large pot of salted water, boil the potatoes until they can be pierced easily with a fork. Drain potatoes and rinse under cold water; set aside to cool. While potatoes are cooking, in a medium saucepan on medium-high heat, sauté the "bacon", onions, and celery in oil until onions are translucent. Add the flour, sugar, salt, and pepper; stir constantly until thickened. Immediately whisk in water and vinegar, stirring constantly until sauce starts to thicken. Pour contents into medium bowl and add the cooled potatoes, tossing together gently. Serve warm or at room temperature. Makes 2 large or 4 small servings.

SPICED POTATO SALAD

Ahh, the mighty potato. So versatile. So yummy. So good!

1½ lb potatoes, diced
1 tsp mustard seeds
2 tsp cumin seeds
2 garlic cloves, minced
1 medium jalapeno pepper, seeded and minced
2 tbsp olive oil
¼ cup fresh cilantro, chopped
1 tsp ground coriander
¼ tsp salt
2 tbsp vegan "mayonnaise" (pg 293)
splash of lime juice (optional)

In a large pot of salted water, boil the potatoes until they can be pierced easily with a fork. Drain potatoes and rinse under cold water; set aside to cool. While potatoes are cooking, in a medium saucepan on medium heat, sauté the mustard seeds, cumin seeds, garlic, and jalapeno in oil until mustard seeds start to pop and crackle. Add the cilantro, coriander, and salt and sauté for an additional minute; stir often to avoid burning. In a medium bowl, add the "mayonnaise" and lime juice, toss all ingredients together, and refrigerate for at least 1 hour before serving. Makes 2 large or 4 small servings.

ROASTED ASPARAGUS POTATO SALAD

Chilled potato salad on a hot summer day, with a glass of something cold and bubbly. Ahhhh – life is good, don't ever forget that!

1 lb new potatoes, quartered
8 large asparagus spears, ends removed and cut into thirds
1 small red onion, finely chopped
1 tbsp olive oil
¼ tsp salt
¼ tsp pepper
2 tbsp red wine vinegar
2 tbsp oil (e.g. flax, hemp, olive)
¼ cup fresh chives, finely chopped

Preheat oven to 450°F (230°C). In a large pot, boil the potatoes until they can be pierced easily with a fork. Drain potatoes and rinse under cold water; set aside to cool. While potatoes are boiling, in an 8x8 baking dish, combine the asparagus, onions, oil, salt, and pepper. Bake for 12-15 minutes. In a medium bowl, place cooled potatoes. Add the cooked vegetables, red wine vinegar, oil, and chives. Toss together gently and refrigerate for at least 1 hour before serving. Makes 2 large or 4 small servings.

LEFTOVER TACO SALAD

This is a fast and delicious meal when you're in a hurry or you don't feel like cooking. – Wolffie, Davie, FL
(What to do with all that leftover chili (pg 163 or 164)? Make a taco salad. Genius!)

2 cups chili (pg 163, 164)
4 cups Romaine lettuce, finely chopped
¼ cup oil & vinegar dressing (pg 94-99) of your choice
1 large tomato, chopped
4 green onions, minced
1 - 2 cups tortilla chips, crushed

In a small saucepan on medium heat, warm up the chili. On each plate, evenly distribute lettuce, drizzle with salad dressing, and add hot chili. Top with tomatoes, onions, and tortilla chips. Makes 2 large or 4 small servings.

DRESSINGS

For me, making salad dressing is like exercising. I hate to do it and can always think of an excuse to get out of it . . . but as with most things, once you do it, you're glad that you did!

CREAMY BASIL DRESSING

The smell of fresh basil is like an aphrodisiac to me. Lay me down in a bed of roses? I don't think so, Jon Bon Jovi. Lay me down in a bed of basil . . . and we'll talk.

> ½ **cup soft or silken tofu**
> 3 **tbsp oil (e.g. flax, olive, hemp)**
> ¼ **cup fresh basil**
> 2 **tsp tamari**
> 1 **tsp rice vinegar**
> ¼ **tsp salt**
> ¼ **tsp sugar**

With a hand blender or in a food processor, blend all the ingredients until smooth and creamy. Makes approx. ¾ cup.

CREAMY FIESTA DRESSING

Originally from Wolffies's Fiesta Macaroni Bean Salad (pg 73), this creamy, tasty dressing is also great as a veggie dip or over a nice green salad.

> ¾ **cups vegan "mayonnaise" (pg 293)**
> 2 **tbsp fresh parsley, minced**
> 1 **tbsp red wine vinegar**
> 1 **tbsp sugar**
> 1 **tsp dried basil**
> ½ **tsp celery seed**
> ½ **tsp paprika**
> ½ **tsp salt**
> ¼ **tsp ground black pepper**
> ¼ **tsp garlic powder**

In a jar or dressing bottle, combine all ingredients. Cap and shake well before using. Makes approx. 1 cup.

FRENCH DRESSING

Bonjour, mes amis!

> **1 tbsp sugar**
> **1 tsp paprika**
> **1 tsp dry mustard**
> **½ tsp salt**
> **¼ tsp ground black pepper**
> **½ cup oil (e.g. flax, olive, hemp)**
> **¼ cup rice vinegar (*or* apple cider vinegar)**

In a jar or dressing bottle, combine all ingredients. Cap and shake well before using. Makes approx. ¾ cup.

TERESA'S DRESSING

This is it – my famous dressing. Creamy and garlicky gingery. – Teresa, Toronto, ON

> **2 tbsp olive oil**
> **2 tbsp oil (e.g. flax, hemp, grapeseed)**
> **1 tbsp dark sesame oil**
> **2 tbsp rice vinegar (*or* apple cider vinegar)**
> **2 tbsp tahini**
> **1 tbsp maple syrup**
> **1 tsp tamari**
> **1 - 3 garlic cloves, minced**
> **1½ inches fresh ginger, finely grated**
> **¼ tsp salt**
> **¼ tsp ground black pepper**

With a hand blender or in a food processor, blend all the ingredients until smooth and creamy. Makes approx. ¾ cup.

CAESAR SALAD DRESSING

Blanched almonds have had their thin husks removed by soaking them in boiled water and removing the husks by hand. You can certainly make them yourself . . . but who wants to go to all that work? They are available in just about every grocery store. As for the dressing, you can't go wrong with a classic. Serve over some freshly chopped Romaine lettuce.

40 blanched almonds
3 large garlic cloves
1 tbsp nutritional yeast
2 tbsp tamari
3 tbsp lemon juice
1 tbsp Dijon mustard
¼ cup water
1 tbsp oil (e.g. olive, flax, hemp)

With a hand blender or in a food processor, blend all the ingredients until smooth and creamy. Makes approx. 1 cup.

CREAMY COLESLAW DRESSING

This wonderful, thick dressing is a treat when used in the Red Bean Coleslaw (pg 84), as a veggie dip, or over a crunchy green salad.

¾ cup vegan "mayonnaise" (pg 293)
¼ cup red wine vinegar
1 tbsp sugar
1 tbsp fresh parsley, minced
1 tsp dried oregano
½ tsp salt
¼ tsp ground black pepper

In a jar or dressing bottle, combine all ingredients. Cap and shake well before using. Makes approx. 1 cup.

CREAMY SOYGURT DRESSING

If you can find soy yogurt in a market near you, then this recipe is for you. It adds just the right amount of tang to this creamy dressing. This recipe is also included with the Cool Cucumber Salad on pg 83.

¼ cup soy yogurt
1 tbsp apple cider vinegar
1 tbsp oil (e.g. flax, olive, hemp)
1 tbsp lemon juice
1 tsp maple syrup
½ inch fresh ginger, finely grated
½ tsp ground cumin
½ tsp ground coriander
⅛ tsp ground black pepper

In a jar or dressing bottle, combine all ingredients. Cap and shake well before using. Makes approx. ¾ cup.

DIJON RED WINE VINAIGRETTE

Simple and classic.

¼ cup red wine vinegar
½ cup oil (e.g. flax, olive, hemp)
1 garlic clove, minced
1 tbsp Dijon mustard
½ tsp salt
⅛ tsp ground black pepper

In a jar or dressing bottle, combine all ingredients. Cap and shake well before using. Makes approx. ¾ cup.

FRESH BASIL & TOMATO VINAIGRETTE

Oh, Basil! You're so fine. You're so fine, you blow my mind.

1 cup fresh basil leaves, packed tightly
1 medium tomato, roughly chopped
¼ cup olive oil
¼ cup oil (e.g. flax, hemp)
1 tbsp lemon juice
1 tbsp red wine vinegar
1 tbsp Dijon mustard

With a hand blender or in a food processor, blend all the ingredients until smooth and creamy. Makes approx. 1 cup.

WOLFFIE'S BALSAMIC VINEGAR DRESSING

Balsamic vinegar is very dark in color, has a sweet, fruity flavor, and can be found in most grocery stores or specialty kitchen shops.

2 tbsp balsamic vinegar
2 tbsp red wine vinegar
3 tbsp maple syrup
¼ cup olive oil
¼ cup oil (e.g. flax, hemp, grapeseed)
1 garlic clove, minced
½ tsp salt
¼ tsp ground black pepper

In a jar or dressing bottle, combine all ingredients. Cap and shake well before using. Makes approx. 1 cup.

QUICH MAPLE GINGER DRESSING

This dressing is perfect when you're pressed for time.

> **1 garlic clove, minced**
> **2 inches fresh ginger, finely grated**
> **¼ cup rice vinegar**
> **2 tbsp dark sesame oil**
> **2 tbsp oil (e.g. flax, olive, hemp)**
> **2 tbsp tamari**
> **1 tbsp maple syrup**
> **1 tbsp sesame seeds, toasted (pg 295)**

In a jar or dressing bottle, combine all ingredients. Cap and shake well before using. Makes approx. ¾ cup.

SESAME MISO VINAIGRETTE

If you'd like to add a little sweet, peppery heat, add some fresh finely grated ginger.

> **3 tbsp water**
> **3 tbsp flax oil**
> **2 tbsp rice vinegar**
> **2 tbsp miso**
> **1 tbsp sugar or maple syrup**
> **1 tbsp tahini**

In a jar or dressing bottle, combine all ingredients. Cap and shake well before using. Makes approx. ¾ cup.

WOLFFIE'S DIJON MAPLE DRESSING

Sweet Jeebus! Shirley wows me again with another rock 'em, sock 'em recipe.

¼ **cup olive oil**
¼ **cup flax oil (*or* hemp, grapeseed, etc.)**
¼ **cup red wine vinegar**
⅓ **cup maple syrup**
1 **tsp paprika**
1 **tsp celery seed**
⅛ **tsp salt**
1 **tsp Dijon mustard**

In a jar or dressing bottle, combine all ingredients. Cap and shake well before using. Makes approx. 1 cup.

STRAWBERRY VINAIGRETTE

Fresh and fruity. This vinaigrette perfectly complements the Baby Spinach Salad on pg 79.

¼ **cup olive oil**
¼ **cup oil (e.g. flax, hemp, grapeseed)**
⅓ **cup rice wine vinegar**
4 - 6 **strawberries, fresh or frozen**
1 **tsp Dijon mustard**
⅛ **tsp salt**
¼ **tsp ground black pepper**

With a hand blender or in a food processor, blend all the ingredients until smooth and creamy. Makes approx. 1 cup.

SWEET BASIL DRESSING

Use this dressing for Wolffie's "Pepperoni" Pasta Salad (pg 87) or over fresh greens. If fresh basil is in season, then use approximately 1 tablespoon fresh, minced basil instead of dried.

1 tbsp balsamic vinegar
1 tbsp red wine vinegar
¼ cup rice vinegar
2 tbsp maple syrup
2 tbsp water
1 tbsp oil (e.g. flax, olive, hemp)
1 tsp dried basil
½ tsp salt
⅛ tsp black pepper
2 tbsp vegan "Parmesan cheese" (optional)

In a jar or dressing bottle, combine all ingredients. Cap and shake well before using. Makes approx. ¾ cup.

SWEET RED WINE VINAIGRETTE

The best and most beautiful things in the world cannot be seen or even touched – they must be felt with the tongue.

3 tbsp apple cider vinegar
3 tbsp red wine vinegar
¼ tsp paprika
1 tbsp sweetener (e.g. sugar, maple syrup)
¼ cup oil (e.g. flax, hemp, grapeseed)
¼ cup olive oil

In a jar or dressing bottle, combine all ingredients. Cap and shake well before using.
Makes approx. ¾ cup.

WOLFFIE'S DELICIOUS DRESSING

This recipe goes with Wolffie's Black Bean and Lentil Salad (pg 72), but is so tasty in its own right that I recommend you try it with a nice crunchy bed of greens. It's yum.

- ¼ **cup olive oil**
- ¼ **cup oil (e.g. flax, hemp, grapeseed)**
- ¼ **cup red wine vinegar**
- ½ **tbsp Dijon mustard**
- ¾ **tsp ground cumin**
- **1 garlic clove, minced**
- ¼ **tsp salt**
- ¼ **tsp ground black pepper**
- **1 tsp sugar**

In a jar or dressing bottle, combine all ingredients. Cap and shake well before using. Makes approx. ¾ cup.

Soups

We worship soup in the Kramer house. Soup is usually regarded as an appetizer, but often our meals feature soup as the main course.

Soup can satisfy on so many levels. It fullfills your body's appetite for vibrant colors and luscious flavors by blending the perfect amount of spices and vegetables, all the while providing you with warmth and nourishment.

There's an old Spanish saying: "Between soup and love, the first is better." I'm down with that.

FRENCHIE ONION SOUP

The only man a girl can depend on is her daddy. – Frenchie

> **1 tbsp vegan margarine** *or* **olive oil**
> **4 medium onions, chopped**
> **1 clove garlic, minced**
> **2 tsp sugar**
> **½ tsp salt**
> **¼ tsp ground black pepper**
> **2½ cups vegetable stock**
> **2 slices bread (e.g. Easy French Bread, pg 269)**
> **½ cup vegan "cheese," grated**

In a medium soup pot on medium heat, sauté the onions in margarine until the onions are translucent. Add the garlic, sugar, salt, and pepper and sauté for an additional 5-7 minutes; stir often to avoid sticking. Add the vegetable stock, then bring to a boil and reduce heat. Simmer for 8-10 minutes. Place each slice of bread into a separate "oven-proof" bowl. Pour soup over top of bread. Sprinkle each bowl with grated "cheese" and place bowls onto a baking sheet in the oven. Set your oven to broil and remove bowls when the "cheese" has melted. Watch carefully to make sure it does not burn. Serve. Makes 2 large or 4 small servings.

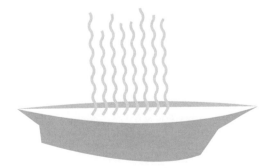

JESSICA'S CURE WHAT AILS YA GARLIC SOUP

Hi Sarah, Here's a recipe I adapted. If you're feeling under the weather, it kills any flu bug that might be buzzing around. – Jessica, Guerneville, CA *(Stinky breath alert! Do not eat before a date. Serve with a nice thick piece of crunchy bread and a fresh green salad.)*

1 small onion, chopped
1 head garlic, minced (approx 4 tbsp)
3 large button mushrooms, finely chopped
1 tbsp olive oil
2 cups vegetable stock
2 tsp tamari
2 tsp miso paste
½ cup "milk"

In a medium soup pot on medium heat, sauté the onions, garlic, and mushrooms in oil until the onions are translucent. Add the stock, then bring to a boil, and reduce heat. In a small bowl, stir together the tamari and miso paste and 2 tablespoons of the hot soup stock as prepared above. Stir until miso is smooth. Add the miso and "milk" to soup. Reheat and serve. Makes 2 large or 4 small servings.

SOBA NOODLE MISO SOUP

Miso can be found in Japanese markets and health food stores and come in a wide variety of flavors, some earthier and nuttier than others. But you really can't go wrong with whichever one you choose; they're all delicious and extremely nutritious – with rich amounts of B vitamins and protein. (Cooking miso will destroy its healthy attributes, so avoid boiling your miso by stirring it into your dish the last few minutes before serving.)

4 cups water
½ sheet nori (seaweed),
   cut *or* torn into small pieces
2 tbsp tamari
1 cup soba noodles

½ block firm or extra firm tofu, cubed
2 cups bok choy, chopped
3 tbsp miso
1 tbsp water
gomashio (garnish) (pg 305)

In a medium soup pot on high heat, bring water to a boil. Add the seaweed and tamari. Remove from heat and let sit 15 minutes. While soup stock is steeping, bring a medium pot of salted water to a boil and cook the soba noodles. Once done, drain, rinse well, and add to soup stock. Add tofu and bok choy and return to heat for 2-3 minutes. In a small bowl, stir together the miso and 3 tablespoons of hot soup stock as prepared above. Stir until miso is smooth. Add miso to the soup, stir well, and serve immediately, garnished with gomashio. Makes 2 large or 4 small servings.

QUICH MISO SOUP FOR ONE

This is one of my favorite recipes to make when I'm feeling under the weather. It's fast, doesn't take much preparation, and will chase the sniffles away. (Cooking miso will destroy its healthy attributes, so avoid boiling your miso by stirring it into your dish in the last few minutes before serving.)

2 cups water
1 clove garlic, peeled and slightly crushed
1 inch piece of ginger, roughly chopped
2 tbsp miso
¼ cup firm or extra firm tofu, cubed
1 small carrot, grated *or* minced
¼ cup green veggies, your choice (e.g. bok choy, baby spinach, peas, kale), chopped

In a medium soup pot on high heat, bring water to a boil. Reduce heat and add the garlic and ginger. Cover with lid and let simmer for 6-8 minutes. Remove garlic and ginger with a slotted spoon and turn off heat. In a small bowl, stir together the miso and 3 tablespoons of the hot soup stock as prepared above. Stir until miso is smooth. Add the miso, tofu, carrots, and green veggies. Cover with a lid and let sit for 3-5 minutes before serving.Makes 1 large serving.

SEAWEED SOUP

Seaweed is high in protein, calcium, and other minerals. This is one of those lickety-split soup recipes that I love to serve in a shallow bowl with some rice crackers.

1 sheet nori seaweed
2½ cups vegetable stock
1 7-oz (200-g) pkg of fresh udon noodles
1 tbsp tamari
splash of lime juice
1 stalk green onion, minced
gomashio (pg 305)

Cut nori sheets into small strips and place into a small soup pot. Add the stock, noodles, and tamari and bring to a boil on stove. Reduce heat and let simmer for 4-6 minutes. Stir in lime juice and green onions. Serve immediately, garnished with gomashio. Makes 2 servings.

HOT & SOUR SOUP

Is it hot? Is it sour? It's both!!

2 cups vegetable stock
1 cup water
1½ tbsp tamari
1 inch fresh ginger, finely grated
1 clove garlic, minced
1 tsp sugar
½ - 1 tsp garlic Asian chili sauce
1 small carrot, grated
½ cup oyster mushrooms, roughly chopped
2 tbsp rice vinegar
¼ lb firm or extra firm tofu, cubed
⅓ cup frozen peas

In a medium soup pot on high heat, bring stock and water to a boil. Reduce heat and add the tamari, ginger, garlic, sugar, chili sauce, carrots, and mushrooms. Simmer for 8-10 minutes. Turn off heat; add the vinegar, tofu, and peas. Cover with lid and let sit for 3-5 minutes before serving. Makes 2 large or 4 small servings.

ON GOLDEN POND MUSHROOM SOUP

Since my partner and I have temporarily moved in with my dad and his wife, I have taken on the somewhat daunting task of feeding four adults – two vegans and two carnies. In the last few weeks I have baked and cooked my way through *The Garden of Vegan* and am quickly running out of synonyms for "delicious"! It has been such a joy to serve food that people love. Since your cookbooks are the only ones that offer a winner every time, I must say that everyone in the Mercer household is a true fan of yours and more than that, I am a dedicated one. I hope you enjoy my recipe for mushroom soup that I veganized from a friend of a friend's cousin. It's a big hit around here. – Krishna Mercer, St. John's, NF

1 small onion, chopped
8 - 10 large white mushrooms, chopped
2 tbsp olive oil
2 tbsp tamari
1 - 3 tsp paprika
1 tsp dried dill
½ tsp salt
½ tsp black pepper
2 tbsp flour
1 cup vegetable stock
1½ cups "milk"

In a medium soup pot on medium heat, sauté the onions and mushrooms in oil until the onions are translucent. Add the tamari, paprika, dill, salt, and pepper, and sauté for an additional 5 minutes; stir often to avoid sticking. Stir in the flour to create a mushroom paste. Slowly add the stock ½ cup at a time, stirring often as it thickens. Add the "milk" and let simmer for 8-10 minutes before serving. Makes 2 large or 4 small servings.

RAUNCHY RED LENTIL SOUP

This warm thick soup can be served with basmati rice or served with Chapati Flat Bread (pg 267).

1 large onion, chopped
1 tbsp olive oil
3 cloves garlic, minced
1 jalapeno chili, seeded and minced
3 cups vegetable stock
1 cup dried red lentils

1 tsp turmeric
1½ tsp ground cumin
½ tsp salt
1 inch fresh ginger, finely grated
2 small tomatoes, chopped
¼ cup fresh cilantro, chopped

In a medium soup pot on medium heat, sauté the onions in oil until translucent. Add the garlic and jalapeno, and sauté for an additional 5 minutes. Add the stock, lentils, turmeric, cumin, salt, and ginger. Bring to a boil, then reduce heat. Cover with lid and simmer for 15 minutes or until the lentils are tender. With a hand blender or food processor, blend half or all of the soup until smooth (be careful when blending hot liquids); return to pot and stir in the tomatoes and cilantro. Cover with a lid, remove from heat, and let stand 2-3 minutes before serving. Makes 2 large or 4 small servings.

COCONUT CURRY RED LENTIL SOUP

There is nothing more comforting then a big bowl of thick soup and a fresh green salad. You can find curry paste in most supermarkets or at your local Asian market.

1 small onion, chopped
1 tbsp olive oil
1 garlic clove, minced
1 celery stalk, chopped
1 small yam, cubed
1 small potato, cubed
2 cups vegetable stock
½ cup dried red lentils
1 tbsp curry paste
½ tsp salt
½ tsp ground black pepper
1 14-oz (398-ml) can coconut milk
¼ cup fresh cilantro, minced

In a medium soup pot on medium heat, sauté the onions in oil until translucent. Add the garlic and celery and sauté for an additional 5 minutes. Add the yams, potatoes, stock, lentils, curry paste, salt, and pepper. Bring to a boil, then reduce heat. Simmer for 15-20 minutes or until the potatoes are cooked. Stir in the coconut milk and with a hand blender or food processor, blend half or all of the soup until smooth (be careful when blending hot liquids). Return to pot, stir in the cilantro, and serve. Makes 2 large or 4 small servings.

CAULIFLOWER RED LENTIL SOUP

A gorgeous and hearty soup that is great on its own, or served over rice.

1 medium onion, chopped
1 tbsp olive oil
1 tbsp fresh ginger, grated
4 cloves garlic, minced
1 tsp cumin seeds
½ tsp red pepper flakes
1 tsp ground turmeric
2½ cups vegetable stock
2 cups cauliflower, cut into bite-sized pieces
2 medium tomatoes, chopped
1 cup dried red lentils
¼ cup fresh cilantro, minced
½ tsp salt

In a medium soup pot on medium heat, sauté the onions in oil until translucent. Add the ginger, garlic, cumin, red pepper, and turmeric and sauté for 2 minutes; stir constantly to avoid sticking. Add the stock, cauliflower, tomatoes, and lentils. Bring to a boil, then reduce heat. Cover with lid and simmer for 15-20 minutes or until veggies and lentils are cooked. Stir in the cilantro and salt, remove from heat, and let sit 5 minutes before serving. Makes 2 large or 4 small servings.

CAULIFLOWER POTATO SOUP WITH NUTMEG

How many vegans does it take to screw in a light bulb? Two! One to change the bulb . . . and one to check for animal ingredients.

1 small onion, chopped
1 large carrot, chopped
1 tbsp olive oil
2 cups vegetable stock
1 medium potato, chopped
2 cups cauliflower, cut into bite-sized pieces
½ tsp ground cumin
¼ tsp ground nutmeg
¼ tsp salt
¼ tsp ground black pepper
1 cup "milk"

In a medium soup pot on medium heat, sauté the onions and carrots in oil until the onions are translucent. Add the vegetable stock, potatoes, cauliflower, cumin, nutmeg, salt, and pepper. Bring to a boil, then reduce heat. Simmer for 10-15 minutes, or until the potatoes are cooked. Stir in "milk" and with a hand blender or food processor, blend half or all of the soup until smooth (be careful when blending hot liquids). Return to pot, reheat, and serve. Makes 2 large or 4 small servings.

LEEK & POTATO SOUP WITH CILANTRO

Leeks have a sweeter and more delicate flavor than onions and are a good source of Vitamin C and iron. The garam masala adds such an inviting aroma, you'll wonder why you didn't double this recipe.

2 large leeks, sliced (white and
    pale green parts only)
1 tbsp olive oil
1 celery stalk, chopped
1 large carrot, chopped
2 cloves garlic, minced

2 medium potatoes, cubed
2 cups vegetable stock
1 tsp garam masala (pg 304)
¼ tsp salt
¼ cup fresh cilantro, chopped
½ - 1 cup vegan "cheese" (optional)

In a medium soup pot on medium heat, sauté the leeks in oil until translucent. Add the celery, carrots, and garlic and sauté for 2-3 minutes. Add the potatoes, stock, garam masala, and salt. Bring to a boil, then reduce heat. Cover with lid and simmer for 15-20 minutes, or until the potatoes are cooked. With a hand blender or food processor, blend half or all of the soup until smooth (be careful when blending hot liquids). Return to pot, stir in the cilantro, and serve with ¼ - ½ cup of "cheese" per bowl as a garnish. Makes 2 large or 4 small servings.

SIMPLE LEEK AND POTATO SOUP

I'm a potato and I'm so hip! This satisfying soup is perfect for cold winter days when all you have in your pantry is potatoes. If you don't have any leeks handy and it's too cold to go to the supermarket, replace the leeks with 1 large onion from your pantry.

2 medium leeks, sliced (white and pale green parts only)
1 tbsp olive oil
2 medium potatoes, cubed
2 cups vegetable stock
¼ tsp salt
¼ tsp ground black pepper

In a medium soup pot on medium heat, sauté the leeks in oil until translucent. Add the potatoes and sauté for 2-3 minutes; stir constantly to avoid sticking. Add the stock, salt, and pepper. Bring to a boil, then reduce heat. Simmer for 20-25 minutes, or until the potatoes are cooked. Serve as is, or if you like a creamier soup, using a hand blender or food processor, blend half or all of the soup until smooth (be careful when blending hot liquids). Return to pot, reheat, and serve. Makes 2 large or 4 small servings.

PARSNIP APPLE SOUP

Serve this happy soup with a side of sautéed kale (pg 148) and a nice big glass of water. It's important to stay hydrated.

½ **cup shallots, minced**
1 leek, sliced (white and pale green parts only)
1 tbsp olive oil
1 large parsnip, peeled and chopped
1 large potato, chopped
2 cups vegetable stock
½ **tsp salt**
½ **tsp pepper**
1 cup "milk"
½ **cup apple juice**

In a medium soup pot on medium heat, sauté the shallots and leeks in oil until translucent. Add the parsnips, potatoes, stock, salt, and pepper. Bring to a boil, then reduce heat. Cover with lid and simmer for 15-20 minutes, or until the potatoes are cooked. With a hand blender or food processor, blend half or all of the soup until smooth (be careful when blending hot liquids). Return to pot and stir in the "milk" and juice. Reheat and serve. Makes 2 large or 4 small servings.

MAURY'S ROASTED ROOT SOUP

Dear Sarah darling: I have to pass this along to you as I'm reeling from it. Maury's latest creation is roasting veggies to make soup. It is the creamiest, yummiest . . . wow. I love you. P.S. We still have mice. – Shoshana, *ShoshanaSperling.com*

1 large yam, cubed
4 small parsnips, cubed (approx. 1 cup)
3 new potatoes, cubed (approx. 1 cup)
1 small onion, chopped
3 cloves garlic, minced
2 tsp dried rosemary
2 tbsp grapeseed oil (or olive)
1½ cup vegetable stock
1 cup "milk"
½ tsp salt
½ tsp pepper

Pre-heat oven to 400°F (205°C). In a medium baking dish, stir together the yam, parsnips, potatoes, onions, garlic, rosemary, and oil until well coated. Bake for 25-30 minutes, or until the veggies can be poked easily with a fork. Just before the veggies are ready, in a medium soup pot, bring the stock to a boil. Reduce heat and add the roasted vegetables. Simmer for 2-3 minutes. Add the "milk" and with a hand blender or food processor, blend half or all of the soup until smooth (be careful when blending hot liquids). Return to pot and stir in the salt and pepper. Reheat and serve. Makes 2 large or 4 small servings.

ROASTED CARROT COCONUT SOUP

Roasting vegetables, especially carrots, will bring out their natural sweetness and intensifies their full rich flavor.

5 - 6 large carrots, diced
1 small onion, chopped
1 garlic clove, minced
1 inch fresh ginger, grated
1 stick fresh lemongrass (tough outer layers removed),
   chopped (use bottom 6 inches only)
½ tsp garam masala (pg 304)
½ tsp ground coriander seeds
2 tbsp olive oil
1 cup vegetable stock
1-14-oz (398-ml) can coconut milk
1 tbsp lime juice
¼ cup fresh cilantro, chopped
½ tsp salt
¼ tsp ground black pepper

Preheat oven to 400°F (205°C). In a medium baking dish, combine the carrots, onions, garlic, ginger, lemongrass, garam masala, coriander, and oil until well coated. Bake for 35-40 minutes, or until carrots are tender. Just before vegetables are done, in a medium soup pot, bring the stock to a boil. Reduce heat and add the roasted vegetables. Simmer for 2-3 minutes. Add the coconut milk and with a hand blender or food processor, blend half or all of the soup until smooth (be careful when blending hot liquids). Return to pot and stir in the lime juice, cilantro, salt, and pepper. Reheat and serve. Makes 2 large or 4 small servings.

QUICK GINGER CARROT SOUP

Walk softly . . . and carry a big carrot.

- **1 small onion, chopped**
- **1 tbsp olive oil**
- **1 small potato, cubed**
- **2 large carrots, chopped**
- **2 inches fresh ginger, grated**
- **2 cups vegetable stock**
- **¼ tsp salt**
- **½ tsp ground pepper**

In a medium soup pot on medium heat, sauté the onions in oil until translucent. Add the potatoes, carrots, and ginger and sauté for 2-3 minutes; stir constantly to avoid sticking. Add the stock, salt, and pepper. Bring to a boil, then reduce heat. Simmer for 15-20 minutes, or until the vegetables are tender. With a hand blender or food processor, blend half or all of the soup until smooth (be careful when blending hot liquids). Return to pot, reheat, and serve. Makes 2 large or 4 small servings.

JEN'S GINGER BUTTERNUT LENTIL SOUP

My kids go nuts for this soup . . . and it's so fast and easy to make! – Jen, Kingston, ON

- **1 small onion, chopped**
- **1 tbsp olive oil**
- **2 inches fresh ginger, grated**
- **2 cups butternut squash, cubed**
- **2 cups vegetable stock**
- **1 14-oz (398-ml) can diced tomatoes**
- **½ cup red lentils**
- **½ tsp salt**
- **½ tsp ground black pepper**

In a medium soup pot on medium heat, sauté the onion in oil until translucent. Add the ginger and squash and sauté for 5 minutes. Add the stock, tomatoes, lentils, salt, and pepper. Bring to a boil, then reduce heat. Simmer for 15-20 minutes or until squash is cooked. With a hand blender or food processor, blend half or all of the soup until smooth (be careful when blending hot liquids). Return to pot, reheat, and serve. Makes 2 large or 4 small servings.

CURRIED GINGER BUTTERNUT SQUASH SOUP

Mmm, mmm, mmmm – squash never tasted so good. Butternut squash is shaped like a giant pear and is a good source of iron and Vitamins A and C.

1 small onion, chopped
1 tbsp oil
1 garlic cloves, minced
2 inches fresh ginger, grated
½ tsp garam masala (pg 304)

¼ tsp curry powder
1 medium potato, chopped
2 cups butternut squash, cubed
2 cups vegetable stock

In a medium soup pot on medium heat, sauté the onions in oil until translucent. Add the garlic, ginger, garam masala, and curry powder; sauté for 2 minutes, stirring often to avoid sticking. Add the potatoes, squash, and stock. Bring to a boil, then reduce heat. Simmer for 15-20 minutes or until vegetables are tender. With a hand blender or food processor, blend half or all of the soup until smooth (be careful when blending hot liquids). Return to pot, reheat, and serve. Makes 2 large or 4 small servings.

CREAM OF TOMATO & BASIL SOUP

I like to serve this recipe with a slice of fresh, Easy French Bread (pg 269) and a small green salad. If you have any leftover rice in the fridge, throw it in. Yum!

1 small red onion
1 tbsp olive oil
½ cup vegetable stock
1 14-oz (398-ml) can crushed tomatoes
½ tsp salt
½ tsp ground black pepper
1 cup "milk"
½ cup fresh basil, roughly chopped
1 tbsp maple syrup

In a medium soup pot on medium heat, sauté the onion in oil until translucent. Add the stock, tomatoes, salt, and pepper. Bring to a boil, then reduce heat. Cover with lid and simmer for 6-8 minutes. Stir in the "milk," basil, and maple syrup. Turn off heat and let sit for 5 minutes before serving. Makes 2 large or 4 small servings.

TRACY & EMMA'S FRESH BASIL TOMATO BREAD SOUP

My friends Tracy and Emma from Victoria, BC sent me this fabulous soup recipe that's perfect to make during late summer when your garden is bursting with fresh basil and ripe tomatoes. Hey, Emma! Remember when we went to Vegas to see The Go-Go's and Kathy Valentine gave you her bass pik?

> **1 garlic clove, minced**
> **¼ cup shallots, minced**
> **1 tbsp olive oil**
> **2½ cups vegetable stock**
> **3 large tomatoes, roughly chopped**
> **¼ tsp salt**
> **½ tsp ground black pepper**
> **1 cup fresh basil, roughly chopped**
> **2 slices bread, stale or toasted, torn into pieces**
> **vegan "Parmesan cheese" (optional)**

In a medium soup pot on medium-low heat, sauté the garlic and shallots in oil until the shallots are translucent. Add the stock, tomatoes, salt, and pepper. Bring to a boil, then reduce heat. Simmer for 5-6 minutes. Turn off heat, stir in basil and bread, and let stand 15 minutes before serving. Serve garnished with optional Parmesan cheese. Makes 2 large or 4 small servings.

TOMATO CABBAGE SOUP

Cabbage is the bomb. It's a great source of Vitamin C, fiber, and some Vitamin A, and best of all it helps prevent scurvy. Ahoy matey! Arrrgh. . . .

> **1 small red onion, minced**
> **½ tbsp caraway seeds**
> **1 tbsp olive oil**
> **2 garlic cloves, minced**
> **½ tbsp paprika**
> **1 14-oz (398-ml) can diced tomatoes**
>
> **2½ cups vegetable stock**
> **2 cups cabbage, finely chopped**
> **¼ tsp salt**
> **¼ tsp ground black pepper**
> **1 tbsp apple cider vinegar**
> **1 tbsp maple syrup**

In a medium soup pot on medium heat, sauté the onions and caraway seeds in oil until onions are translucent. Add the garlic and paprika and sauté for 2-3 minutes; stir often to avoid sticking. Add the tomatoes, stock, cabbage, salt, and pepper. Bring to a boil, then reduce heat. Cover with lid and simmer for 15-20 minutes. Stir in the vinegar and maple syrup and serve immediately. Makes 2 large or 4 small servings.

BEAUTY & THE BEET BORSCHT

Everybody get on your feet! We know you can dance to the beet!

1 small onion, chopped
1 tbsp olive oil
1 celery stalk, chopped
1 small carrot, chopped
1 14-oz (398-ml) can stewed tomatoes
2½ cups vegetable stock
1 cup cabbage, finely chopped

1 small or medium beet, cubed
2 garlic cloves, minced
½ tsp dried dill
¼ tsp salt
¼ tsp ground black pepper
Faux Sour Cream (pg 293)

In a medium soup pot on medium heat, sauté the onions in oil until translucent. Add the celery and carrots and sauté for 2-3 minutes. Add the tomatoes, stock, cabbage, beets, garlic, dill, salt, and pepper. Bring to a boil, then reduce heat. Cover with lid and simmer for 15-20 minutes, or until beets are cooked. Serve with a nice big dollop of "sour cream." Makes 2 large or 4 small servings.

MARGO'S VEGGIE PEANUT STEW

Hey Sarah, I've got a super delicious recipe for you, if you're into peanutty soups. It's so good, I can't stand it!
– Margo, Ann Arbor, MI

1 large onion, chopped
1 tbsp olive oil
1 large carrot, chopped
½ inch fresh ginger, grated
½ tsp salt
¼ tsp cayenne pepper to taste
1 large sweet potato, chopped
1½ cups vegetable stock
⅓ cup peanut butter
1 cup tomato juice
⅓ cup roasted peanuts (pg 295)

In a medium soup pot on medium heat, sauté the onions in oil until translucent. Add the carrots, ginger, salt, and cayenne and sauté for 5 minutes. Add the sweet potatoes and stock and bring to a boil, then reduce heat. Cover with lid and simmer for 10-15 minutes, or until the vegetables are tender. Stir in the peanut butter and tomato juice and with a hand blender or food processor, blend half or all of the soup until smooth (be careful when blending hot liquids). Return to pot, reheat, and serve garnished with roasted peanuts. Makes 2 large or 4 small servings.

VANESSA'S LENTIL-QUINOA STEW

Here's a recipe for ya! I just made it up tonight. Enjoy! – Vanessa, Surrey, BC

1 small onion, chopped
1 tbsp olive oil
1 celery stalk, diced
1 small carrot, diced
1 garlic clove, minced
2½ cups vegetable stock
½ cup dry red lentils
¼ cup quinoa
½ tsp dried basil
½ tsp dried oregano
½ tsp salt
½ tsp ground black pepper
1 medium tomato, diced
¼ cup fresh cilantro, minced
1 tbsp apple cider vinegar

In a medium saucepan on medium heat, sauté the onions in oil until translucent. Add the celery, carrots, and garlic and sauté for 5 minutes. Add the stock, lentils, quinoa, basil, oregano, salt, and pepper. Bring to a boil, then reduce heat. Cover with lid and simmer for 20-25 minutes or until the lentils are tender. In a food processor or with a hand blender, blend half the soup until smooth (be careful when blending hot liquids). Return to pot, stir in the tomatoes, cilantro, and vinegar, reheat and serve. Makes 2 large or 4 small servings.

SARAH'S GREEN SPLIT PEA SOUP

This hearty, healthy recipe will stick to your ribs and keep you warm on cold winter days when, like Don Henley, all you want to do is dance.

1 small onion, chopped
1 large carrot, chopped
1 celery stalk, chopped
1 tbsp oil
1 garlic clove, minced
1 medium potato, chopped
1 small turnip (approx. ½ cup), finely chopped
½ tsp turmeric
pinch of dried rosemary
1 tsp salt
½ tsp ground black pepper
2½ cups vegetable stock
½ cup dried green split peas

In a medium soup pot on medium heat, sauté the onions, carrots, and celery in oil until the onions are translucent. Add the remaining ingredients and bring to a boil, then reduce heat. Cover with lid and simmer for 40-45 minutes (stirring occasionally), or until peas are cooked. Makes 2 large or 4 small servings.

ADAM'S YELLOW SPLIT PEA CHOWDER

This wonderful recipe came via e-mail from Adam in Red Deer, AB.

1 small onion, chopped
2 medium carrots, chopped
2 celery stalks, chopped
1 tbsp olive oil
3 cups vegetable stock

¼ cup brown rice
¼ cup yellow split peas
½ tsp dried basil
½ tsp salt

In a medium soup pot on medium heat, sauté the onions, carrots, and celery in oil until the onions are translucent. Add the stock, rice, peas, basil, and salt. Bring to a boil, then reduce heat. Cover with lid and simmer for 45 minutes, or until rice and peas are cooked. With a hand blender or food processor, blend half or all of the soup until smooth (be careful when blending hot liquids). Return to pot, reheat and serve. Makes 2 large or 4 small servings.

MOCKED CLAM CHOWDER

Oh, the poor clam . . . it can't get any respect.

1 large onion, chopped
1 tbsp olive oil
1 celery stalk, chopped
1 large carrot, chopped
1½ cups vegetable stock *or* **water**
4 medium new potatoes, diced
1 tsp dried thyme
½ tsp ground black pepper
½ pound medium *or* **firm tofu, cubed**
2 tsp tamari
1 tsp powdered kelp
½ tsp ground black pepper
1 tbsp olive oil
1 cup "milk"
¼ cup faux bacon bits (optional)

In a medium soup pot on medium heat, sauté the onions in oil until translucent. Add the celery and carrots and sauté for 5 minutes. Add the stock, potatoes, thyme, and pepper. Bring to a boil, then reduce heat. Cover with lid and simmer for 15-20 minutes, or until potatoes are tender. While the soup simmers, in a frying pan on medium-high heat, sauté the tofu, tamari, kelp, and pepper in oil, tossing frequently until tofu is browned and crispy. Once cooked, set aside. With a hand blender or food processor, blend half or all of the soup until smooth (be careful when blending hot liquids). Return to pot, add the "milk" and tofu, and reheat. Serve garnished with faux bacon bits. Makes 2 large or 4 small servings.

CHUNKY VEGETABLE CHOWDER

This is the perfect recipe for when you're in a hurry and only have a few items in the vegetable crisper to throw together.

1 tbsp olive oil	**2 cups vegetable stock**
1 small onion, chopped	**1 tsp dried oregano**
1 celery stalk, chopped	**¼ tsp ground nutmeg**
1 large carrot, chopped	**½ tsp salt**
1 inch fresh ginger, grated	**½ tsp ground black pepper**
1 large potato, cubed	

In a medium soup pot on medium heat, sauté the onions in oil until translucent. Add the celery, carrots, and ginger and sauté for 2-3 minutes. Add the potatoes, stock, oregano, nutmeg, salt, and pepper. Bring to a boil, then reduce heat. Cover with lid and simmer for 15-20 minutes, or until the potatoes are tender. Makes 2 large or 4 small servings.

CHUNKY CORN CHOWDER

Thick. Warm. Wonderful. . . .

1 small onion, minced
1 tbsp olive oil
1 large celery stalk, chopped
1 large carrot, chopped
1 large leek, sliced (white and pale green parts only)
3 garlic cloves, minced
1 large potato, cubed
2 cups vegetable stock
½ tsp salt
½ tsp ground black pepper
pinch of ground nutmeg
1 cup "milk"
1 cup corn, fresh or frozen

In a medium soup pot on medium heat, sauté the onions in oil until translucent. Add the celery, carrots, leeks, and garlic and sauté for 5 minutes. Add the potato, stock, salt, pepper, and nutmeg. Bring to a boil, then reduce heat. Simmer for 15-20 minutes or until the potatoes are tender. With a hand blender or food processor, blend half or all of the soup until smooth (be careful when blending hot liquids). Return to pot and stir in the "milk" and corn. Turn off heat and let sit for 5 minutes before serving. Makes 2 large or 4 small servings.

CINDY O'S "CHICKEN" & RICE SOUP FOR THE SOUL

Hi Sarah: This recipe is dedicated to soy-intolerant vegans who get sick and crave home style chicken soup or to anyone who just might have a hankering for chicken & rice soup *without the soul* . . . I cut my "Mock Chicken" dough into small bite-sized chunks. They will grow in size as you cook them, so don't worry. The dough also absorbs the flavor from the soup so no worries about needing to season it. This soup is super yummy. Enjoy! – Cindy O., Vancouver, BC *(Gluten flour is high-protein, hard-wheat flour treated to remove most of the starch. Available at most health food stores, you can also make it with regular untreated flour. Check out the recipes on pg 284 for details.)*

"Chicken":

2 tbsp instant vital gluten flour
2 tbsp water

Soup:

1 small onion, chopped
1 tbsp olive oil
1 celery stalk, chopped
1 medium carrot, chopped
1 - 2 garlic cloves, minced
2½ cups vegetable stock or faux chicken vegetable stock
½ tsp ground marjoram
½ tsp dried thyme
¼ tsp salt
¼ tsp ground black pepper
¼ cup basmati rice

In a medium bowl, stir together the gluten flour and water. Mix immediately with a fork to form the dough. When it becomes thick, use your hands and knead 10-15 times. Form dough into a tube shape and cut into small cubes. Set aside. In a medium saucepan on medium heat, sauté the onions in oil until translucent. Add the celery, carrots, and garlic and sauté for an additional 5 minutes. Add the stock, "chicken" cubes, marjoram, thyme, salt, pepper, and basmati rice. Bring to a boil, then reduce heat. Cover with lid and simmer for 15-20 minutes, or until rice is cooked. Makes 2 large or 4 small servings.

KATHLEEN'S MOM'S TORTILLA CHIP SOUP

Hey Sarah, I have a great recipe for tortilla soup from my Mom. It can be doubled and used as an inexpensive meal for many guests. I am a poor college student and it has fed many! – Kathleen, Santa Barbara, CA
(Reduce the amount of green chilies if you want to reduce the heat of the soup.)

1 small onion, chopped
1 tbsp olive oil
1 garlic clove, minced
1 small orange bell pepper, chopped
1 3.8-oz (114-ml) can green chilies, chopped
2½ cups vegetable stock
¾ cup corn, fresh *or* **frozen**
½ cup fresh cilantro, chopped
1 19-oz (540-ml) can black beans, drained
½ tsp chili powder
½ tsp dried basil
¼ tsp salt
¼ tsp ground black pepper
1 5.5-oz (156-ml) can tomato paste
tortilla chips

In a medium saucepan on medium heat, sauté the onions in oil until translucent. Add the garlic, bell peppers, and chilies and sauté for 2-3 minutes. Add the stock, corn, cilantro, beans, chili powder, basil, salt, pepper, and tomato paste. Stir together well. Bring to a boil, then reduce heat. Cover with lid and simmer for 15-20 minutes. Place several tortilla chips in the bottom of each soup bowl before serving. Makes 4 servings.

BLACK BEAN TORTILLA CHIP SOUP WITH AVOCADO TOMATO SALSA

Black beans are an excellent source of fiber as well as a great source of protein. Topped with nutrient rich avocado salsa, you can't go wrong with this hot meal in a bowl.

Soup:
1 small onion, minced
1 tbsp olive oil
1 celery stalk, chopped
1 medium carrot, chopped
2 garlic cloves, minced
2 cups vegetable stock
1 19-oz (540-ml) can black beans, drained
1½ tsp chili powder
1 tsp dried oregano
½ tsp salt

Garnish:
1 medium tomato, chopped
1 avocado, cubed
¼ cup cilantro, minced
1 stalk green onion, minced
1 tbsp oil (e.g. flax, hemp, olive)
2 tsp fresh lime juice
enough tortilla chips for 2 people

In a medium soup pot on medium heat, sauté the onions in oil until translucent. Add the celery, carrots, and garlic and sauté for 2-3 minutes. Add the stock, beans, chili powder, oregano, and salt. Bring to a boil, then reduce heat. Cover with lid and simmer for 15-20 minutes. While the soup simmers, in a medium bowl, stir together the tomatoes, avocados, cilantro, green onions, oil, and lime juice. Set aside. With a hand blender or food processor, blend half or all of the soup until smooth (be careful when blending hot liquids). Return to pot and reheat. Serve topped with a generous helping of avocado salsa and tortilla chips. Makes 2 large or 4 small servings.

Entrées

Entrées are the cornerstone of any meal; they must be substantial, flavorful, and leave you feeling full and satisfied. This chapter is broken up into 3 parts: noodle dishes, dishes served with rice, and of course the ever-popular miscellany section. Don't forget to balance your entrées with a lovely salad and/or a side dish.

NOODLE DISHES

Pasta is traditionally made with wheat, but now you can find all sorts of noodles made from rice, corn, kamut, and other types of grains. See what varieties your local health food store carries and experiment. You might just find something new to enjoy. Check out pg 27 in the Kitchen Wisdom section for some pasta-making tips.

CLAIRE'S MACARONI & CHEEZE

I hope you like this recipe! – Claire, CoquetteFauxFurriers.com (When it comes to "food therapy," there's nothing more comforting in the world than the combination of pasta and a "cheese" sauce. This simple sauce can be whipped up in a few minutes and can be served over a number of different items: veggies, nachos, etc. I make this recipe with Vegan Rella and sometimes add sautéed vegetables like mushrooms and leeks or bite sized broccoli florettes.)

> **dry pasta, enough for 2 people**
> **3 tbsp vegan margarine**
> **3 tbsp flour**
> **½ tsp salt**
> **¼ tsp ground black pepper**
> **1½ cups vegan "milk"**
> **1 cup vegan "cheese," grated**
> **½ tsp Dijon mustard (optional)**

In a large pot of salted water, boil the pasta. While pasta is cooking, in a small saucepan on medium heat, melt the margarine. Once margarine is liquefied, remove from heat (don't turn the burner off) and add the flour, salt, and pepper and whisk until smooth. Place saucepan back onto burner and slowly add ½ cup of "milk," whisking constantly until thickening occurs. Once thick, repeat action with remaining "milk" ½ cup at a time. Cook sauce over medium heat, whisking constantly until thickened and smooth. Add the "cheese" and Dijon mustard and cook for an additional 5 minutes, whisking until smooth and well blended. Remove from heat and set aside. Drain noodles and return to the pot. Toss the cheese sauce with the noodles and serve immediately. Makes 2 large or 4 small servings. Sauce makes approx. 2 cups.

ROASTED CHERRY TOMATO PASTA

I like to use mozzarella-style Vegan Rella for this recipe, as it adds a more tart flavor than other vegan "cheeses." But experiment, and see which "cheese" suits you best. This recipe may seem complicated, but it's not at all. Trust me. Just make it, eat it, and then send me an e-mail to say thanks: *thankyousarah@govegan.net.*

26 - 28 ripe cherry tomatoes, halved
1 tbsp olive oil
2 slices bread, roughly chopped
¼ cup vegan "cheese," grated
3 tbsp olive oil
2 garlic cloves

½ tsp salt
½ tsp ground black pepper
dry pasta, enough for 2 people
¼ cup fresh basil, tightly packed
    and roughly chopped

Preheat the oven to 400°F (205°C). Toss the sliced tomatoes in oil and place in an 8x8-inch pan, cut side up. In a food processor, blend the bread, "cheese," oil, garlic, salt, and pepper. Sprinkle the breadcrumb mixture evenly over the tomatoes and bake for 20 minutes. While tomatoes are in the oven, boil pasta in a large pot of salted water. Drain noodles and return to the pot. Add the cooked tomatoes and basil to the noodles and toss together well. Serve immediately. Makes 2 large or 4 small servings.

ROASTED CHERRY TOMATO PASTA WITH KALAMATA OLIVES & CAPERS

This subtle, tasty recipe can be made beforehand and stirred into hot pasta at your convenience. For added flavor and texture, try throwing in ¼ cup of toasted walnuts or pine nuts (pg 295). It's nummy-liscious!

20 - 24 cherry tomatoes, halved
2 tbsp olive oil
2 garlic cloves, minced
2 tsp balsamic vinegar
⅛ teaspoon hot red pepper flakes
1½ tsp dried oregano

dry pasta, enough for 2 people
¼ cup pitted Kalamata olives,
    roughly chopped
2 tbsp capers, drained
¼ cup vegan "cheese," grated (optional)

Preheat the oven to 400°F (205°C). Toss the sliced tomatoes in oil with garlic, balsamic vinegar, red pepper flakes, and oregano and place in an 8x8-inch pan, cut side up. Bake for 20 minutes. While tomatoes are in the oven, boil pasta in a large pot of salted water. Drain noodles and return to the pot. Add the cooked tomatoes, olives, capers, and "cheese" to the noodles and toss together well. Serve immediately. Makes 2 large or 4 small servings.

PASTA WITH 5-MINUTE ROASTED RED PEPPER PESTO

Roasted red peppers come in a jar and are usually in the pickle section of your local supermarket. If I want to add extra weight to this recipe, I throw in a little tofu or Faux Chicken (pg 287).

dry pasta, enough for 2 people
¾ cup roasted red peppers, drained
⅓ cup walnuts
½ cup fresh basil, tightly packed
¼ cup fresh parsley, tightly packed
1 garlic clove
¼ cup olive oil

In a large pot of salted water, boil the pasta. While pasta is cooking, in a food processor or blender, blend together the red peppers, walnuts, basil, parsley, and garlic. Slowly add the olive oil while blending until well mixed and set aside. Drain noodles and return to the pot. Add the pesto to the noodles and toss together well. Serve immediately. Makes 2 large or 4 small servings.

PASTA WITH FRESH 5-MINUTE BASIL TOMATO SAUCE

This simple, fresh, no-cook sauce can be whizzed together in a matter of minutes. Take some time to stop and smell the basil – you'll be happy that you did! To add a little weight to this sauce, I'll sometimes throw in ½ pound of cubed tofu.

dry pasta, enough for 2 people
4 medium tomatoes, roughly chopped
2 tbsp olive oil
2 garlic cloves
¼ cup fresh basil, tightly packed
½ tsp salt
½ tsp ground black pepper

In a large pot of salted water, boil the pasta. While pasta is cooking, chop one of the tomatoes and set aside for later. In a blender or food processor, blend together the remaining tomatoes, oil, garlic, basil, salt, and pepper until chunky. Drain and return noodles to pot. Add the sauce and reserved chopped tomatoes to the noodles and toss together well. Serve immediately. Makes 2 large or 4 small servings.

GERRY'S QUICK BROCCOLI & HOT CHILI PEPPER PASTA

Broccoli is high in Vitamins C and A, calcium, and fiber. Wow. Your Mum was right, eat your broccoli! It's good for you. Gerry and I love this recipe when we're in a hurry and need a quick, easy to prepare meal.

dry pasta, enough for 2 people
1 large head of broccoli, finely chopped
¼ tsp hot red pepper flakes
⅓ cup flax oil (*or* other oil of your choice)

In a large pot of salted water, boil the pasta. While pasta is cooking, steam the broccoli until it turns bright green and can be poked easily with a fork. Set aside. Drain and return noodles to the pot. Add the broccoli, red pepper flakes, and oil to the noodles and toss together well. Serve immediately. Makes 2 large or 4 small servings.

PUNK-KIN PASTA

A lovely alternative to tomato sauce, this tasty pasta will have you wishing you doubled the recipe so you could have leftovers. If you can't find veggie "sausage," use diced veggie burgers, mock meat of your choice (pg 285-289), or nothing at all: the sauce is so yum, it can easily stand alone.

dry pasta, enough for 2 people
1 medium onion, chopped
1 cup veggie "sausage," sliced
1 tbsp olive oil
1 14-oz (398-ml) can unsweetened pumpkin purée
½ tsp salt
½ tsp ground black pepper
¼ - ½ cup vegetable stock (optional)
½ cup vegan "cheese," grated (optional)

In a large pot of salted water, boil the pasta. While pasta is cooking, in a large saucepan on medium-high heat, sauté the onions and "sausage" in oil until onions become translucent. Add the pumpkin, salt, and pepper and simmer for 5-7 minutes. This sauce can be quite thick, so to thin it out, add ¼ cup vegetable stock at a time until you've reached the desired consistency. Drain noodles and return to the pot. Add the sauce to the noodles and toss together well. Serve immediately garnished with "cheese." Makes 2 large or 4 small servings.

SPAGHETTI & TOFU BALLS

It's all about timing, people! If you're looking to save time, the tofu balls can be made ahead of time and freeze well for future use. But if you get into multi-tasking like I do, prepare the tofu balls while your sauce is simmering on one burner and your noodles are doing their thing on another, then toss the tofu balls into the tomato sauce and voilà! You're ready to rumble. If you want a chunkier sauce check out the Fast & Fresh Tomato Sauce on pg 178.

dry pasta, enough for 2 people

Tofu balls:
½ cup firm tofu, mashed or crumbled
¼ cup flour
½ tbsp tahini (*or* nut butter)
1 tbsp tamari
⅛ cup parsley, minced
1 very small onion, minced
¼ tsp dry mustard
⅛ tsp ground black pepper
¼ cup flour (for coating)
2 tbsp olive oil

Pasta Sauce:
1 tbsp olive oil
1 small onion, chopped
1 small carrot, chopped
1 celery stalk, chopped
2 garlic cloves, chopped
1 14-oz (398-ml) can tomato sauce
½ tbsp dried basil
½ tsp salt
1 tsp sweetener (e.g. maple syrup, sugar)
¼ cup fresh parsley, minced
1 tbsp red wine vinegar

To prepare tofu balls: In a large bowl, stir together the tofu, ¼ cup flour, tahini, tamari, parsley, onions, mustard, and pepper. Place ¼ cup flour onto a small plate and roll ½ tsbp tofu mixture into a ball and coat with flour. In a frying pan on medium heat, fry tofu balls in oil until browned all over. Set aside. In a large pot of salted water, boil the pasta. While pasta is cooking, in a medium saucepan on medium-high heat, sauté the onions in oil until translucent. Add the carrots, celery, and garlic and sauté for an additional 4-6 minutes or until carrots start to soften. Add the tomato sauce, basil, salt, and sweetener, and let simmer over medium-low heat for 15-20 minutes. When ready to serve, turn off heat and stir in the parsley, vinegar, and tofu balls. Let stand 5 minutes before serving over pasta. Makes 2 large or 4 small servings. Makes approx. 8-10 tofu balls.

PORTOBELLO CANNELLONI WITH SUN-DRIED TOMATO WHITE SAUCE

This recipe is time-consuming – I won't kid you. But it's worth the extra effort. If you can find "oven-ready" cannelloni, you can skip the step of boiling the pasta which makes things MUCHO easier. You can also serve this dish smothered in a number of different sauces and some vegan "cheese" melted on top, but I think this Sun-Dried Tomato White Sauce is purr-fect.

Pasta stuffing:
10 - 12 cannelloni tubes
¾ lb Portobello mushrooms, roughly chopped
1 small onion, roughly chopped
1 small potato, roughly chopped
¼ tsp salt
¼ tsp ground black pepper
2 tbsp vegan margarine

Sauce:
¼ cup vegan margarine
¼ cup flour
2 cups "milk"
1 cup vegan "cheese," grated
6 large sun dried tomatoes, finely chopped
¼ tsp salt
¼ tsp ground black pepper

Preheat oven to 350°F (175°C). Lightly oil an 8x8-inch baking dish and set aside. In a large pot of salted water, boil the pasta until "just cooked." Drain and rinse noodles in cold water cooled and set aside. In a food processor, blend mushrooms, onions, potatoes, salt, and pepper until finely chopped. In a large frying pan on medium-high heat, sauté the chopped vegetables in margarine for 6-8 minutes. Remove from heat and with a small spoon stuff each pasta tube with the filling and lay in baking dish. Set aside. To prepare the sauce: in a small saucepan on medium heat, melt the margarine. Once margarine is liquefied, remove from heat (don't turn the burner off) and add the flour and whisk until smooth. Place saucepan back onto burner and slowly add ½ cup "milk," whisking constantly until thickening occurs. Once thick, repeat action with remaining "milk," ½ cup at a time. Cook sauce over medium heat, whisking constantly until thickened and smooth. Add the "cheese," tomatoes, salt, and pepper and cook for an additional 5 minutes, whisking until smooth and well blended. Pour sauce over pasta tubes and bake for 20-25 minutes. Makes 2 large or 4 small servings. Sauce makes approx. 3 cups.

DILIP'S STUFFED MANICOTTI WITH ROASTED RED PEPPER & PORCINI MUSHROOM SAUCE

Dilip from Chapel Hill, North Carolina has been a *GoVegan.net* supporter since the very beginning. This incredible recipe takes a bit more time than other recipes in this book and there are a few extra steps, but it's well worth the effort. Thanks for sharing, Dilip!

8 tubes manicotti pasta

Sauce:
1 small onion, chopped
1 tbsp olive oil
¼ cup roasted red pepper, finely chopped
½ cup dried porcini mushrooms (*or* ½ lb fresh), chopped
1 14-oz (398-ml) can tomato sauce
1 garlic clove, minced
¼ tsp salt
¼ tsp ground black pepper
1 tsp fresh rosemary, chopped

Stuffing:
1 small onion, chopped
¾ cup fresh spinach, chopped
½ lb medium tofu, drained
1 tbsp lemon juice
½ tsp dried oregano
1½ tsp dried basil
1 tsp salt
½ tsp ground black pepper

Preheat oven to 350°F (175°C). In a large pot of salted water, boil the pasta until al dente (firm to the bite). Drain and rinse in cold water and set aside. In a medium saucepan, sauté the onions in oil until translucent. Add the red peppers, mushrooms, tomato sauce, garlic, salt, pepper, and rosemary. Bring to a boil, then reduce heat. Cover with lid and simmer until sauce is needed. To prepare the stuffing: In a food processor, blend the onions, spinach, tofu, lemon juice, oregano, basil, salt, and pepper until smooth. Set aside. Spoon a thin layer of tomato sauce on the bottom of a 9x13-inch baking dish. With a small spoon, carefully stuff each pasta tube with the filling and lay in baking dish. Cover pasta with remaining tomato sauce and bake for 20-30 minutes before serving. Makes 2 large or 4 small servings. Sauce makes approx. 2 cups.

GERRY'S ARTICHOKE HEART & BASIL PASTA

My hubby loves his pasta. He made this recipe up one night when I didn't feel like cooking. Gosh, I'm a lucky girl.

dry pasta, enough for 2 people
⅓ cup pine nuts, toasted (pg 295)
2 garlic cloves, minced
1 tbsp olive oil
1 large tomato, chopped
1 6-oz (170-ml) jar marinated artichoke hearts, drained and chopped
¼ cup fresh basil, roughly chopped
¼ tsp dried oregano
¼ tsp salt
¼ tsp ground black pepper

In a large pot of salted water, boil the pasta. While pasta is cooking, in a large saucepan on medium-low heat, sauté the pine nuts and garlic in oil until garlic starts to soften. Watch carefully so it doesn't burn. Add the tomatoes, artichokes, basil, oregano, salt, and pepper and heat thoroughly. Drain noodles and return to the pot. Add the sauce to the noodles and toss together well. Serve immediately. Makes 2 large or 4 small servings.

PEACEFROG'S ARTICHOKE HEART PASTA

I was trying to replicate a meal from one of my favorite Italian restaurants. It turned out delish and was so easy! I think penne noodles work best with this dish. – Carla aka Peacefrog, Greencastle, PA

> **dry pasta, enough for 2 people**
> **4 large garlic cloves, minced**
> **4 large button mushrooms, roughly chopped**
> **2 tbsp olive oil**
> **1 6-oz (170-ml) jar marinated artichoke hearts, drained and chopped**
> **8 sun-dried tomatoes, roughly chopped**
> **¼ cup vegetable stock**
> **1 large tomato, roughly chopped**
> **1 cup fresh basil, tightly packed and roughly chopped**
> **¼ cup fresh parsley, roughly chopped**

In a large pot of salted water, boil the pasta. While pasta is cooking, in a large saucepan on medium-low heat, sauté the garlic and mushrooms in oil until mushrooms start to soften. Add the artichoke hearts, sun-dried tomatoes, and vegetable stock. Bring to a boil, then reduce heat and let simmer for 5 minutes. Drain noodles and return to the pot. Add the artichoke hearts sauce, chopped tomatoes, basil, and parsley. Toss together well and serve immediately. Makes 2 large or 4 small servings.

JEN'S CREAMY BASIL & SUN-DRIED TOMATO PASTA

This is a wonderful sauce recipe from my good friend Jen in Kingston, Ontario. It can be whipped up in a flash while you're waiting for your pasta to cook. Where Jen lives, fresh basil can be scarce during winter, so she buys frozen cubes of basil from the supermarket. She used 4 cubes in place of the fresh.

> **dry pasta, enough for 2 people**
> **7 - 8 sun-dried tomatoes**
> **1 300-g (10.56-oz) pkg of firm silken**
> **   or soft tofu**
>
> **2 - 3 garlic cloves**
> **¼ cup fresh basil, tightly packed**
> **½ tsp salt**
> **2 cups broccoli, cut into bite-sized pieces**

In a large pot of salted water, boil the pasta. While the pasta is cooking, in a blender or food processor, blend the sun-dried tomatoes, tofu, garlic, basil, and salt until smooth. Set aside. When pasta is almost done, add the broccoli to the pasta water and cook for an additional 2-3 minutes. Drain noodles and broccoli and return cooked to the pot. Add the basil sauce and toss together well. Serve immediately. Makes 2 large or 4 small servings.

MARIANNE'S GOULASH

Marianne from Gansevoort, New York, sent me this incredible goulash recipe, which makes my hubby feel like he's back in the trailer park he grew up in. It makes quite a large quantity, but I didn't want to cut it in half and have you end up with half a can of tomato paste leftover. I love to serve this with a fresh green salad and then send Gerry off to work in the morning with the goulash leftovers for lunch.

4 cups elbow noodles, uncooked
1 small onion, chopped
2 celery stalks, chopped
2 tbsp olive oil
1 pkg or 1½ cups mock ground "beef"
2 tbsp "Needs a Little Extra" Spice (pg 305)
1 14-oz (398-ml) can diced tomatoes
1 5.5-oz (156-ml) can tomato paste

In a medium pot of salted water, boil the pasta. While pasta is cooking, in a large saucepan on medium heat, sauté the onions and celery in oil until onions are translucent. Add the ground "beef," spices, tomatoes, and tomato paste and simmer until celery is cooked. Drain noodles and add to the "beef" mixture. Stir together until well combined and serve immediately. Makes 4 large or 6 small servings.

MATTHEW'S SPICY TOMATO PEANUT & KALE PASTA

I don't know what came over me to throw these ingredients together to make this dish, but I'm glad I did. It's always a hit and super simple to make. – Matthew, Santa Cruz, CA (*I was very reluctant to try this recipe at first because it sounded so odd, but it has now become a Kramer favorite. It's so easy even a husband can make it! The Asian chili garlic sauce can be found in any Asian market and at most grocery stores. If you can't find it, throw in something else spicy like Tabasco or hot sauce to add some heat.*)

dry pasta, enough for 2 people
1 10-oz (295-ml) can tomato juice, unsweetened
2 cups kale, finely chopped
2 tbsp peanut butter (*or* nut butter of choice)
1 tsp Asian chili-garlic sauce

In a large pot of salted water, boil the pasta. While pasta is cooking, in a medium pot on medium-high heat, cook the tomato juice and kale for 6-8 minutes or until kale is tender. Stir in the peanut butter and the chili sauce until smooth and simmer for an additional 2 minutes. Drain and return noodles to the pot. Add the sauce to the noodles and toss together well. Serve immediately. Makes 2 large or 4 small servings.

MOCK BEEF & RICE NOODLE TOSS

You can use the homemade teriyaki marinade on pg 300 or if you're lazy like me, buy a bottle of it at your local Asian grocer or supermarket. The less work the better, I always say! You can also use plain tofu for this recipe, but the chewy mock "beef" adds a little something-something to this yummy-licious recipe.

⅓ cup Teriyaki Marinade (pg 300)
1 cup Faux Beef (pg 288), roughly chopped
rice noodles, enough for 2 people
1 tbsp dark sesame oil
1 small red onion, chopped
2 inches fresh ginger, grated
3 garlic cloves, minced
¾ cup frozen peas *or* **edamame beans**

In a medium bowl, marinate the "beef" in teriyaki marinade for 15-20 minutes. In a large pot of salted water, boil the rice noodles. Drain, rinse with hot water, and return to the pot. Toss noodles with a splash of dark sesame oil and set aside. In a wok or large saucepan on medium-high heat, sauté the onions, ginger, and garlic in oil until onions start to soften. Add the "beef" and marinade and sauté for 3-5 minutes. Toss in the peas, turn off the heat, cover with lid, and let sit 5 minutes before serving over noodles. Makes 2 large or 4 small servings.

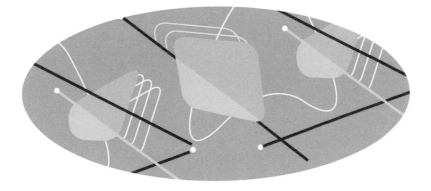

PHEBE'S MUSHROOM STROGANOFF

Hi Sarah: I've had your cookbook *The Garden of Vegan* since my last birthday and have tried a few of the recipes (yum!) but I had never read the introductions before. I read them today while leafing through the book, and was seized by a desire to tell you how inspirational you are in a non-preachy, non-threatening way. What I really want to do is send you a recipe, in hopes that you will love it annnnnd . . . if you ever write a third cookbook, you may want to, you know, add it. – Phebe, Thunder Bay, ON *(Consider it done! This recipe is best served over broad noodles or over rice.)*

dry pasta, enough for 2 people
1 small onion, finely chopped
5 large button mushrooms, chopped
3 garlic cloves, minced
1 cup Faux Chicken *or* **Beef, cubed (pg 287-288)**
2 tbsp olive oil
1 cup "milk"
2 tbsp flour
1 tbsp vegan Worcestershire sauce
1 tbsp tamari
1 10.5-oz (300-g) pkg soft *or* **silken tofu**
⅛ cup fresh parsley
¼ tsp salt
½ tsp ground black pepper

In a large pot of salted water, boil the pasta. While pasta is cooking, in a large saucepan on medium heat, sauté the onions, mushrooms, garlic, and mock "meat" in oil until onions are translucent. While onions are cooking, in a food processor, combine the "milk," flour, Worcestershire sauce, tamari, tofu, parsley, salt, and pepper together and blend until smooth. Once onions are cooked, add tofu mixture to saucepan, then reduce heat. Cover with lid and simmer for 6-8 minutes. Drain noodles and return to the pot. Add the stroganoff to the noodles and toss together well. Serve immediately. Makes 2 large or 4 small servings.

RED LENTIL PASTA

Holy time saver, Bat-Girl! This pasta can be made faster then Bruce Wayne getting into his costume and is chock full of protein and vitamins. Use whatever noodle suits your fancy.

dry noodles (enough for 2 people)
1 small onion, chopped
1 tbsp olive oil
2 garlic cloves, minced
¾ cup vegetable stock
½ cup red lentils
1 large tomato, chopped
¼ tsp ground cinnamon
¼ tsp salt
¼ tsp ground black pepper
½ cup toasted cashews (pg 295)

In a large pot of salted water, boil the noodles. While noodles are cooking, in a medium saucepan on medium heat, sauté the onions in oil until translucent. Add the garlic, stock, lentils, tomatoes, cinnamon, salt, and pepper. Bring to a boil, then reduce heat; simmer for 10-12 minutes or until lentils are cooked. In a food processor, blend half or all of the sauce until smooth (be careful when blending hot liquids); return to pot. Reheat and serve over noodles garnished with cashews. Makes 2 large or 4 small servings.

RICE ENTREES

Like all grains, make sure you rinse the rice thoroughly under cold running water and then remove any debris or discolored grains that you find. Rinsing rice will also prevent the rice from sticking. For more rice tips, check out pg 27 in the Kitchen Wisdom section.

TERESA'S GARLIC SHOOT STIR-FRY

When my friend Teresa came to town and we went to the local farmer's market, grabbed some veggies, and made up this recipe when we got home. Garlic shoots or garlic scapes are available in late spring and can be found in most grocery stores or Asian markets. They are an incredible, snake-like, green shoot that grows from the center of the garlic plant in late spring. They are trimmed away to allow the garlic bulbs to fully develop and add a subtle garlic flavor to any meal. This recipe uses Shoshana's Spectacular All-Purpose Tahini Sauce, which you can use on just about anything. Yum.

brown rice (*or* **grain of your choice), enough for 2 people**

Sauce:
½ cup shallots, roughly chopped (*or* **1 small onion)**
2 garlic cloves, roughly chopped
1 tbsp dark sesame oil
¼ cup lemon juice
3 tbsp tamari
⅓ cup tahini
1 tbsp maple syrup (*or* **other sweetener)**
¼ cup water
¼ cup olive oil
¼ cup oil (e.g. flax, hemp, grapeseed)

Stir-fry:
½ lb firm tofu, cubed
1 tbsp dark sesame oil
1 tbsp tamari
1 tsp ground black pepper
1 cup snap *or* **sweet peas, stems removed and chopped in half**
1 cup garlic shoots, roughly chopped
2 cups red Swiss chard, roughly chopped

In a medium pot, cook the rice accordingly. While rice is cooking, in a small saucepan on medium heat, sauté the shallots and garlic in oil until shallots are translucent. In a blender or food processor, blend the remaining sauce ingredients (including the shallots) until smooth and creamy. Pour back into pot and keep warm on stove until needed. In a wok or large saucepan on medium-high heat, sauté the tofu in oil until tofu starts to brown. Add the tamari, pepper, peas, and garlic shoots; sauté for 5 minutes. Turn off heat, add the Swiss chard, and cover with lid. Let sit 5 minutes before serving. Serve vegetables over rice, topped with tahini sauce. Makes 2 large or 4 small servings. Sauce makes approx. 1½ cups.

CINNAMON-SPICED ROASTED VEGGIES WITH COUSCOUS

This yummy entrée can easily be made into a side dish by omitting the couscous as a base. Whatever, dude – it's all good.

Veggies:
¼ cup shallots, roughly chopped
1 small red bell pepper, chopped
1 small sweet potato, cubed
1 small butternut squash, cubed (approx. 2 cups)
1 tsp coarse salt
1 tsp ground coriander
2 tsp ground cumin
½ tsp ground cinnamon
3 tbsp oil

Couscous:
¾ cup water
¾ cup couscous

Preheat oven to 375°F (190°C). In a 9x13-inch baking dish, toss together the shallots, red peppers, sweet potatoes, squash, salt, coriander, cumin, cinnamon, and oil until well coated. Bake for 40-45 minutes, or until veggies can be pierced easily with a fork. About 5 minutes before vegetables are done, in a small pot, bring water to a boil. Stir in couscous, turn off heat. Cover with lid and let sit for 5 minutes. Fluff couscous with a fork and portion out onto plates, then top with roasted vegetables. Serve immediately. Makes 2 large or 4 small servings.

WENDY'S LENTIL & BROWN RICE CASSEROLE

This recipe is from my dear friend Wendy and takes approximately an hour and a half to make. But don't let that turn you off! It's a great recipe to make on lazy days; you can go read a book, do some laundry or weed your garden whiles it bakes. Despite the time, this recipe is über easy to make and is one of my all-time favorite dishes. It goes fabulously with a fresh baguette and a green salad.

¾ **cup dried red lentils**
¾ **cup brown rice**
1 medium onion, chopped
3 cups vegetable stock

1 14-oz (398-ml) can crushed tomatoes
½ **tsp dried basil**
½ **tsp dried oregano**
¾ **cup vegan "cheese" (optional), grated**

Preheat oven to 350°F (175°C). In a large casserole dish, combine the lentils, rice, onions, stock, tomatoes, basil, oregano, and stir it together. Cover with lid and bake for 1½ hours (stirring every half-hour). Remove lid, sprinkle "cheese" on top of casserole, and broil uncovered until "cheese" has melted. (Keep an eye on it so it doesn't burn. Makes 2 large or 4 small servings.

VEGGIE GOULASH

Goulash is defined in the dictionary as a mixture of many different elements: a hodgepodge. I love that word. Say it over and over a few times and you'll start laughing out loud. You can't help yourself. Hodgepodge . . . hodgepodge. No? Is it just me? Serve this veggie dish over brown rice, quinoa, or any other favorite grain as a main meal or as a complementary side dish.

brown rice (or **grain of your choice),**
  enough for 2 people
1 small onion, chopped
1 tbsp olive oil
2 garlic cloves, minced
½ **tsp ground marjoram**
1 large tomato, diced
1 cup cauliflower, cut into bite-sized florets

1 large carrot, chopped
1 small zucchini (approx. 1 cup), chopped
1 14-oz (398-ml) can pinto beans
1 cup vegetable stock
1 - 2 tsp paprika (you decide the heat)
½ **tsp salt**
½ **tsp ground black pepper**

In a medium pot, cook the rice accordingly. While rice is cooking, in a large saucepan on medium-high heat, sauté the onions in oil until translucent. Add the garlic and marjoram and sauté for 2 minutes. Add the tomatoes, cauliflower, carrots, zucchini, beans, stock, paprika, salt, and pepper. Bring to a boil, then reduce heat. Simmer for 20-25 minutes or until the carrots are tender. Serve over rice. Makes 2 large or 4 small servings.

ALOO GOBI POTATOES & CAULIFLOWER

Did you know that cauliflower has almost as much Vitamin C as an orange? Who knew? Serve this dish over Quick Vegetable Rice (pg 190), with plain short grain brown rice or flatbread.

1 small onion, chopped
1 inch fresh ginger, grated
1 hot pepper, finely chopped (you decided the heat)
2 tbsp olive oil
2 garlic cloves, minced
1 tsp garam masala (pg 304)
½ tsp ground cumin
½ tsp cayenne
½ tsp salt
¼ tsp turmeric
½ cup vegetable stock *or* **water**
1 medium potato, cubed
1½ cups cauliflower, cut into bite-sized florets
¼ cup fresh cilantro, roughly chopped
¼ cup pre-shucked edamame beans *or* **peas**

In a large saucepan on medium heat, sauté the onions, ginger, hot peppers, and garlic in oil until the onions are translucent. Add the garam masala, cumin, cayenne, salt, and turmeric; sauté for 2 minutes, stirring constantly to avoid sticking. Add the stock and potatoes, and stir until well-coated. Cover with lid and cook for 8-10 minutes, stirring occasionally. Add cauliflower and cook for an additional 8-10 minutes. Stir in the cilantro and edamame, remove from heat, and let sit for 5 minutes before serving. Makes 2 large or 4 small servings.

ALOO MATTAR POTATOES & PEAS

Serve over plain rice or with a flatbread (pg 267). It can also be served as a side dish to complement a larger meal.

> **brown rice (or grain of your choice), enough for 2 people**
> **1 medium onion, finely chopped**
> **2 tbsp olive oil**
> **1 inch fresh ginger, finely grated**
> **1 tsp garam masala (pg 304)**
> **½ tsp paprika**
> **¼ cup vegetable stock**
> **1 large potato, cubed**
> **1 large tomato, minced**
> **½ tsp salt**
> **½ cup frozen peas**
> **1 tbsp fresh cilantro, minced**

In a medium pot, cook the rice accordingly. While rice is cooking, in a large saucepan on medium heat, sauté the onions in oil until translucent. Add the ginger, garam masala, and paprika and sauté for 2 minutes; stir constantly to avoid sticking. Add the stock, potatoes, tomatoes, and salt, and stir until well coated. Cover with lid and cook for 8-10 minutes, stirring occasionally. Once potatoes are cooked, stir in the peas and cilantro; remove from heat and let sit for 5 minutes before serving. Makes 2 large or 4 small servings.

COUSIN NATASHA'S EVERYTHING BUT THE KITCHEN SINK VEGETABLE CURRY

My cousin Tash gave me this recipe, and now I give it to you. Tash says: 'I love this recipe, when I have veggies in the fridge that aren't at their prime. I've thrown in eggplant, turnips, whatever I have on hand. Serve this recipe over a bed of rice and enjoy.'

brown rice (*or* grain of your choice), enough for 2 people
1 small onion, chopped
3 tbsp olive oil
1 small sweet potato, cubed
1 large carrot, chopped
2 - 3 garlic cloves, minced
1 cup vegetable stock
½ small red bell pepper, chopped
½ small zucchini, chopped
1 14-oz (398-ml) can chickpeas (garbanzo beans), rinsed and drained
1 tsp ground turmeric
1 tbsp curry powder
1 tsp ground cinnamon
¾ tsp cayenne
½ tsp salt
¼ cup raisins
1 cup spinach, roughly chopped

In a medium pot, cook the rice accordingly. While rice is cooking, in a large saucepan on medium heat, sauté the onions in oil until translucent. Add the sweet potatoes, carrots, and garlic and sauté for 2 minutes; stir occasionally to avoid sticking. Add the stock, red peppers, zucchini, chickpeas, turmeric, curry, cinnamon, cayenne, and salt. Stir well. Reduce heat and cover with lid. Cook for 10-15 minutes, or until vegetables are tender. Stir in the raisins and spinach, remove from heat, and let sit for 5 minutes before serving. Makes 2 large or 4 small servings.

INDER & VANDNA'S PUNJABI PEPPERS & TOFU

Inder and Vandna Bedi from *ViaVegan.com* are the creators of Matt and Nat Handbags. They sent me this incredible recipe which you can serve over rice or with Naan bread.

- **brown rice (***or* **grain of your choice), enough for 2 people**
- **½ lb firm tofu, cubed**
- **1 small onion, chopped**
- **1 tbsp olive oil**
- **1 small green bell pepper, chopped**
- **1 small red bell pepper, chopped**
- **1 tsp salt**
- **1 tsp hot chili powder**
- **1 tsp garam masala (pg 304)**
- **1 large tomato, finely chopped**

In a medium pot, cook the rice accordingly. While rice is cooking, in a wok or large saucepan on medium-high heat, sauté the tofu and onions in oil until onions are translucent and tofu starts to brown. Add the green and red peppers, salt, chili powder, garam masala, and tomatoes. Reduce heat and cover with lid. Simmer for 4-6 minutes or until vegetables are tender. Serve over rice. Makes 2 large or 4 small servings.

EGGPLANT BHARTA

Salting an eggplant to remove bitterness is really only necessary if the eggplant is older; if it's young or fresh, then it is not needed. But if you're not sure, then lightly salt your cubed eggplant, and let sit for 10-15 minutes. Rinse under cold water and pat dry with a paper towel before you start cooking.

- **brown rice (***or* **grain of your choice), enough for 2 people**
- **1 small eggplant, peeled and cubed**
- **1 small onion, chopped**
- **½ cup vegetable stock**
- **3 cloves garlic, minced**
- **2 inches fresh ginger, grated**
- **1 tbsp ground cumin**
- **1 tsp ground coriander**
- **½ tsp ground cinnamon**
- **½ tsp turmeric**
- **¼ tsp cayenne**
- **1 small hot pepper (you decide the heat)**
- **4 roma tomatoes, finely chopped**
- **¼ cup fresh cilantro, chopped**

In a medium pot, cook the rice accordingly. While rice is cooking, in a large saucepan on medium-high heat, combine the eggplant, onions, and stock; cover with lid and cook for 5-7 minutes, or until the eggplant starts to soften and reduce. Add the garlic, ginger, spices, and hot peppers; sauté for an additional 2 minutes. Reduce heat. Add the tomatoes and cilantro, re-cover, and let simmer for an additional 5 minutes before serving over rice. Makes 2 large or 4 small servings.

EGGPLANT PARMESAN

The sauce in this recipe is the Quick All-Purpose Garlic Tomato Sauce on pg 179, but you can cut down your cooking time by using a store-bought tomato sauce, rather than making it from scratch. This recipe is best served over brown rice, but any grain will do. It's worth the time it takes: it's so yum!

brown rice (*or* grain of your choice), enough for 2 people

Sauce:
2 large garlic cloves, minced
2 tbsp olive oil
1 14-oz (398-ml) can diced tomatoes
1 5.5-oz (156-ml) can tomato paste
1 tsp sweetener (e.g. maple syrup, sugar)
¼ tsp salt
¼ tsp ground black pepper

Eggplant:
1 medium eggplant, cut into ½ inch slices
1 - 2 tsp salt
¼ cup flour
¼ cup cornmeal
3 tbsp olive oil
¾ cup vegan "cheese"
¾ cup vegan parmesan "cheese"

In a medium pot, cook the rice accordingly. In a medium saucepan on medium-low heat, sauté the garlic in oil until translucent. Add the tomatoes, tomato paste, sweetener, salt, and pepper; bring to a boil. Reduce heat and let simmer for 15-20 minutes. Remove from heat and set aside when done. Lay eggplant slices onto a plate or cutting board and sprinkle with salt. Let sit for 10-15 minutes. In a small bowl, stir together the flour and cornmeal. Rinse eggplant under cold water and pat dry with paper towel. Dip each slice of eggplant into the flour mixture, making sure both sides are well-coated. Heat the oil in a medium frying pan and cook 3-4 eggplant slices at a time; make sure that both sides are browned evenly. Set aside and continue until all eggplant slices are browned. Preheat oven to 400°F (205°C). In an 8x8-inch baking dish, spoon ½ cup of tomato sauce evenly onto the bottom of dish. Lay down a layer of eggplant followed by ¼ cup "cheese" and a ¼ cup Parmesan "cheese." Then put down a layer of eggplant, top with tomato sauce and the "cheeses." Place on top a final layer of eggplant, tomato sauce, and the "cheeses." Bake for 30-35 minutes. Serve eggplant over rice. Makes 2 large or 4 small servings. Sauce makes approx. 2 cups.

BLESSED BROCCOLI & TOFU STIR-FRY

Serve this stir-fry over brown rice or some wild rice if you're in the mood for a different and nuttier flavor.

brown rice (*or* grain of your choice), enough for 2 people
1 small red onion, roughly chopped
½ lb firm tofu, cubed
4 large button mushrooms, chopped
1 tbsp dark sesame oil
1 large carrot, chopped
1 cup broccoli, cut into bite-sized florets
1 tbsp tamari

In a medium pot, cook the rice accordingly. While rice is cooking, in a wok or large frying pan on medium-high heat, sauté the onions, tofu, and mushrooms in oil until the onions are translucent and tofu starts to brown. Add the carrots, broccoli, and tamari. Cover with lid, then reduce heat. Simmer for 4-6 minutes or until vegetables are tender. Serve over rice. Makes 2 large or 4 small servings.

BOUNTIFUL BEANS & BROWN RICE

There is nothing quite like the marriage of beans and rice. Not only is it an economical way of having a perfect protein in your tummy, but it tastes good too!

brown rice (*or* grain of your choice),
**   enough for 2 people**
1 small onion, chopped
1 celery stalk, chopped
1 small green bell pepper, chopped
½ small jalapeno pepper, minced
1 tbsp olive oil
1 clove garlic, minced
½ tsp chili powder

½ tsp ground cumin
¼ tsp salt
¼ tsp ground black pepper
1 large tomato, chopped
1 14-oz (398-ml) can pinto beans,
**   drained and rinsed**
½ cup vegetable stock
¼ cup fresh cilantro, minced

In a medium pot, cook the rice accordingly. While rice is cooking, in a large saucepan on medium-high heat, sauté the onions, celery, green peppers, and jalapenos in oil until onions are translucent. Add the garlic, chili powder, cumin, salt, and pepper; sauté for an additional 1-2 minutes. Add the tomatoes, beans, and stock. Bring to a boil, then reduce heat. Simmer for 10-15 minutes. Turn off heat and stir in cilantro. Cover with lid and let sit for 5 minutes before serving over rice. Makes 2 large or 4 small servings.

CURRY FENNEL CAULIFLOWER BAKE

"Sarah, I hope you enjoy this family favorite recipe. Even the meat eaters in my family like it!" – Colleen, Las Vegas, NV

brown rice (*or* grain of your choice), enough for 2 people
3 cups cauliflower, cut into bite-sized florets
1 small red onion, chopped
1 garlic clove, minced
½ pound medium or firm tofu, cubed or crumbled
2 tbsp olive oil
1 tsp curry powder
1 tsp garam masala (pg 304)
1 tsp fennel seeds
1 tsp salt
½ tsp ground black pepper
½ cup frozen peas *or* edamame beans
¼ cup fresh cilantro, roughly chopped

Preheat oven to 400°F (205°C). In a medium pot, cook the rice accordingly. While rice is cooking, in a 9x13-inch baking pan, toss together the cauliflower, red onions, garlic, tofu, oil, curry, garam masala, fennel seeds, salt, and pepper. Bake for 30 minutes, stirring every 10 minutes to avoid burning. Once cooked, stir in the peas and cilantro. Turn off the oven and let sit for 5 minutes before serving over rice. Makes 2 large or 4 small servings.

EILEEN'S SESAME GINGER STIR-FRY

Sarah, here's my little fast and tasty contribution to the new book. I made it up one night using things that were in my fridge, when my boy and me were ravenous for something quick to eat. Oh, and by the way, you rock! – Eileen, Toronto, ON

brown rice (*or* grain of your choice), enough for 2 people
1 small onion, chopped
½ block medium *or* firm tofu, cubed
4 large button mushrooms, chopped
1 tbsp dark sesame oil
3 tbsp tahini

1 tbsp water
2 cloves garlic, minced
1 inch fresh ginger, grated
½ small red bell pepper, chopped
¼ cup bean sprouts
¼ tsp salt
¼ tsp ground black pepper

In a medium pot, cook the rice accordingly. While rice is cooking, in a wok or large frying pan on medium-high heat, sauté the onions, tofu, and mushrooms in oil until the onions are translucent and tofu starts to brown. In a small bowl, stir together the tahini and water until smooth. Set aside. Add the garlic, ginger, and red peppers to the frying pan and sauté for 2-3 minutes. Add the tahini, bean sprouts, salt, and pepper. Cover with lid, reduce heat, and simmer for 4-6 minutes. Serve over rice. Makes 2 large or 4 small servings.

EMIRA'S SPEEDY GOURMET KALE & TOFU DELIGHT

Sarah: As such a long time fan of both books, I constantly tell myself to write in with recipes, but I never have the time. Today, I'm giving it a shot. This is a quick and easy way of preparing kale that has made my boyfriend (among those who are deeply suspicious of kale) actually request kale for dinner. Enjoy! – Emira, Vancouver, BC

brown rice (*or* grain of your choice), enough for 2 people
½ lb tofu (flavored *or* plain), cubed
2 tbsp olive oil
1 large garlic clove, minced
4 cups kale, chopped

¼ tsp hot red pepper flakes
¼ tsp salt
¼ tsp ground black pepper
1 tbsp balsamic vinegar
¼ cup pine nuts, toasted (pg 295)

In a medium pot, cook the rice accordingly. While rice is cooking, in a wok or large saucepan on medium-high heat, sauté the tofu in oil until tofu starts to brown. Add the garlic, kale, red pepper flakes, salt, pepper, and balsamic vinegar. Cover with lid and sauté for an additional 5 minutes. Garnish with pine nuts and serve over rice. Makes 2 servings.

MAGNIFICENT MIXED BEANS & BULGUR

Bulgur seems to be shrouded in mystery most of the time. It has a billion different spellings (bulgar, bulghur, and burghul to name a few), and it's often confused with cracked wheat, but it takes less to time to prepare. Because of its quick cooking time bulgur can be stirred into just about any dish to add a little extra oomph. In this recipe bulgur is combined with mixed beans, which as we all know, makes a perfect protein. Yippee!

1 small onion, chopped
2 cups eggplant, chopped
½ small red bell pepper, chopped
2 garlic cloves, minced
2 tbsp olive oil
1 19-oz (540-ml) can mixed beans, rinsed and drained
1 cup vegetable stock
½ cup bulgur
½ tsp salt
½ tsp ground black pepper
1 large tomato, chopped
½ tsp dried mint (*or*** fresh if you have it)**

In a medium saucepan on medium-high heat, sauté the onions, eggplant, red peppers, and garlic in oil until the onions are translucent; stir occasionally to avoid sticking. Add the beans, stock, bulgur, salt, and pepper. Reduce heat and cover with lid. Cook for 5-8 minutes or until bulgur is cooked. Stir in the tomatoes and mint, turn off heat, and let sit 5 minutes before serving. Makes 2 large or 4 small servings.

VEGETABLE BIRYANI

This is a favorite dish that a colleague of mine brings to potlucks. – Kim, via the Internet *(This recipe can be served as a main course with Chapati Flat Bread [pg 267] and the Cool Cucumber Salad [pg 83], or as a side dish as part of a bigger meal.)*

1 small onion, chopped
1 tbsp oil
2 cloves garlic, finely chopped
½ tsp ground cinnamon
¼ tsp ground turmeric
¼ tsp ground black pepper
¼ tsp ground ginger
½ tsp salt
1 large carrot, chopped
1 14-oz (398-ml) can chickpeas (garbanzo beans), rinsed and drained
¼ cup dried red lentils
½ cup basmati rice
2½ cups water
1 large tomato, finely chopped
½ cup frozen peas
1 tbsp fresh mint, minced
¼ cup plain soygurt (optional)

In a large saucepan on medium-high heat, sauté the onions in oil until translucent. Add the garlic, cinnamon, turmeric, pepper, ginger, and salt; sauté for 1-2 minutes, stirring often to avoid sticking. Add the carrots, chickpeas, lentils, rice, and water. Bring to a boil, then reduce heat. Cover with lid and simmer for 15-20 minutes, or until rice is cooked. Turn off heat, stir in the tomatoes, peas, and mint and let stand for 5 minutes before serving. Serve with a dollop of soygurt. Makes 2 large or 4 small servings.

SHIRLEY'S CAJUN RED BEANS & RICE

This dish can be served as an entree, but also makes a nice side dish for a larger meal.

> **1 medium onion, chopped**
> **1 large celery stalk, chopped**
> **1 small green bell pepper, chopped**
> **1 tbsp olive oil**
> **1½ cups vegetable stock** *or* **water**
> **1 14-oz (398-ml) diced tomatoes, including liquid**
> **½ - 1 tsp Cajun spice (pg 303)**
> **¼ tsp ground black pepper**
> **2 tsp sweetener (e.g. sugar, maple syrup)**
> **1 cup white basmati rice** *or* **quick cooking rice**
> **1 14-oz (398-ml) can kidney beans, drained and rinsed**

In a medium saucepan on medium-high heat, sauté the onions, celery, and green peppers in oil until tender. Add the stock, tomatoes, Cajun spice, pepper, and sweetener. Bring to a boil, then reduce heat. Stir in rice and simmer for 15-20 minutes or until rice is cooked. Stir in kidney beans and cook until heated through. Makes 2 large or 4 small servings.

MISCELLANEOUS ENTRÉES
TYLER & PHOEBE'S PERFECT PESTO PIZZA

Hi Sarah! Here is a pizza recipe from Phoebe and me. This is our version of what was our favorite non-vegan pizza before we stopped eating dairy, from a local Italian food place. It's very simple and very good. – Tyler, an American living somewhere in Canada *(The Faux Feta Cheese recipe tastes best when you let it marinate for at least an hour or more, so prepare it in the morning if you're planning on making pizza that evening. If you don't have time to make a crust from scratch, buy a large loaf of bread, cut in half lengthwise, and cover both halves with ingredients.)*

Pesto sauce:
3 cups fresh basil, tightly packed
¼ - ½ cup pine nuts, toasted (pg 295)
2 - 4 garlic cloves
½ tsp salt
½ tsp ground black pepper
½ cup olive oil

Toppings:
1 pizza crust (pg 300-301)
½ cup shallots, chopped
½ tbsp olive oil
1 cup baby spinach
1 - 2 cups vegan "cheese," grated
Faux Feta Cheese (pg 292)

Preheat oven to 450°F (230°C). Place prepared pizza crust on baking sheet and set aside. To prepare sauce: in a food processor, blend together the basil, pine nuts, garlic, salt, and pepper. Slowly add the olive oil, while blending, until well mixed. Set aside. In a large saucepan on medium heat, sauté the shallots in oil until translucent and set aside. Spread the pesto sauce evenly over pizza crust. Evenly add the spinach and shallots. Add a layer of "cheese," topped with faux feta "cheese." Bake for 10-12 minutes. Let cool 5 minutes before cutting and serving. Makes 1 large pizza. Pesto sauce makes approx. 1 cup.

VEGGIE POT PIE

This recipe uses the All-Purpose Crust (pg 262) cut in half. The dough needs to be refrigerated for at least an hour before you can use it, so prepare it in the morning if you're going to make the pot pie for dinner. This is one of those comfort food recipes that makes you wish you had a corncob pipe and a pocketknife to whittle with.

Crust:
1 cup flour
½ tsp salt
⅓ cup vegan margarine
2 tbsp "milk"

Filling:
1 small onion, chopped
1 tbsp olive oil
2 celery stalks, chopped
1 large carrot, chopped
½ red bell pepper, chopped
1 medium potato, finely chopped
⅓ cup frozen peas
¼ cup red lentils
1 cup vegetable stock
½ tsp salt
¼ tsp ground black pepper
¼ tsp sage
¼ tsp thyme
¼ tsp cayenne pepper
2 tbsp flour
½ cup "milk"

To prepare the dough: in a food processor, blend the flour and salt together. Add the margarine and pulse until mixture resembles a coarse meal. Add "milk" and blend until well combined and dough forms. Remove dough, roll into a ball, and wrap in plastic. Refrigerate for at least 1 hour before using. Preheat oven to 400°F (205°C). Lightly oil a deep dish 10-inch pie plate or an 8x8-inch baking dish and set aside. In a large saucepan on medium heat, sauté the onions in oil until translucent. Add the celery, carrots, and bell peppers and sauté for an additional 2-3 minutes. Add the potatoes, peas, lentils, stock, salt, pepper, sage, thyme, and cayenne pepper. Bring to a boil, then reduce heat; cover with lid and simmer for 4-6 minutes or until lentils are soft. Stir in the flour and milk and simmer until sauce begins to thicken. Transfer cooked vegetables to baking dish. Roll out dough and place evenly over top of vegetables and bake for 20-25 minutes. Makes 2 large or 4 small servings.

TIP-TOP TOFU LOAF

Is there any other word in the English language that is less appetizing than the word "loaf"? Despite the name, this easy dish can be thrown together and on your table to eat in about an hour. It makes a hardy main course when accompanied with Cumin Fried Potatoes (pg 192) or Dijon Mustard Brussels Sprouts (pg 185), or slice it into wedges and served as a sandwich filler.

2 tbsp olive oil
1 cup medium-firm tofu, drained
1 small onion, roughly chopped
2 garlic cloves, roughly chopped
2 tbsp ketchup
2 tbsp tamari
1 tbsp Dijon mustard
¼ cup fresh parsley, minced
¼ tsp ground black pepper
½ cup rolled oat flakes *or* **breadcrumbs**
1 tbsp tahini

Preheat oven to 350°F (175°C). Oil a 9-inch loaf pan with the olive oil (leaving excess on the pan) and set aside. In a food processor, blend together the tofu, onions, garlic, ketchup, tamari, mustard, parsley, pepper, oat flakes, and tahini until well mixed. Pour into baking dish, pressing down evenly into baking pan. Bake for 55-60 minutes. Let cool 10 minutes before removing from pan and serving. Makes approx. 2 large or 4 small servings.

GROOVY GARDEN VEGETABLE CASSEROLE

The crazy kids in the *GoVegan.net* chatroom have been begging me to come up with more casserole recipes. I'm like, "What? Is this the 1970s? I thought casseroles were out of style." I guess if you wait long enough, everything comes back around to haunt you. Luckily for you, this one isn't as painful as that polyester pantsuit that you wore to your 8th grade graduation party.

Filling:
1 medium onion, chopped
1 tbsp olive oil
1 garlic clove, chopped
2 cups kale, finely chopped
2 cups broccoli, finely chopped
1 cup parsnip, finely chopped
1 large carrot, chopped
¼ cup vegetable stock *or* **water**
1 tbsp tamari
½ tsp salt

Topping:
3 slices of bread, roughly chopped
½ cup vegan "cheese," grated (optional)
½ cup firm tofu
2 tbsp olive oil
1 tbsp tamari
1 tsp dried basil
1 tsp dried oregano
1 tsp Asian chili garlic sauce (*or* **other hot sauce)**
¼ tsp salt
¼ tsp ground black pepper

Preheat oven to 350°F (175°C). Lightly oil an 8x8-inch baking dish and set aside. In a large saucepan on medium heat, sauté the onions in oil until translucent. Add the garlic, kale, broccoli, parsnips, carrots, stock, tamari, and salt. Cover with a lid and simmer for 4-6 minutes, or until carrots start to soften. While vegetables are simmering, in a food processor, blend the bread, "cheese," tofu, oil, tamari, basil, oregano, hot sauce, salt, and pepper until smooth. Transfer cooked vegetables to baking dish. Spread tofu mixture evenly over top of vegetables and bake for 20-25 minutes. Makes 2 large or 4 small servings.

PINTO BEAN CASSEROLE WITH TORTILLA CHIP CRUST

Oh, the pinto bean. Pinto is Spanish for "painted." These beans are high in fiber, and rich in protein, calcium, and iron. When you weigh the pros against the inappropriate flatulence, I think beans always win out in the end – either one!

1 19-oz (540-ml) can pinto beans, drained and rinsed
1 small onion, chopped
1 small green bell pepper, chopped
1 tbsp olive oil
1 garlic clove, minced
1 tbsp pickled jalapenos, minced
2 tsp chili powder
½ tsp ground cumin
2 medium tomatoes, chopped
¼ cup vegetable stock
3 - 4 cups tortilla chips, crushed
1 cup vegan "cheese"
Faux Sour Cream (pg 293), optional

Preheat oven to 400°F (205°C). Pour beans into a lightly oiled 8x8-inch baking dish and mash well with a potato masher or a fork, then set aside. In a large saucepan on medium heat, sauté the onions and green peppers in oil until onions are translucent. Add the garlic, jalapenos, chili powder, cumin, tomatoes, and stock. Cover with a lid and simmer 2-4 minutes. While vegetables are simmering, in a medium bowl, crush the tortilla chips with your hand or a potato masher and set aside. Add vegetable mixture to the pinto beans and stir well. Cover with an even layer of tortilla chips and bake for 25 minutes. Remove from oven, add a layer of "cheese," and bake for an additional 5 minutes. Serve with a dollop of Faux Sour Cream. Makes 2 large or 4 small servings.

KAREN'S MEXICAN BURRITO PIE

Here's an "easy as pie" recipe for you. One of my favorite meals is bean burritos, which are fairly easy to make. This is a variation on the burrito and is even easier to throw together (I think) – and a little "tidier" if you're serving it to guests. – Karen, Northwood, NH *(If you can't find pinto beans, you can use any kind of beans you like [e.g. black beans, kidney, mixed] in this delicious versatile recipe.)*

1 large, very ripe avocado
1 garlic clove, minced
2 - 3 green onions, finely chopped
1 tbsp Faux Sour Cream (pg 293)
1 tbsp lemon juice
1 19-oz (540-ml) can pinto beans, drained and rinsed
1 cup salsa (pg 63, 297)
2 tbsp pickled jalapenos, minced
1 tsp chili powder
½ tsp ground cumin
5 - 8 inch flour tortillas
1½ cups vegan "cheese," grated

Preheat oven to 350°F (175°C). In a small bowl, mash together the avocados, garlic, green onions, "sour cream," and lemon juice until smooth. Set aside. In a medium bowl, mash together the pinto beans, salsa, jalapenos, chili powder, and cumin. Set aside. Lightly oil a deep dish 8-inch pie plate and start to layer. Lay down a tortilla, then half the bean mixture. Follow with another tortilla, half the avocado mixture and ½ cup "cheese." Continue with an additional tortilla, the remaining bean mixture, another tortilla, the remaining avocado mixture, ½ cup "cheese," and a final tortilla. Cover with tinfoil and bake for 25 minutes. Remove cover, top with remaining "cheese," and bake for an additional 5 minutes. Cut pie into wedges and serve. Makes 4 servings.

BLACK BEAN & SWEET POTATO BURRITOS

This recipe takes a few more minutes than most other recipes in this book, but it's well worth the extra time. It makes 4 burritos because I didn't want you to only use half a can of beans (only to have the other half rot away in the back of your refrigerator). The burritos freeze well for later, or you can take them to work the next day for lunch. You'll need a potato masher for this recipe.

2 medium sweet potatoes (approx. 4 cups), diced
1 small onion, finely chopped
1 tbsp olive oil
1 19-oz (540-ml) can black beans, drained and rinsed
1 cup vegetable stock
2 garlic cloves, minced
1½ tbsp chili powder
2 tsp ground mustard
1 tsp ground cumin
½ tsp salt
4 large flour tortillas
¼ cup salsa (pg 63, 297)
1 cup vegan "cheese," grated (optional)

In a large pot of salted water, boil the sweet potatoes. While sweet potatoes are cooking, in a medium saucepan on medium heat, sauté the onions in oil until translucent. Add the black beans, stock, garlic, chili powder, mustard, cumin, and salt; simmer, uncovered, over medium-high heat for 15 minutes. Drain water from sweet potatoes; return sweet potatoes to pot and mash with a potato masher. Set aside. Once bean mixture is done, mash with potato masher and set aside. Take 4 tortilla shells and lay on counter. Spread out onto each tortilla: 1 tbsp salsa, ¼ of the sweet potatoes, ¼ of the beans, and ¼ of the "cheese." Roll up each burrito and serve as is, or bake in oven until crisp. Makes 4 burritos.

SLOPPY JANE'S

Quick, easy, and sloppy. Just like Jane.

1 small onion, chopped
1 tbsp olive oil
1 small green bell pepper, chopped
1 lb medium *or* **firm tofu, crumbled** *or* **mashed**
1 14-oz (398-ml) can tomato sauce
1 tbsp chili powder
½ tsp salt
¼ tsp pepper
½ tbsp prepared mustard
1 tbsp maple syrup *or* **sweetener**
2 tbsp vegan Worcestershire sauce
¼ cup basmati rice
1 large pickle, chopped

In a large saucepan on medium heat, sauté the onions in oil until translucent. Add the green peppers and tofu and sauté for 2 minutes, stirring constantly to prevent sticking. Add the tomato sauce, chili powder, salt, pepper, mustard, maple syrup, Worcestershire sauce, and rice. Cover, reduce heat, and simmer for 15-20 minutes or until rice is cooked; stir occasionally to prevent sticking. Once cooked, stir in pickles and serve over toasted buns or bread. Makes 2 large or 4 small servings.

TU-NO OPEN-FACE SANDWICH

TuNA? Just say Tu-NO! This sandwich filling is great on a big chunk of bread, or try toasting it with some vegan "cheese" on top to bring back those white trash memories of visiting Grandma in the double-wide.

½ cup tempeh, cubed *or* **crumbled**
¼ cup Faux Mayonnaise (pg 293)
2 tbsp pickle relish
¼ tsp dried dill weed
¼ tsp ground cumin
¼ tsp kelp

½ tbsp tamari
1 tsp lime juice
1 celery stalk, chopped
1 small garlic clove, minced
2 tsp sunflower seeds
4 slices bread, toasted

In a medium bowl, stir together the tempeh, "mayonnaise," relish, dill, cumin, kelp, tamari, lime juice, celery, garlic, and sunflower seeds. Serve even amounts over toasted bread. Makes 2 large or 4 small servings.

CURRY ALMOND BURGERS

Serve these tasty burgers on a bun topped with some mango chutney and with a nice green side salad. If you can't find any mock "ground beef," you can also use well crumbled firm tofu in its place, but add a little more curry powder for extra flavor.

> 1½ cups mock "ground beef"
> 3 green onions, finely chopped
> 1 garlic clove, finely chopped
> 2 inches fresh ginger, grated
> ⅓ cup slivered almonds
> ¼ cup bread crumbs
> 1 tbsp curry powder
> ¼ tsp salt
> egg replacer to equal 1 egg (pg 296)

In a medium bowl, stir together all ingredients until well mixed. With hands, divide and shape firmly into 4 patties. In a lightly oiled frying pan on medium-high heat, fry patties for 5-10 minutes or until browned on both sides. Serve immediately. Makes 4 patties.

MAMA MAYHEM'S TOFU EXTRAVAGANZA

I always make this for our Super Bowl football parties, and it's always a huge hit at any potluck. Even my friends who are afraid of tofu love this recipe. – Mary, Knoxville, TN *(Serve this multi-purpose recipe on buns, as a dip, in a tortilla wrap, over toast, as a side dish . . . shall I go on?)*

> 1 block firm tofu, drained
> ¼ cup tamari
> 1 tbsp nutritional yeast
> ¼ cup Faux Mayonnaise (pg 293)
> ⅓ cup walnuts, chopped
> ¼ of a small red onion, minced
> 2 - 3 large dill pickles, minced
> ½ tsp celery seed
> ½ tsp dried dill weed

In a large bowl, mash the tofu until well crumbled. Add the remainder of the ingredients and stir together well. Keep chilled until ready to serve. Makes approx. 2½ cups.

COCONUT CURRIED VEGGIES

There's nothing I like better than a meal made in one pot – easy to make, easy to clean up. Eat it out of the pot, for all I care! The less dishes to do at the end of the meal, the better.

1 medium onion, roughly chopped
1 tbsp olive oil
1 small hot pepper, finely chopped (you decide the heat)
1 medium red bell pepper, diced
2 - 3 garlic cloves, minced
2 tsp curry powder
½ tsp dried thyme
½ tsp black pepper
½ tsp salt
1 cup vegetable stock
1 cup jasmine rice
1 14-oz (398-ml) can red kidney beans, rinsed and drained
1 13.5-oz (384-ml) can coconut milk

In a large saucepan on medium heat, sauté the onions in oil until translucent. Add the hot peppers, red peppers, garlic, curry, thyme, pepper and salt and sauté for 2 minutes; stir constantly to prevent sticking. Add the stock, rice, beans, and coconut milk. Cover and simmer on medium heat for 15-20 minutes or until rice is cooked, stirring occasionally to prevent sticking. Makes 2 large or 4 small servings.

FESTIVE STUFFED BUTTERNUT SQUASH

This recipe takes a little longer, but it's perfect for when you have a little more time to spend on dinner. You can prepare the stuffed squash ahead of time then serve this festive meal garnished with Merciful Miso Gravy (pg 182). Remember to count your blessings!

½ cup brown rice
1 cup water
1 small/medium butternut squash
1 medium onion, chopped
1 garlic clove, minced
1 celery stalk, chopped
½ small green bell pepper, chopped
1 tbsp olive oil
¼ tsp dried basil
¼ tsp dried oregano
¼ tsp ground cumin
1 tbsp tamari
3 tsp tahini
¼ tsp salt
¼ tsp ground black pepper
½ cups walnuts, chopped
¼ cup pecans, chopped
1 slice bread, cubed

Preheat oven to 350°F (175°C). In a medium pot, cook the rice and water accordingly. While rice is cooking, wash the outside of the squash thoroughly. Cut the squash in half (lengthwise), scoop out the seeds, and place squash cut side down on a lightly oiled baking sheet. Bake in the oven for 20-35 minutes or until squash is tender. Remove squash from the oven (do not turn off oven) and place on cooling racks. Let sit until squash cools down enough to handle, then scoop out flesh (reserve squash shells for later) and place into a large bowl. Set aside. In a large saucepan on medium-high heat, sauté the onions, garlic, celery, and green peppers in oil until onions are translucent. Combine the butternut squash with the cooked vegetables, cooked brown rice, basil, oregano, cumin, tamari, tahini, salt, pepper, walnuts, pecans, and bread and stir together well. Stuff mixture into hollowed-out squash shells. Return shells to baking sheet and bake for 15-20 minutes. Makes 2 large or 4 small servings.

SARAH'S CHILI-CON-BULGUR

My husband says he always feels bad when he taste-tests my new chili recipes. He says I'll never top the chili in *How It All Vegan!* But a girl can try, right? If you can't find any bulgur you can use rice; just cook chili until rice is done.

1 medium onion, minced
1 tbsp olive oil
1 large carrot, chopped
1 celery stalk, chopped
1 medium green bell pepper, chopped
2 garlic cloves, minced
1 14-oz (398-ml) can diced tomatoes
3½ cups vegetable stock
¾ cup bulgur

1 19-oz (540-ml) can beans (your choice), drained and rinsed
¼ cup tamari
1½ tsp chili powder
1½ tsp dried oregano
1 tsp ground cumin
½ tsp pepper
¼ tsp salt

In a large saucepan on medium heat, sauté the onions in oil until translucent. Add the carrots, celery, green peppers, and garlic and sauté for an additional 2-3 minutes. Add the remaining ingredients, bring to a boil, then reduce heat. Simmer for 25-30 minutes, stirring occasionally to prevent sticking. Makes 4 servings.

TASTY TEMPEH CHILI

Tempeh is a fermented soybean cake, which may not sound appealing, but don't be scared! Tempeh has an earthy nutty flavor, and like tofu, is high in protein. You can find it in your local health food store and some grocery stores.

1 small onion, chopped
1 tbsp olive oil
1 cup tempeh, cubed
1 garlic clove, minced
3 large tomatoes, chopped
1 14-oz (398-ml) can tomato sauce
1 14-oz (398-ml) can kidney beans, drained and rinsed

¼ cup frozen corn niblets
1 tbsp tamari
1 tsp molasses
1½ tsp chili powder
1 tsp groundcumin
¼ tsp salt
½ cup vegan "cheese" (optional)

In a large saucepan on medium heat, sauté the onions in oil until translucent. Add the tempeh and garlic and sauté for an additional 2-3 minutes. Add the tomatoes, tomato sauce, kidney beans, corn, tamari, molasses, chili powder, cumin, and salt. Bring to a boil, then reduce heat; cover with lid and simmer for 15-20 minutes. Serve each bowl of chili topped with a "cheese" garnish. Makes 2 large or 4 small servings.

SHERRI'S BLACK BEAN CHILI

This soup can bring tears to your eyes depending on how many chilies you use. The apple juice is an excellent balance to the heat. – Sherri, Winnipeg, MB *(Serve this wonderful chili with Basic Baking Powder Biscuits [pg 271] and a nice green salad.)*

1 small onion, chopped
1 tbsp olive oil
½ small red bell pepper, chopped
1 cup water *or* **vegetable stock**
1 cup apple juice
½ tsp dried oregano
½ tsp ground cumin
½ tsp salt
¼ tsp cayenne pepper
1 3.8-oz (114-ml) can pickled green chilies (reduce amount to reduce heat)
1 19-oz (540-ml) can black beans, drained and rinsed
1 5.5-oz (156-ml) can tomato paste
¼ cup basmati rice
¼ cup fresh cilantro, minced
½ cup vegan "cheese," grated (optional)

In a large saucepan on medium heat, sauté the onions in oil until translucent. Add the red peppers and sauté for an additional 2-3 minutes. Add the water, juice, oregano, cumin, salt, cayenne, and green chilies. Bring to a boil, then reduce heat, and simmer for 5 minutes. Stir in the beans, tomato paste, and rice. Cover with lid and simmer for 15-20 minutes or until rice is cooked; stir occasionally to prevent from sticking. Stir in cilantro just before serving and top each bowl of chili with a "cheese" garnish. Makes 2 large or 4 small servings.

STUFFED CABBAGE ROLLS

These cabbage rolls take a little while to make, but they're worth the effort. The suggested sauce recipe is the Quick All-Purpose Garlic Tomato Sauce (pg 179), but you can cut down your cooking time by using a jar of tomato sauce instead. Don't forget to use any leftover cabbage for soup or in your vegetable stock.

1 small head of green cabbage

Filling:
¼ cup bulgur
¼ cup boiling water
1 small onion
2 garlic cloves, minced
3 large button mushrooms, finely chopped
1 tbsp olive oil
1 tbsp tamari
⅛ tsp paprika
⅛ tsp black ground pepper
⅛ tsp cayenne
3 tbsp walnuts, finely chopped
½ cup cooked cabbage, finely chopped

Sauce:
2 large garlic cloves, minced
2 tbsp olive oil
1 14-oz (398-ml) can diced tomatoes
1 15.5-oz (156-ml) can tomato paste
1 tsp sweetener (e.g. maple syrup, sugar)
¼ tsp salt
¼ tsp ground black pepper

Preheat oven to 350°F (175°C). Remove core from cabbage and steam whole head for 20 minutes. Set aside to cool. Remove 6 large leaves and set aside. While cabbage is steaming, in a small bowl, pour boiling water over bulgur. Cover with lid and set aside. In a medium saucepan on medium heat, sauté the onions, garlic, and mushrooms in oil until onions are translucent. Add the tamari, paprika, pepper, cayenne, walnuts, and bulgur and sauté for 6-8 minutes. Add ½ cup of the chopped, cooked cabbage and set aside. To prepare the sauce: In a medium saucepan on medium-low heat, sauté the garlic in oil until translucent. Add the tomatoes, tomato paste, sweetener, salt, and pepper and bring to a boil. Reduce heat and let simmer over low heat for 15-20 minutes. Assemble cabbage rolls by dividing filling among the 6 leaves. Roll each leaf and arrange in a lightly oiled 8x8-inch baking dish. Spoon tomato sauce evenly over top and bake for 20-25 minutes. Makes 2 large or 4 small servings. Sauce makes approx. 2 cups.

EMILY'S "MEAT" LOAF

Hey Sarah: I swear this is the best vegan "meat loaf" I've ever had, and I've tried them all. Any leftovers also make great sandwiches. This recipe is named for Emily the cow, who jumped a 5-foot fence to escape the slaughterhouse. – Wolffie, Davie, FL *(This is one of those great recipes that you can throw together in advance. Pop it in the oven when you get home, and while your loaf is "loafing", make yourself a nice spinach salad. Don't forget your greens!)*

1 small onion, finely chopped
2 celery stalks, finely chopped
1 small carrot, finely chopped
1 garlic clove, minced
1 tbsp olive oil
2 slices bread, roughly chopped
1 cup walnuts
5 - 6 veggie burgers *or* **1½ cups mock ground "beef," crumbled**
½ tsp salt
¼ tsp ground black pepper
½ tsp dried oregano
½ tsp dried basil
1 tbsp nutritional yeast flakes
1 tbsp tahini *or* **nut butter (your choice)**
1 tbsp tamari
2 tbsp vegan Worcestershire sauce
1 cup vegan "cheese," finely grated
¼ - ½ cup ketchup

Preheat oven to 350°F (180°C). Lightly oil an 8-inch loaf pan and set aside. In a large saucepan on medium-high heat, sauté the onions, celery, carrots, and garlic in oil until onions are translucent. Set aside to cool. In a food processor, blend the bread and walnuts and set aside. In a large bowl, combine the sautéed vegetables, bread mixture, "beef," salt, pepper, oregano, basil, nutritional yeast, tahini, tamari, Worcestershire sauce, and "cheese." Mix together until well blended. Press firmly into loaf pan and bake for 30 minutes. Pour ketchup evenly over top of loaf and bake for an additional 10 minutes. Remove from oven and let sit 5 minutes before serving. Makes 4-6 servings.

JAY-LO'S FRIED "CHICKEN"

When you prepare your Faux Chicken cutlets (pg 287), shape and cut them so they resemble a chicken breast. (Tee hee – I said breast.) This is my good friend Jason's recipe, which he makes for BBQs at his house. It's delish and quite a dish . . . just like Jay!

¼ **cup flour**
½ **tsp paprika**
½ **tsp salt**
½ **tsp ground black pepper**
½ **cup "milk"**
Faux Chicken cutlets (pg 287)
3 - 4 tbsp olive oil

In a shallow dish, stir together the flour, paprika, salt, and pepper and set aside. In a small bowl, pour "milk" and set aside. Dip "chicken" into flour, then dip in "milk," and then into the flour again. In a large frying pan on medium-high heat, fry "chicken" in oil until well browned on both sides. Makes 2 large or 4 small servings.

MUSHROOM "SAUSAGE" PIZZA

Vegetarian pizza has gotten so much more interesting with the widespread availability of mock "meat" and "cheese" products!

1 pizza crust (pg 300-301)
½ **cup tomato sauce (pg 178-179)**
½ **cup Faux Sausage, chopped (pg 285)**
4 - 6 shitake mushrooms, thinly sliced
¼ **cup red onions, thinly sliced**
½ **cup vegan "cheese," finely grated**

Preheat oven to 450°F (230°C). Place prepared pizza crust on baking sheet. Spread tomato sauce evenly over crust. Evenly add the "sausage," mushrooms, and onions, and top with an even layer of "cheese." Bake for 15-20 minutes. Let cool 5 minutes before cutting and serving. Makes 1 large pizza.

PORTOBELLO POT PIE

Portobello mushrooms have a wonderful earthy flavor and add a "meaty" texture to this pot pie. This recipe uses the All-Purpose Crust recipe (pg 262) cut in half – but don't sweat it; I've already done the math for you. The dough needs to be chilled for at least an hour before you can use it. To make things easier, prepare the dough in the morning if you're going to make the pot pie for dinner.

Crust:

1 cup all-purpose *or* **pastry flour**
½ tsp salt
⅓ cup vegan margarine
2 tbsp "milk"

Filling:

1 medium onion, chopped
2 large Portobello mushrooms, stems removed, cubed
4 - 6 button mushrooms, chopped
1 tbsp olive oil
1 small potato, cubed
1 celery stalk, chopped
1 medium carrot, chopped
2 tbsp tamari
½ tsp dried thyme
1 tsp dried sage
¾ cups vegetable stock
2 tbsp flour

To prepare the crust: In a food processor, blend the flour and salt together. Add the margarine and pulse until mixture resembles a coarse meal. Add "milk" and blend until well combined and dough forms. Remove dough, roll into a ball, and wrap in plastic; chill for at least 1 hour before using. Preheat oven to 350°F (180°C). Lightly oil a deep 10-inch pie plate or an 8x8-inch baking dish and set aside. In a large saucepan on medium heat, sauté the onions and mushrooms in oil until onions are translucent. Add the potatoes, celery, carrots, tamari, thyme, sage, and stock. Bring to a boil then reduce heat. Cover with lid and simmer for 4-6 minutes or until potatoes can be poked easily with a fork. Stir in the flour and simmer until sauce begins to thicken. Transfer cooked vegetables to baking dish. Roll out the chilled dough and place evenly over top of vegetables. Bake for 20-25 minutes. Let sit 5 minutes before serving. Makes 4 servings.

WOLFFIE'S SOUTHWESTERN CORN CASSEROLE

A wonderfully easy recipe that satisfies on so many levels and goes perfectly with the Wolffie's Spinach Walnut Salad (pg 78) or Edamame & Asparagus Couscous Salad (pg 83). To cut back on the heat, omit the jalapeno pepper.

½ cup + 2 tbsp "milk"
2 tsp apple cider vinegar
½ cup soft or silken tofu
2 tbsp vegan margarine
2 tsp sugar
1 12-oz (341-ml) can corn niblets, drained
⅓ cup flour
⅓ cornmeal
½ tsp baking soda
1 tsp salt
1 medium onion, chopped
1 3.8-oz (114-ml) can chopped green chilies, including liquid
1 small jalapeno pepper, minced (optional)

Preheat oven to 325°F (160°C). Lightly oil an 8x8-inch baking dish and set aside. In a food processor, combine the "milk," vinegar, tofu, margarine, sugar, and ½ can of corn; blend until smooth and set aside. In a medium bowl, stir together the flour, cornmeal, baking soda, and salt. Stir in the tofu mixture, reserved corn, onions, chilies, and jalapeno peppers. Pour evenly into the baking dish and bake for 55-60 minutes. Makes 2 large or 4 small servings.

TOFU ROAST

This is one of those recipes that requires a bit of time but for special occasions it's perfect. Serve with gravy (pg 181-182) and Dijon Mustard Brussels Sprouts (pg 185) and thank your lucky stars that you're surrounded by so much love. Cheesecloth is inexpensive and can be found in any grocery or kitchen store; you will need it to help mold the tofu into the correct shape and to help squeeze out any excess moisture.

2 lbs firm *or* **extra-firm tofu**
2 tbsp tamari
1 tsp dried sage

Stuffing:
1 small onion, minced
4 large button mushrooms, chopped
1 small carrot, diced
1 celery stalk, minced
1½ tbsp olive oil
½ cup golden raisins
2 garlic cloves, minced
2 tbsp tamari
1 tsp dried sage
1 tsp rosemary
½ tsp thyme
3 cups bread, cubed
¼ cup walnuts, roughly chopped
1 cup vegetable stock

Basting sauce:
¼ cup dark sesame oil
¼ cup olive oil
¼ cup tamari
1 tbsp miso paste
2 tbsp juice (cranberry *or* **orange)**
1 tsp Dijon mustard
½ tsp liquid smoke (optional)
¼ tsp ground black pepper

Carefully squeeze the tofu to remove as much water as possible. Line a large colander with dampened cheesecloth so that the cheesecloth hangs over the sides. Place colander on a large plate. Roughly chop tofu, place inside colander, and cover with cheesecloth. Place something heavy (e.g., 2 unopened soy milk boxes) on top of the cheesecloth in order to press any remaining liquid out of the tofu. Let sit for an hour. In a large saucepan, sauté the onions, mushrooms, carrots, and celery in oil until onions are translucent. Add the raisins, garlic, tamari, sage, rosemary, thyme, bread, walnuts, and stock and simmer for 5-6 minutes or until liquid has been absorbed. Set aside. In a food processor, blend the drained tofu, tamari, and sage until smooth. Remove ½ cup of the tofu and set aside for later. Return the remaining blended tofu to the cheesecloth-covered colander and press it down against the edges of the colander – leaving a 1-inch thick shell, creating a "bowl" shape. Add your cooked stuffing to center of the tofu bowl and press reserved tofu over top to cover stuffing. Smooth tofu over so stuffing is sealed inside. Carefully bring up the edges the cheesecloth, tying the cheesecloth VERY tightly together, and place colander on a large plate. Place a smaller plate on top of roast and put weight back on top of the cheesecloth in order the press any remaining liquid out of the tofu. Let sit in refrigerator for at least 3 hours (overnight is better). Preheat oven to 450°F (230°C). To prepare basting sauce: In a small bowl, whisk together the sesame oil, olive oil, tamari, miso paste, juice, Dijon mustard, liquid smoke, and pepper. Set aside. Line a baking pan with tin foil. Remove roast from fridge and carefully remove from cheesecloth. Place roast upside down on baking sheet and baste with half the basting sauce. Cover with foil and bake for 1 hour. Reduce heat to 350°F (175°C). Remove foil, and baste with remaining sauce. Bake for an additional 30 minutes, basting every 10 minutes with run-off sauce. Carefully transfer roast to serving platter. Makes 6-8 servings.

THE JOINT'S "CHEESE BURGER" PIZZA

Our hippie friend Jeff (don't let the dreadlocks scare you) and his beautiful wife Keeley run a pizza place right next to The Tattoo Zoo called The Joint. We eat there almost every single day; they serve a vegetarian "Cheese Burger Pizza" that is so crazy, you're going to love it.

1 pizza crust (pg 300-301)
¾ cup tomato sauce
1 - 2 pickles, thinly sliced
¼ small onion, thinly sliced
1 cup mock ground "beef"
1 cup vegan "cheese," grated
2 tbsp - ¼ cup prepared mustard

Preheat oven to 450°F (230°C). Place prepared pizza crust on baking sheet. Spread tomato sauce evenly over crust. Evenly distribute the pickles and onions, then a layer of "ground beef," topped with "cheese." Top with desired amount of mustard over cheese and bake for 15-20 minutes. Let cool 5 minutes before cutting and serving. Makes 1 large pizza.

TOMATO WALNUT-CRUSTED FRIED "CHICKEN"

This wonderful faux "meat" recipe is best when served over your favorite whole grain with a nice side of steamed veggies.

4 Faux Chicken *or* **Faux Turkey cutlets (pg 287, 289)**
3 tbsp olive oil

Marinade:
1 5.5-oz (156-ml) can tomato paste
2 tbsp red wine vinegar
½ cup juice (e.g. orange, cranberry)
2 garlic cloves, minced
1 tsp dried rosemary
2 tsp No-Salt Shaker (pg 303)

Crust:
1 cup walnuts
½ cup flour
1 tbsp dried rosemary
½ tsp salt
½ tsp ground black pepper

In a small bowl, stir together the tomato paste, vinegar, juice, garlic, rosemary, and No-Salt. Place "chicken" cutlets on a large plate and pour marinade over top, making sure that both sides are coated well. Marinade for a least 1 hour before cooking. In a food processor, blend together the walnuts, flour, rosemary, salt, and pepper until smooth. Pour into a shallow dish and dip marinated "chicken" into flour, coating both sides. In a large frying pan on medium-high heat, fry "chicken" in oil until well browned on both sides. Makes 2 large or 4 small servings.

BAKED CHILI WITH CORNBREAD BISCUIT TOPPING

Onward and upward! – Wolffie, Davie, FL *(This recipe makes a large amount! But I didn't want to cut the recipe in half and leave you with all sorts of cans of half used beans and tomatoes in your fridge. So be prepared for leftovers, or better yet – call some friends over and have a party.)*

Chili:
- 1 large onion, chopped
- 1 large green bell pepper, chopped
- 2 tbsp olive oil
- 1½ cups mock ground "beef," crumbled
- 1 14-oz (398-ml) can tomato sauce
- 1 14-oz (398-ml) can diced tomatoes
- 1 19-oz (540-ml) can beans, your choice (e.g. black, kidney)
- 1 12-oz (341-ml) can corn niblets, drained
- 1 3.8-oz (114-ml) can pickled green chilies (reduce amount to lessen heat)
- 1 tsp salt
- 2 tsp unsweetened cocoa powder
- 2 tbsp chili powder
- 2 tbsp molasses
- ½ tsp ground cumin
- ½ tsp garlic powder

Topping:
- 1 cup + 2 tbsp "milk"
- 1 tbsp apple cider vinegar
- 1 cup flour
- 1 cup cornmeal
- 2 tbsp sugar
- 2 tsp baking powder
- ½ tsp salt
- 2 tbsp oil

Preheat oven to 400°F (205°C). Lightly oil a 9x13-inch baking dish and set aside. In a large saucepan on medium heat, sauté the onions and green peppers in oil until onions are translucent. Add the remainder of the chili ingredients and simmer for 5-10 minutes. To prepare topping: In a small bowl, while chili is cooking, stir together the "milk" and vinegar. Set aside. In a medium bowl, stir together the flour, cornmeal, sugar, baking powder, and salt. Add the oil and "milk" mixture, stirring together gently until "just mixed." Transfer chili from pot to baking dish and spoon biscuit batter evenly on top of chili. Bake, uncovered, for 15-20 minutes. Makes 6-8 servings.

Sauces

So many sauces . . . such little time. All these sauces have recipes that accompany them, but they are also terrific on their own. So experiment and try with serving them with different entrees.

CLAIRE'S "CHEEZE" SAUCE

I hope you like this recipe! – Claire, *CoquetteFauxFurriers.com (This simple, cheesy sauce can be whipped up in a few minutes and can be served over: veggies, nachos, or pasta. I make this recipe with Vegan-rella and sometimes add sautéed vegetables like mushrooms and leeks or bite-sized broccoli florettes.)*

3 tbsp vegan margarine
3 tbsp flour
½ tsp salt
¼ tsp ground black pepper
1½ cups vegan "milk"
1 cup vegan "cheese," finely grated
½ tsp Dijon mustard (optional)

In a small saucepan on medium heat, melt the margarine. Once margarine is liquefied, remove from heat (don't turn the burner off) and add the flour, salt, and pepper; whisk until smooth. Place saucepan back onto burner and slowly add ½ cup of "milk," whisking constantly until thickening occurs, then add remaining "milk" ½ cup at a time. Cook sauce over medium heat, whisking constantly until thickened and smooth. Add the "cheese" and Dijon mustard and cook for an additional 5 minutes, whisking until smooth and well blended. Serve. Makes approx. 2 cups.

WOLFFIE'S NUTRITIONAL YEAST "CHEESE" SAUCE

This recipe is for the Wolffie's BLT Brunch Casserole (pg 43), but can be used over anything that you want for that "cheesy" flavor.

½ cup nutritional yeast flakes
2 tbsp flour
½ tsp salt
1 cup water

2 tsp oil
1½ tsp Dijon mustard
1½ tsp tamari

In a small saucepan, whisk all the ingredients together. Bring to a boil, then reduce heat. Simmer for 2-4 minutes, stirring constantly. Makes approx. 1½ cups.

SHOSHANA'S SPECTACULAR ALL-PURPOSE TAHINI SAUCE

Here's a wonderful sauce that I pour it over lentils, quinoa or steamed veggies. It's awesome. −Shoshana, *TheMonkeyBunch.com (This fantastic and nutritious recipe can be poured over a stir-fry like Teresa's Garlic-Shoot Stir-fry [pg 138], or used as a gravy over potatoes or veggies, or as a salad dressing [when chilled]. It's spectacular!)*

½ cup shallots *or* 1 small onion, roughly chopped
2 garlic cloves, roughly chopped
1 tbsp dark sesame oil
¼ cup lemon juice
3 tbsp tamari
⅓ cup tahini
1 tbsp maple syrup
¼ cup vegetable stock
¼ cup olive oil
¼ cup oil (e.g. flax, hemp, grape seed)

In a small saucepan on medium heat, sauté the shallots and garlic in oil until shallots are translucent. In a blender or food processor, blend the shallots and the remaining ingredients until smooth and creamy. Makes approx. 1½ cups.

TYLER & PHOEBE'S PERFECT PESTO SAUCE

This recipe is used in Tyler & Phoebe's Perfect Pesto Pizza recipe (pg 152), but hell . . . I hate to waste a good recipe. Try it tossed with hot noodles, as a sandwich spread, with Perfect Pesto Potato Salad (pg 88), or eat it with a spoon. Basil never tasted so good.

3 cups fresh basil
¼ - ½ cup pine nuts, toasted (pg 295)
2 - 4 garlic cloves
½ tsp salt
½ tsp ground black pepper
½ cup olive oil

In a blender or food processor, blend together the basil, pine nuts, garlic, salt, and pepper. Slowly add the oil, while blending, until well mixed. Makes approx. 1 cup.

5-MINUTE ROASTED RED PEPPER PESTO

You can find prepared roasted red peppers in a jar, usually in the pickle section of your local supermarket. You can serve this sauce over noodles or on pizza, or on anything else that tickles your fancy.

¾ cup roasted red bell peppers, drained
⅓ cup walnuts
½ cup fresh basil, tightly packed
¼ cup fresh parsley, tightly packed
1 garlic clove
¼ cup olive oil

In a blender or food processor, blend together the red peppers, walnuts, basil, parsley, and garlic. Slowly add the oil, while blending, until well mixed. Makes approx. 1½ cups.

FAST & FRESH TOMATO SAUCE

This is a simple and lovely recipe to make when your garden is bursting with fresh tomatoes. This sauce freezes well . . . but odds are it won't be around that long. It can be thinned out with some vegetable stock, or you can serve it as is.

1 small onion, minced
1 tbsp olive oil
1 garlic clove, minced
6 medium tomatoes, chopped
1 5.5-oz (156-ml) can tomato paste
¼ cup vegetable stock
1 tbsp molasses
½ tsp dried basil
½ tsp dried oregano
½ tsp fennel seeds
1 tsp salt
¼ tsp ground black pepper

In a medium saucepan on medium-high heat, sauté the onions in oil until translucent. Add the remaining ingredients and bring to a boil, then reduce heat. Cover with lid and let simmer for 15-20 minutes. Makes approx. 4 cups.

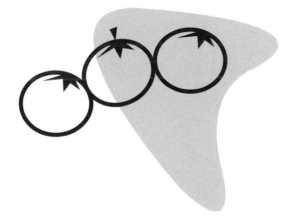

FRESH 5-MINUTE BASIL TOMATO SAUCE

This simple, fresh no-cook sauce can be whizzed together in a matter of minutes. Take some time to stop and smell the basil – you'll be happy that you did! To add a little weight to this sauce, I'll sometimes throw in ½ pound of cubed tofu.

> **4 medium tomatoes, roughly chopped**
> **2 tbsp olive oil**
> **2 garlic cloves**
> **¼ cup fresh basil, tightly packed**
> **½ tsp salt**
> **½ tsp ground black pepper**

Chop one of the tomatoes and set aside for later. In a blender or food processor, blend together the remaining tomatoes, olive oil, garlic, basil, salt, and pepper until chunky. Add the sauce and reserved chopped tomatoes to the noodles and toss together well. Serve immediately. Makes approx. 2 cups.

QUICH ALL-PURPOSE GARLIC TOMATO SAUCE

Once this sauce is done simmering, you can throw in some fresh basil leaves for added oomph. It can be thinned out with some vegetable stock, or you can serve it as is.

> **2 large garlic cloves, minced**
> **2 tbsp olive oil**
> **1 14-oz (398-ml) can diced tomatoes**
> **1 5.5-oz (156-ml) can tomato paste**
> **1 tsp sweetener (e.g. maple syrup, sugar)**
> **¼ tsp salt**
> **¼ tsp ground black pepper**

In a medium saucepan on medium-low heat, sauté the garlic in oil until translucent. Add the tomatoes, tomato paste, sweetener, salt, and pepper and bring to a boil. Reduce heat and let simmer for 15-20 minutes. Makes approx. 2 cups.

SIMPLE SPAGHETTI TOMATO SAUCE

This recipe is from the Spaghetti and Tofu Balls recipe on pg 129.

1 small onion, chopped
1 tbsp olive oil
1 small carrot, chopped
1 celery stalk, chopped
2 garlic cloves, minced
1 14-oz (398-ml) can tomato sauce
½ tbsp dried basil
½ tsp salt
1 tsp sweetener (e.g. maple syrup, sugar)
¼ cup fresh parsley, minced
1 tbsp red wine vinegar

In a medium saucepan on medium-high heat, sauté the onions in oil until translucent. Add the carrots, celery, and garlic; sauté for an additional 2 minutes. Add the tomato sauce, basil, salt, and sweetener and let simmer for 15-20 minutes. Turn off heat, stir in the parsley and vinegar. Let sit 5-6 minutes before serving. Makes approx. 2 cups.

DILIP'S ROASTED RED PEPPER & PORCINI MUSHROOM SAUCE

This quick and easy tomato sauce is best served over Dilip's stuffed Manicotti Pasta on pg 131. Porcini mushrooms have a strong, woody flavor that will have you doubling this recipe and sharing it with friends.

1 small onion, chopped
1 tbsp olive oil
¼ cup roasted red bell pepper, finely chopped
½ cup dried porcini mushrooms (or ½ lb fresh)
1 14-oz (398-ml) can tomato sauce
1 garlic clove, minced
¼ tsp salt
¼ tsp ground black pepper
1 tsp fresh rosemary

In a medium saucepan, sauté the onions in oil until translucent. Add the red peppers, mushrooms, tomato sauce, garlic, salt, pepper, and rosemary. Bring to a boil, then reduce heat. Cover with lid and simmer for 10-12 minutes. Makes approx. 2 cups.

MALLOREIGH'S MUSHROOM GRAVY

I love to eat this over mashed potatoes or a bowl full of fries with some shredded soy cheese. Vegan poutine!
– Malloreigh, Victoria, BC

2 tbsp vegan margarine
4 - 6 button mushrooms, finely chopped
3 tbsp flour
1 tbsp nutritional yeast
¼ tsp ground black pepper
1 tsp tamari
1 cup vegetable stock

In a medium saucepan on medium-high heat, sauté the mushrooms in margarine until soft. Add the flour, nutritional yeast, pepper, and tamari; stir constantly until thickened. Whisk in stock ¼ cup at a time, stirring constantly until thickened. Blend in food processor if you want smooth gravy or serve as is. Makes approx. 1½ cups.

MERCIFUL MISO GRAVY

This gravy is great over mashed potatoes, steamed veggies, or over your favorite entrée like the Veggie Pot Pie (pg 153). Using vegan margarine instead of oil gives it more of a "buttery" flavor.

1 tbsp miso
2 tbsp "milk"
1 small onion, minced
2 tbsp vegan margarine
1 garlic clove, minced
¼ tsp ground thyme
¼ tsp salt
¼ tsp ground black pepper
3 tbsp flour
1 cup "milk"

In a small bowl, whisk together the miso and 2 tbsp "milk." Set aside. In a medium saucepan on medium-high heat, sauté the onions in margarine until translucent. Add the garlic, thyme, salt, pepper, and flour; stir constantly until thickened. Whisk in "milk" ¼ cup at a time, whisking constantly until thickened. Turn off heat, stir in miso sauce, and cover with a lid. Let sit 5 minutes before serving. Makes approx. 1½ cups.

RED LENTIL SAUCE

This quick lentil sauce can be served over noodles or over steamed veggies and rice.

1 small onion, chopped
1 tbsp olive oil
2 garlic cloves, minced
¾ cup vegetable stock
½ cup dried red lentils
1 large tomato, chopped
¼ tsp ground cinnamon
¼ tsp salt
¼ tsp ground black pepper

In a medium saucepan on medium heat, sauté the onions in oil until translucent. Add the garlic, stock, lentils, tomatoes, cinnamon, salt, and pepper. Bring to a boil, then reduce heat. Simmer for 10-12 minutes or until lentils are cooked. In a blender or food processor, blend half or all of the sauce until smooth (be careful when blending hot liquids); return to pot. Makes 2½ cups.

SPICY NUT DRESSING

This fabu recipe goes perfectly in the Noodle Salad recipe on pg 80, but can also be used as a quick sauce over hot noodles or a stir-fry or as a dip for Shook 'N' Cook Tofu (pg 57).

⅓ **cup nut butter (your choice)**
¼ **cup vegetable stock**
3 tbsp rice vinegar
3 tbsp tamari
1½ **tbsp sweetener (e.g. sugar, maple syrup)**
1 tbsp dark sesame oil
2 inches fresh ginger, finely grated
½ **tsp cayenne pepper**

In a small bowl, whisk together the nut butter, stock, rice vinegar, tamari, sweetener, sesame oil, ginger, and cayenne. Makes approx. 1 cup.

SUN-DRIED TOMATO WHITE SAUCE

This quick and easy tomato sauce goes perfectly with the Portobello Cannelloni on pg 130. You can also toss it over noodles, potatoes or steamed veggies. The possibilities are endless.

¼ **cup vegan margarine**
¼ **cup flour**
2 cups vegan "milk"
1 cup vegan "cheese," finely grated
6 large sun-dried tomatoes, finely chopped
¼ **tsp salt**
¼ **tsp ground black pepper**

In a small saucepan on medium heat, melt the margarine. Once margarine is liquefied, remove from heat (don't turn the burner off) and add the flour; whisk until smooth. Place saucepan back onto burner and slowly add "milk" ½ cup at a time, whisking constantly until thickening occurs. Once thick, repeat action with remaining "milk." Cook sauce over medium heat, whisking constantly until thickened and smooth. Add the "cheese," tomatoes, salt, and pepper and cook for an additional 5 minutes, whisking until smooth and well blended. Makes approx. 3 cups.

Side Dishes

Side dishes are the icing on the cake. The bow on the top of a present. The cream in your coffee. They add a little extra something-something to your meal. Choose a side dish that will complement your entrée and you're set!

SESAME ROASTED ASPARAGUS

Roasting is a quick and delightful way to bring out the natural nutty and sweet flavors in asparagus. It's perfect when served as a side with Dilip's Stuffed Manicotti (pg 131) or along side a nice bowl of Leek & Potato Soup (pg 109).

> **1 lb fresh asparagus, ends removed**
> **2 tsp dark sesame oil**
> **¼ - ½ tsp coarse salt**
> **1 tbsp sesame seeds, toasted (pg 295)**

Preheat oven to 475°F (245°C).In a large bowl toss the asparagus, oil, salt, and sesame seeds together until well coated. Lay on a baking sheet and bake for 10-12 minutes. Serve immediately or at room temperature. Makes 2 large or 4 small servings.

DIJON MUSTARD BRUSSELS SPROUTS

When we were kids, my dad was always trying to get us to eat Brussels sprouts. Why? Because they're good for you. No more back talk . . . EAT!

> **1 lb (approx. 25) Brussels sprouts**
> **2 tsp mustard seeds**
> **2 tbsp vegan margarine** *or* **oil (e.g. flax, hemp)**
> **½ cup shallots, minced**
> **1 tsp Dijon mustard**
> **¼ tsp salt**
> **¼ tsp ground black pepper**

Trim ends off sprouts and cut each one in half. In a steamer, steam sprouts for 6-8 minutes or until they can be poked easily with a fork. Set aside. While sprouts are steaming, in a large frying pan on medium-high heat, dry toast the mustard seeds until they are lightly toasted and start to pop. Reduce heat to medium and add the margarine, shallots, and Dijon mustard; sauté until shallots are translucent. Add the sprouts, salt, and pepper; toss until well coated and reheated. Serve warm. Makes 2 large or 4 small servings.

STEVE & ZIPPORAH'S GREEN BEAN ZASMASHKA

My buddy Zipporah sent me this fantastic side dish that can be whipped up in a matter of minutes. I have no idea what Zasmashka means, but it must mean good!

3 slices bread, roughly chopped (*or* **¾ cup breadcrumbs)**
1 lb green beans, ends removed and cut into thirds
3 tbsp vegan margarine

In a food processor, blend the bread until fine. In a medium saucepan on medium-high heat, sauté the breadcrumbs and margarine until breadcrumbs begin to brown. Set aside. Steam beans for 3-4 minutes until they are bright green and can be pierced easily with a fork. Toss beans and breadcrumbs together and serve immediately. Makes 2 large or 4 small servings.

VEGANICA.COM CAJUN SWEET POTATO FRIES

I always just randomly whip this recipe up and I don't use precise measurements, so here's the version from my head. If you want to tweak the amounts, feel free. – Derek, *Veganica.com (Hooooo doggy, these are some spicy fries! If you find Derek's Cajun spice too spicy, try it with the kinder gentler "Needs A Little Extra" Spice (pg 305). And while you're at it, check out Veganica.com. It's a wicked online art gallery for vegan/vegetarian artists. If you look carefully, you can see some of my photography!)*

1 large sweet potato
2 tbsp olive oil
½ - 1 tbsp Cajun Spice (pg 303) (you decide the heat)

Preheat oven to 400°F (205°C). Wash the sweet potatoes and cut into fry-size wedges. Place wedges in a large bowl and toss with the oil and spice until well coated. Spread out flat and evenly on baking sheet. Bake for 10 minutes, flip, and bake an additional 5 minutes. Remove from oven and let sit 5 minutes before serving. Serve with ketchup or other favorite condiment. Makes 2 large or 4 small servings.

HARVARD BEETS

Here's a great side dish that can be made fast, fast, fast. – Wolffie, Davie, FL

¼ **cup maple syrup**
¼ **cup apple cider vinegar**
2 tsp cornstarch
¼ **tsp salt**
⅛ **tsp ground cloves**
1 14-oz (398-ml) can diced beets, drained

In a medium saucepan on medium-high heat, stir together the maple syrup, vinegar, cornstarch, salt, and cloves. Cook until thickened, stirring constantly. Stir in the beets and simmer for 2-3 minutes or until beets are warmed through. Makes 2 large or 4 small servings.

SWEET 'N' SOUR RED CABBAGE

I love this dish . . . it has the perfect combination of sweet and sour. – Wolffie, Davie, FL

¼ **cup apple cider vinegar**
3 tbsp sugar
1 tbsp molasses
1 small head red cabbage, shredded (4-5 cups)
1 small onion, chopped
½ **tbsp oil**
1 small Granny Smith apple, chopped
2 tbsp water
1 tbsp red wine vinegar
½ **tsp salt**
¼ **tsp ground black pepper**
⅛ **tsp ground cloves**

In a large bowl, stir together apple cider vinegar, sugar, and molasses until sugar is dissolved. Add cabbage and toss until well coated. Set aside. In a large pot on medium heat, sauté the onions in oil until translucent. Add the apples, water, red wine vinegar, salt, pepper, cloves, and marinated cabbage (including liquid). Bring to a boil, then reduce heat. Simmer for 20-25 minutes, stirring occasionally. Makes 4 servings.

HOLY FRIJOLES BEANS

This is great served with cornbread muffins, wrapped in a flour tortilla, or as a simple side dish. – Wolffie, Davie, FL

1 small onion, chopped
2 - 4 garlic cloves, minced
½ - 1 small jalapeno pepper, seeded and minced
1 tbsp olive oil
1 19-oz (540-ml) can pinto beans, drained and rinsed
1 large tomato, chopped
¾ cup vegetable stock
1 tsp salt
1 tsp maple syrup
1 tsp liquid smoke
½ cup fresh cilantro, roughly chopped

In a large saucepan on medium heat, sauté the onions, garlic, and jalapenos in the oil until onions are translucent. Add the beans, tomatoes, stock, salt, maple syrup, and liquid smoke. Bring to a boil, then reduce heat. Simmer, uncovered, for 20 minutes or until liquid has reduced. Stir in cilantro, let sit 5 minutes, and serve. Make 2 large or 4 small servings.

YAM PECAN BAKE

This is a great side dish to serve on festive occasions with recipes like Tofu Roast (pg 170) or Festive Stuffed Butternut Squash (pg 162) or even with the Veggie Pot Pie (pg 153). Remember, your body needs good quality carbs to live a happy, healthy life. No matter what "they" say . . . and tell them I think diets are for suckers.

Filling:
1 small onion, chopped
2 cloves garlic, minced
1 tbsp olive oil
3 cups assorted greens (e.g. kale, spinach, chard), chopped
1 large yam, cubed (approx. 4 cups)
½ tsp salt
½ tsp ground black pepper
½ tsp ground sage
½ tsp ground thyme
1 cup vegetable stock

Crust:
2 slices bread
1 cup pecans
2 tsp olive oil

Preheat oven to 425°F (220°C). In a large saucepan on medium heat, sauté the onions and garlic in oil until onions are translucent. Add the greens, turn off heat, cover with lid, and let sit for 5 minutes. Meanwhile, place the yams, salt, pepper, sage, thyme, and stock into an 8x8-inch baking dish. Stir in the greens mixture and toss together well. Cover with lid or tinfoil and bake for 30 minutes. While yams are baking, blend the bread, pecans, and oil in a food processor until it's an even meal. Sprinkle pecan mixture over yams and bake uncovered for an additional 15 minutes. Makes 2 large or 4 small servings.

CUMIN-SPICED BROWN RICE

You can cut your cooking time down by using a faster-cooking rice like basmati or jasmine, but brown rice is an excellent source of fiber and Vitamin B, so it's worth the wait.

1 small onion
2 tsp cumin seeds
1 tbsp olive oil
1 cup brown rice
2 cup vegetable stock *or* **water**
¼ tsp black pepper
2 tbsp fresh parsley, finely chopped

In a medium saucepan on medium heat, sauté the onions and cumin seeds in oil until onions are translucent. Stir in the rice, stock, and pepper. Bring to a boil, reduce heat, cover with lid and simmer for 40-45 minutes or until rice is cooked. Stir in parsley and serve. Makes 2 large or 4 small servings.

QUICK VEGETABLE RICE

This fragrant rice is best served with Aloo Gobi Potatoes and Cauliflower (pg 141), but can also be used as a side dish to complement just about any entrée.

1 tbsp oil
1 small onion
½ tsp ground cumin
¼ tsp garam masala (pg 304)
½ cup basmati rice
1 cup water
½ cup frozen mixed vegetables

In a medium saucepan on medium heat, sauté the onions in oil until translucent. Add the cumin and garam masala and sauté for an additional 2 minutes, stirring occasionally to avoid sticking. Stir in the rice, water, and vegetables. Bring to a boil, then reduce heat. Cover with lid and simmer for 10-15 minutes or until rice is cooked. Makes 2 large or 4 small servings.

MASHED PARSNIPS & POTATOES

A little twist on an old favorite.

> **1 large potato, cubed**
> **2 cups parsnips, cubed**
> **1 tbsp vegan margarine**
> **½ cup "milk"**
> **1 tsp ground cumin**
> **½ tsp salt**
> **¼ tsp ground black pepper**

In a large pot of salted water, boil the potatoes and parsnips until they can be poked easily with a fork. Drain and return to pot. Add the margarine, "milk," cumin, salt, and pepper and mash until you've reached the desired consistency. Makes 2 large or 4 small servings.

SPICED POTATOES

Need a little spice in your life? Who doesn't? Enter Mr. Potato stage left.

> **2 large potatoes, cubed**
> **½ tsp cumin seeds**
> **1 hot chili pepper, minced (you decide the heat)**
> **1 inch fresh ginger, finely grated**
> **1 tbsp olive oil**
> **¼ cup fresh cilantro, finely chopped**
> **2 tbsp oil (e.g. flax, hemp)**
> **½ tsp chili powder**
> **¼ tsp salt**

In a large pot of salted water, boil the potatoes until they can be poked easily with a fork. Drain and return to pot. While potatoes are boiling, in a small saucepan, sauté the cumin seeds, chili peppers, and ginger in oil until the peppers start to soften. Add the chili mixture, cilantro, oil, chili powder, and salt to the potatoes and toss together well. Makes 2 large or 4 small servings.

CUMIN FRIED POTATOES

A perfect dish to serve alongside Tip-Top Tofu Loaf (pg 154).

> 1½ tsp cumin seeds
> 1 tbsp olive oil
> 1 small onion, chopped
> 1 large potato, cubed
> ½ cup frozen peas
> ¼ tsp salt

In a large saucepan on medium-high heat, dry toast the cumin seeds until they start to pop and brown, watching carefully so they don't burn. Carefully add the oil, onions, and potatoes to saucepan. Cover with lid and sauté until potatoes are browned (stirring occasionally to avoid sticking) and can be pierced easily with a fork. Turn off heat, add the peas and salt, and cover with a lid. Let sit 5 minutes before serving. Makes 2 large or 4 small servings.

MASHED POTATOES WITH KALAMATA OLIVES

Kalamata olives are Greek in origin and have a intense, rich, fruity flavor that is unmatched by any other olive.

> 3 large potatoes, cubed
> ⅓ cup "milk"
> 3 tbsp vegan margarine
> ½ tsp salt
> ½ tsp ground black pepper
> ⅓ cup Kalamata olives, sliced
> 2 tbsp flax oil

In a large pot of salted water, boil the potatoes until they can be poked easily with a fork. Drain and return to pot. Add the "milk," margarine, salt, and pepper and mash until the desired consistency is reached. Stir in the olives and serve garnished with flax oil. Makes 2 large or 4 small servings.

ROASTED KALAMATA PARSNIPS

Roasting veggies is one of my favorite ways of preparing root vegetables, and parsnips are one of my faves. Often ignored because of their unique flavor, I think they deserve a better reputation. So try them without judgment. Parsnips are the way of the future!

2 cups parsnips, chopped
2 cups butternut squash, chopped
1 large carrot, chopped
½ tsp salt
½ tsp ground black pepper
2 tbsp olive oil
½ cup Kalamata olives, sliced
¼ cup vegan "Parmesan cheese" (optional)

Preheat oven to 450°F (230°C). In a medium baking dish, toss together the parsnips, squash, carrots, salt, pepper, and oil until well coated. Bake for 25-30 minutes or until veggies can be poked easily with a fork. Toss with Kalamata olives and "Parmesan cheese" and serve immediately. Makes 2 large or 4 small servings.

CINNAMON-SPICED ROASTED VEGGIES

This yummy side dish can easily be made into an entrée by adding couscous as a base. Check out the recipe on pg 139.

¼ cup shallots, roughly chopped
1 small red bell pepper, chopped
1 small sweet potato, cubed
1 small butternut squash, cubed (approx. 2 cups)
1 tsp coarse salt
1 tsp ground coriander
2 tsp ground cumin
½ tsp ground cinnamon
3 tbsp oil

Preheat oven to 375°F (190°C). In a 9x13-inch baking dish, toss together the shallots, red peppers, potatoes, squash, salt, coriander, cumin, cinnamon, and oil until well coated. Bake for 40-45 minutes or until veggies can be poked easily with a fork. Makes 2 large or 4 small servings.

MAURY'S ROASTED ROOT VEGETABLES

This recipe can easily be turned into a deliciously thick soup when you follow the directions on pg 111.

1 large yam, cubed
1 cup parsnips, cubed
3 new potatoes, cubed (approx. 1 cup)
1 small onion, chopped
3 garlic cloves, minced
2 tsp dried rosemary
½ tsp salt
½ tsp ground black pepper
2 tbsp grapeseed oil (*or* olive)

Pre-heat oven to 400°F (205°C). In a medium baking dish, toss together all the ingredients until well coated. Bake in oven for 25-30 minutes or until veggies can be poked easily with a fork. Makes 2 large or 4 small servings.

ROASTED HOLIDAY VEGETABLES

This looks beautiful when it comes out of the oven . . . very colorful and glazed. – Wolffie, Davie, FL (*These robust veggies are perfect for holiday dinners.*)

1 large carrot, chopped
1 small potato, diced
1 small sweet potato, diced
1 cup squash, cubed
1 small onion, roughly chopped
1 tbsp olive oil
1 tbsp molasses
1 tbsp water
1 tsp salt
⅛ tsp ground black pepper
¼ tsp cinnamon

Preheat oven to 425°F (220°C). In a medium baking dish, toss together all the ingredients until well coated. Bake in oven for 25-30 minutes or until veggies can be poked easily with a fork. Makes 2 large or 4 small servings.

ROASTED ROOT VEGETABLES

There are many things that make me happy . . . and roasting vegetables is one of them.

3 new potatoes *or* **1 large potato, cubed**
1 large carrot, chopped
1 small onion, chopped
2 garlic cloves, minced
1 large beet, cubed
1 tsp dried rosemary
1 tsp ground thyme
½ tsp salt
½ tsp ground black pepper
2 tbsp olive oil

Preheat oven to 400°F (205°C). In a medium baking dish, toss together the all ingredients until well coated. Bake in oven for 25-30 minutes or until veggies can be poked easily with a fork. Makes 2 large or 4 small servings.

Desserts

Ahh, dessert. If you think being vegan means you can't be decadent, you need to read on. Remember that vegan baking is just like conventional baking – you must follow the recipe exactly, and measure your ingredients with care – but there are a few different rules you must follow for your treats to turn out tasty. Just like the baked goods chapter, all of the recipes in this chapter are made with all-purpose flour unless otherwise stated. Don't forget to always use fresh ingredients. Purchase small amounts of baking soda, baking powder, and yeast because these items have a short shelf life and using stale ingredients can result in baking mishaps.

For recipes that call for baking soda and baking powder, be sure to preheat your oven before you mix the liquid and dry ingredients together. The baking soda and baking powder start activating as soon as the liquid ingredients hit them – so have your oven ready! Once the recipe is prepared, make sure to put your dough in the oven immediately. Remember to handle your dough with care. Stir gently until the ingredients are "just mixed." If you overmix the dough, your dessert may not rise the way you want it to.

My oven's internal thermometer is off by about 25°F (4°C) and that's a huge difference. Use a stand-alone oven thermometer to ensure you're baking at the correct temperature. They're inexpensive and you can purchase them in any kitchen or housewares store.

Check for readiness by inserting a toothpick or knife into the center of your baked goods before you remove them from the oven. If it comes out clean, then you are good to go. If it comes out gooey, then bake another 2-4 minutes and test again.

Check out pg 29 for other cooking tips. Now preheat your oven and let's make us some desserts!

DELICIOUS TREATS
NOT FOR THE FAINT OF HEART
HOT CHOCOLATE

This is a very serious hot chocolate that would make Johnny Depp wish he were my gypsy husband. Make me proud and be sure you purchase Fair Trade cocoa/chocolate.

3 tbsp unsweetened cocoa powder	⅛ tsp salt
3 tbsp sugar	pinch of ground cinnamon
2½ cups "milk"	pinch of cayenne pepper
¼ tsp vanilla extract	vegan marshmallows (pg 290) (optional)

In a medium saucepan, whisk together the cocoa, sugar, "milk," vanilla, salt, cinnamon, and cayenne pepper. Bring to a boil, stirring constantly. Remove from heat and whisk until frothy. Pour evenly into mugs and top with marshmallows, vegan whipped "cream" or cocoa powder. Makes 2 large or 4 small servings.

VEGAN FRUIT JUICE-FLAVORED JELL-O-TIN

J-e-l-l-o-t-i-n! Vegan gelatin is available at stores that carry kosher products or online at stores like *FoodFightGrocery.com* or *VeganEssentials.com*. You can also use an equal amount of agar agar instead of vegan gelatin, but it's not quite the same. For fun, stir in goodies like sliced fruit or sliced marshmallows (pg 290) once the liquid has cooled down a little. (This recipe also appears in the faux fare chapter.)

2 cups fruit juice (your choice)
1 envelope (1 tbsp) vegan gelatin
¼ cup sugar
pinch of salt

In a medium saucepan, whisk together all the ingredients. Bring to a boil, reduce heat, and simmer for 1 minute. Pour into a shallow glass bowl or individual serving bowls and refrigerate for 4-6 hours before serving. Makes approx. 2 cups.

CINNAMON DOUGHNUT HOLES

I can't say enough about these. They're very light. – Wolffie, Davie, FL *(Oooh. I bet if Tim Horton had tasted these, he would have given up hockey and opened a doughnut stand . . .wait, he did!)*

Coating:
¼ cup vegan margarine, melted
1 tsp ground cinnamon
½ cup sugar

Doughnuts:
1⅓ flour
1 cup crispy rice-type cereal, coarsely crushed
2 tbsp sugar
1 tbsp baking powder
½ tsp salt
¼ cup vegetable shortening
½ cup "milk"

Preheat oven to 425°F (220°C). In a small saucepan, melt the margarine. Once liquefied, pour into a small bowl and set aside. In a small bowl, stir together the cinnamon and sugar and set aside. In a medium bowl, whisk together the flour, cereal, sugar, baking powder, and salt. Cut in shortening, until mixture resembles coarse crumbs. Stir in "milk" until well blended and start rolling dough into 1-inch balls with your hands. Dip each ball in the melted margarine and then coat in the cinnamon-sugar. Place them in a lightly oiled 8x8-inch baking pan so the balls are touching one another and bake for 16-18 minutes. Remove from oven and let cool before removing from pan. Makes 20-24 doughnut holes.

VESANTO'S CHOCO-CURRANT CRANBERRY SQUARES

Here's a tasty recipe from the *Food Allergy Survival Guide* by V. Melina, J. Stepaniak, and D. Aronson. This book shows how adults and children can be well-nourished despite food sensitivities, and provides recipes that are entirely free of the major allergens: dairy products, eggs, gluten, tree nuts, peanuts, soy, yeast, fish, shellfish, and wheat. It clarifies links between diet and conditions such as arthritis, asthma, Attention Deficit Hyperactivity Disorder (ADHD), candida, depression, dermatitis, digestive disorders, fatigue, and headaches. These squares are an ideal combination of dried fruit, chocolate, and cereal that you can stir together in minutes. (Vesanto Melina is one of my all-time favorite people; her books are so helpful and chock full of information. Due to my chocolate intolerance, I made this recipe with ¼ cup of carob and it turned out perfectly. This recipe also appears in the appies and snacks chapter.)

½ **cup maple syrup** *or* **rice syrup**
¼ **cup seed** *or* **nut butter (e.g., tahini, almond butter)**
2½ **squares (2.5-oz) semisweet baking chocolate**
⅓ **cup dried currants**
⅓ **cup cranberries**
1¼ **cups puffed rice-type cereal**
1¼ **cups flakes-type cereal**

Lightly oil a 4x9-inch loaf pan and set aside. In a large pot, stir together the syrup, nut butter, and chocolate on medium-low heat until melted; stir often to prevent burning. Once evenly melted and mixed, remove from heat and add the currants, cranberries, and cereals; mix together until well coated. With damp hands, press mixture firmly and evenly into loaf pan and refrigerate for at least 30 minutes to set. Makes 8 squares.

JAE'S PEANUT BUTTER FUDGE

Hi Sarah, I have this awesome recipe for peanut butter fudge from my grandfather (well . . . he doesn't know I veganized it) – and potluckers seem to like it so I thought I would share it with you. It's amazingly simple if you have a candy thermometer so you know when you've reached the "soft ball" stage. I'm sure you can explain it better than me. I hope you like it. – Jae, Halifax, NS *(When your candy thermometer [available in most grocery or kitchen stores] reaches 235°F [115°C], the syrup is at the "softball" stage, meaning that when you drop a bit of it into a glass of cold water, it will form a soft ball. Please take all the necessary precautions when dealing with hot recipes like this. Stay safe.)*

2 cups sugar
½ cup "milk"
¾ cup peanut butter
½ tsp vanilla extract

Lightly oil a 9-inch loaf pan and set aside. In a medium pot on high heat, stir together the sugar and "milk" until it reaches a boil. Stop stirring and allow temperature to reach 235°F (115°C) (remember that the thermometer should not touch the bottom of pot, but rest in the boiling liquid). Remove from heat. Stir in the peanut butter and vanilla, and stir together vigorously until smooth. Pour into loaf pan and refrigerate for at least an hour before removing from loaf pan and cutting into chunks. Makes approx. 2 cups.

WOLFFIE'S NO-FAIL CHOCOLATE MARSHMALLOW FUDGE

This is one fabulous fudge! – Wolffie, Davie, FL *(Make sure you have all your ingredients chopped, measured, and ready to go before you turn on the stove. You will need a candy thermometer for this recipe.)*

1¼ cup sugar
⅓ cup "milk"
2 tbsp vegan margarine
½ oz (½ square) unsweetened baking chocolate, finely chopped

½ cup vegan chocolate chips
1 tsp vanilla extract
¼ cup walnuts, finely chopped
½ cup vegan marshmallows (pg 290), finely chopped

Lightly oil a 9-inch loaf pan and set aside. In a medium pot on high heat, stir together the sugar and "milk" until it reaches a boil. Stop stirring and allow to reach 235°F (115°C) (remember that the thermometer should not touch the bottom of the pot, but rest in the boiling liquid), then remove from heat. Add the margarine, baking chocolate, chocolate chips, and vanilla extract and stir vigorously until smooth. Quickly stir in the walnuts and marshmallows and immediately pour into loaf pan. Refrigerate for at least an hour before removing from loaf pan and cutting into chunks. Makes approx. 2 cups.

MINT CHOCOLATE FUDGE

Be still my beating heart! I think I've eaten too much sugar. You will need a candy thermometer for this recipe.

- 1¼ cups sugar
- ⅓ cup "milk"
- 2 tbsp vegan margarine
- ½ tsp salt
- ¾ cup vegan chocolate chips
- 1 tsp mint extract

Lightly oil a 9-inch loaf pan and set aside. In a medium pot on high heat, stir together the sugar and "milk" until it reaches a boil. Stop stirring and allow to reach 235°F (115°C) (remember that the thermometer should not touch the bottom of the pot, but rest in the boiling liquid), then remove from heat. Add the margarine, salt, chocolate chips, and mint extract and stir together vigorously until smooth. Pour into loaf pan and refrigerate for at least an hour before removing from loaf pan and cutting into chunks. Makes approx. 2 cups.

TERESA'S CAROB-ALMOND TRUFFLES

Oh, Teresa. How you have ruined me – this recipe is to die for. While these truffles are a little time consuming, they are not difficult at all to make . . . and holy cow! Yum-City. I'm sure you could also make these with chocolate chips, but you gotta love carob.

- 1 cup carob chips
- ¼ cup "milk"
- ⅓ cup vegan margarine
- ½ tsp vanilla extract
- ½ cup almonds, toasted (pg 295)

In a medium bowl, place carob chips and set aside. In a small saucepan, bring the "milk," margarine, and vanilla to a boil. Remove from heat and pour over carob chips. Let stand 5 minutes before stirring until smooth. Place bowl in fridge for 45 minutes, stirring every 15 minutes. Once chilled, lay a piece of parchment paper or wax paper on cookie sheet. Drop rounded teaspoonfuls of mixture onto paper and repeat process until done. Place cookie sheet into refrigerator for 1 hour. Coarsely chop the toasted almonds. Remove cookie sheet from fridge and roll each mound into a firm ball and then roll in almonds to coat. Return to cookie sheet. Store truffles in refrigerator until you're ready to serve. Makes 16-20 truffles.

CHOCOLATE WALNUT TRUFFLES

Truffles are traditionally made with butter and cream, but who needs all that when you have compassionate alternatives? To make your truffles more authentic, you can add a dash or two of a liqueur or coffee, finely chopped fruit or mint extract; use your imagination. A melon baller makes this recipe even easier to prepare, but a regular ol' spoon works just as well. This is MESSY work, so be prepared to have sticky hands!

> ½ **cup "milk"**
> **1 cup vegan chocolate chips**
> **1 tsp vanilla extract**
> ½ **cup walnuts, finely chopped**
> **2 tbsp unsweetened cocoa powder**

In a small saucepan, bring the "milk" to a boil. Reduce heat and add chocolate chips, stirring constantly to avoid sticking. Stir until completely melted and very smooth. Stir in the vanilla, pour into a bowl, and refrigerate for at least 12 hours. If you're in a hurry, place in the freezer for 3-4 hours. On a shallow plate, stir together the walnuts and cocoa powder and set aside. Lay a piece of parchment paper or wax paper on a cookie sheet and set aside. With a melon baller or a small spoon, scoop out truffle mixture and quickly roll into small ball with your hands. Transfer to walnut/cocoa mixture and roll around until completely covered. Set on cookie sheet and continue with remaining truffle mixture. Return truffles to refrigerator for at least 3 hours before serving. Makes 12 truffles.

DEBBIE'S PEANUT BUTTER COCONUT SQUARES

Hi Sarah: You wonderful vegan cook, you! I have a recipe for peanut butter squares that you may enjoy trying. Very simple, but incredibly delicious. – Debbie, Goderich, ON *(Because of my peanut/chocolate intolerance, I make this recipe with cashew butter and carob chips and it turns out just as yum!)*

Squares:
2 cups corn flake-type cereal
1 cup crispy rice-type cereal
2 tbsp shredded coconut, unsweetened
1 cup peanut butter
½ cup maple *or* **brown rice syrup**
1 tsp vanilla extract

Topping:
1 cup vegan chocolate chips (optional)
3 tbsp "milk" (optional)

Lightly oil an 8x8-inch pan and set aside. In a large bowl, stir together the two cereals and coconut. Set aside. In a small pot on medium heat, melt the peanut butter, syrup, and vanilla until soft and smooth. Pour peanut sauce into cereal mixture and stir until well blended. Spoon into pan and press down evenly. In a small double boiler, melt the chocolate chips and "milk" on medium heat, stirring until smooth and creamy. Pour evenly over peanut butter squares and refrigerate for at least 1 hour before serving. Makes 4 large or 6 small squares.

DANIYELL'S PEANUT BUTTER & CHOCOLATE BARS

My buddy Danielle from Ottawa, Ontario makes wicked desserts.

Bars:
2½ cups puffed rice-type cereal
¾ cup peanut butter
1 cup sugar
¼ cup vegan margarine
1 tsp vanilla extract

Topping:
¾ cup vegan chocolate chips
3 tbsp vegan margarine

Lightly oil an 8x8-inch baking pan, and set aside. Place cereal in a large bowl and set aside. In a large pot on medium-low heat, stir together the peanut butter, sugar, margarine, and vanilla until melted and smooth, stirring often to prevent burning. Pour into cereal and stir together until well blended. Press cereal firmly and evenly into pan and set aside. In a small pot on medium-low heat, combine the chocolate chips and margarine until melted and smooth, stirring often to prevent burning. Pour evenly over cereal and refrigerate for at least 1 hour before serving. Makes 8-16 squares.

WHITE CHOCOLATE ALMOND BARK

Vegan white chocolate chips are available in some health food stores and online stores like *VeganEssentials.com*, and holy mother are they ever good. This recipe can also be made with dark chocolate or carob, but it's worth the extra postage to get the white.

2 cup vegan white chocolate chips
½ cup almonds, toasted (pg 295) and roughly chopped
½ cup raisins, finely chopped (optional)

On a large plate, place a piece of parchment paper or wax paper and set aside. In a small double boiler on medium-low heat, melt the chocolate chips, stirring until smooth and creamy. Stir in the almonds and raisins and spoon out evenly and thinly on paper. Refrigerate for at least 1 hour before breaking into pieces. Makes approx. 3 cups.

PEANUT BUTTER PECAN BARK

I made up this recipe last night and I thought you would enjoy it. – Ashley, Asheville, NC

1 square (1-oz) unsweetened baking chocolate
2 tbsp peanut butter *or* **other nut butter**
1 tbsp tahini
2 tbsp maple syrup
1 tbsp sugar
½ tsp vanilla extract
½ tsp ground cinnamon
½ cup pecans, finely chopped

On a large plate, place a piece of parchment paper or wax paper and set aside. In a medium pot on medium-low heat, combine the chocolate, peanut butter, tahini, maple syrup, and sugar until melted, stirring often to prevent burning. Once evenly melted and mixed, remove from the heat and stir in the vanilla, cinnamon, and pecans. Spoon out evenly and thinly on paper. Refrigerate for at least 1 hour before breaking into pieces. Makes approx. 2 cups.

WOLFFIE'S COW PIES

This is the only part of the cow I'll eat. – Wolffie, Davie, FL *(Dear Lord, Wolffie. Couldn't you have come up with a better name?)*

2 cups vegan chocolate chips
1 tbsp vegetable shortening *or* **vegan margarine**
½ cup raisins
½ cup walnuts, finely chopped

Lay a piece of parchment paper or wax paper on a cookie sheet and set aside. In a medium saucepan on medium-low heat, melt the chocolate and vegetable shortening. Once melted, remove from heat and stir in the raisins and walnuts. Drop rounded tbspfuls of mixture onto paper and repeat process until done. Refrigerate for at least 1 hour before serving. Makes approx. 24 treats.

BANANA COCONUT PUDDING

Bananas are an excellent source of B6, plus high in Vitamin C and fiber. My husband says, "Who cares about vitamins and fiber – this pudding is wicked good." Serve as is or topped with maple syrup and "milk."

1 13.5-oz (400-ml) coconut milk, canned
2 tbsp sugar
½ tsp ground cardamom
¼ tsp salt
2 large bananas, sliced

In a medium saucepan, bring the coconut milk, sugar, cardamom, and salt to a boil. Reduce heat and add the bananas. Simmer for 12-15 minutes, stirring occasionally to avoid sticking. Mash bananas with back of fork or potato masher before portioning into bowls. Makes 2 large or 4 small servings.

BREAKFAST BROWN RICE PUDDING

This is a great way to use leftover rice and can be served for breaky or dessert garnished with fresh fruit. Feeling nutty? Add coconut milk instead of "milk" and garnish with toasted sesame seeds. This recipe also appears in the breakfast chapter.

1 cup COOKED brown rice
1 cup "milk"
2 tbsp raisins
1 tbsp maple syrup
½ tsp vanilla extract
⅛ tsp cinnamon

In a medium saucepan, combine all ingredients and bring to a boil. Reduce heat and simmer for 15-20 minutes. Serve hot or cold. Makes 1 large or 2 small servings.

MIXED BERRY PUDDIN'

Pink and thick. Just how I like my puddin'.

> **1 cup mixed berries (your choice)**
> **1 cup "milk"**
> **1 tbsp vanilla extract**
> **⅓ cup sugar**
> **3 tbsp cornstarch**
> **⅛ tsp salt**

In a food processor, blend together the fruit, "milk," and vanilla until smooth and set aside. In a medium saucepan, stir together the sugar, cornstarch, and salt. Whisk in ¼ cup of "milk" mixture to make a paste. Stir in the remaining "milk" mixture and bring to a boil, stirring constantly. Reduce heat and simmer for 1 minute or until pudding starts to thicken. Portion evenly into shallow glass bowl or individual serving bowls. Cover with plastic wrap and refrigerate for at least 2 hours before serving. Makes 2 large or 4 small servings.

MOM'S CHOCOLATE PUDDING

I use a heavy bottom pan for this recipe (heavy bottom is what you'll be if you eat too much of this). Enjoy.
– Wolffie, Davie, FL

> **⅓ cup sugar**
> **3 tbsp cornstarch**
> **3 tbsp unsweetened cocoa powder**
> **⅛ tsp salt**
> **2 cups "milk"**
> **2 tsp vanilla extract**

In a medium saucepan, stir together the sugar, corn starch, cocoa powder, and salt. Whisk in ¼ cup of "milk" to make a paste. Stir in the remaining "milk" and vanilla and bring to a boil, stirring constantly. Reduce heat and simmer for 1 minute or until pudding starts to thicken. Portion evenly into shallow glass bowl or individual serving bowls. Cover with plastic wrap and refrigerate for at least 2 hours before serving. Makes 2 large or 4 small servings.

CHOCOLATE CRANBERRY MOUNDS

These sweet chocolate mounds of yummy goodness are perfect for when the lady of the house wants something to nosh on as she lays in bed surrounded by pillows and fashion magazines. You also can drop them into candy moulds if you want to create pretty shapes.

4 squares (4 oz) unsweetened baking chocolate
½ cup maple syrup
1 tsp vanilla extract
¼ cup dried cranberries, finely chopped
½ cup almonds, toasted (pg 295), finely chopped

Lay a piece of parchment paper or wax paper on cookie sheet and set aside. In a small saucepan on medium-low heat, melt the chocolate and maple syrup. Once melted, remove from heat and add the vanilla, cranberries, and almonds, stirring until mixed. Drop rounded tbspfulls of mixture onto paper and repeat process until done. Refrigerate for at least 1 hour before serving. Makes approx. 16 treats.

ESTRELLASOAP.COM PEANUT BUTTER FUDGIE MOUNDS

Jesse from *EstrellaSoap.com* sent me some of his amazing soaps. Have you tried them yet? My favorite is Pink Grapefruit. They smell good enough to eat! He also sent along this fudgie sweet treat recipe. Good stuff!

1 cup sugar
1 tbsp unsweetened cocoa powder
¼ cup "milk"
¼ cup vegan margarine
¼ cup peanut butter
1¼ cups quick oats

Lay a piece of parchment paper or wax paper on cookie sheet and set aside. In a large saucepan, stir together the sugar and cocoa powder. Add the "milk" and margarine and bring to a boil. Reduce heat and simmer for 2 minutes, stirring constantly to avoid sticking. Remove from heat and stir in the peanut butter and oats. Let stand for 2-5 minutes. Drop rounded tbspfuls of mixture onto paper and repeat process until done. Refrigerate for at least 1 hour before serving. Makes approx. 8-12 treats.

STEPHANIE'S ASTEROIDS

Sarah: Here's a quick and easy dessert recipe that I hope you enjoy. I can't wait to see the new book! I have your first two and love them! – Stephanie, Weatherford, TX *(These sweet treats can be made even more decadent with the addition of a little bit of cocoa powder or chocolate chips. Yum!)*

> **1½ cups quick oats**
> **1 tsp ground cinnamon**
> **2 tbsp shredded coconut, unsweetened**
> **1 cup sugar**
> **¼ cup peanut butter (*or* other nut butter)**
> **¼ cup "milk"**

In a medium bowl, combine the oatmeal, cinnamon, and coconut and set aside. In a small pot on medium heat, heat the sugar, peanut butter, and "milk" until soft and smooth, stirring often to avoid burning. Pour peanut sauce into oats and stir until well blended. Form mixture into balls and place on a plate or cookie sheet. Refrigerate for at least 1 hour before serving. Makes 8 large or 16 small Asteroids.

FIONA'S QUICK BANANA ICE CREAM

Hi Sarah: I still love your two cookbooks. My boyfriend and I are currently on a weight loss/healthy eating drive and so I am adapting some of your recipes to cut down on added fat; I'm trying to get most of the fat I need from nuts, etc. (instead of chocolate as I was before). Tonight I adapted the coffee ice cream recipe from *How It All Vegan!* and it turned out to be a lovely treat after our huge veggie curry; so I wanted to share it with you. – Fiona, Accrington, England *(Peeling and slicing your banana before you freeze it makes this recipe mucho easier to prepare.)*

> **1 large frozen banana, sliced**
> **2 tbsp apple sauce**
> **¼ cup "milk"**
> **2 tsp instant coffee powder *or* grain beverage**

With a food processor, blend all the ingredients until smooth and creamy. Serve immediately or place in freezer to harden a little before serving. Makes 1 large or 2 small servings.

QUICK MIXED BERRY ICE CREAM

A quick and easy way to get that ice cream fix without having to spend a fortune.

> **2 cups frozen mixed berries (your choice)**
> **2 tbsp maple syrup** *or* **other sweetener**
> **¾ - 1 cup "milk"**

In a food processor, combine the berries and maple syrup. While food processor is running, add "milk" ¼ cup at a time until you have reached the desired consistency. Serve immediately or place in freezer to harden a little before serving. Makes approx. 2 large or 4 small servings.

QUICK "ANYTHING GOES" ICE CREAM

Frozen fruit in your freezer and a need to eat something ice creamy? Everyone knows – anything goes!

> **2 cups frozen fruit (your choice)**
> **2 tbsp maple syrup** *or* **other sweetener**
> **¾ - 1 cup "milk"**

In a food processor, combine the fruit and maple syrup. While food processor is running, add "milk" ¼ cup at a time until you have reached the desired consistency. Serve immediately or place in freezer to harden a little before serving. Makes approx. 2 large or 4 small servings.

BROWNIES AND COOKES

ESPRESSO BROWNIES

My husband wants everyone to know that it's called espresso, not eXpresso! I like to ice these brownies with the Chocolate Cake Glaze on pg 260.

1½ cups flour	1½ cups "milk"
½ cup unsweetened cocoa powder	1 shot espresso
1½ cup sugar	⅓ cup oil
1½ tsp baking soda	½ cup walnuts, roughly chopped
1 tsp baking powder	¼ cup vegan chocolate chips
1 tsp salt	

Preheat oven to 325°F (165°C). Lightly oil an 8x8-inch baking pan and set aside. In a medium bowl, stir together the flour, cocoa powder, sugar, baking soda, baking powder, and salt. Add the "milk," espresso, oil, walnuts, and chocolate chips and mix together gently until "just mixed." Pour evenly into baking pan and bake for 55-60 minutes or until a toothpick or knife comes out clean. Let cool completely before icing or cutting into squares. Makes 6-8 brownies.

WOLFFIE'S CHOCOLATEY MOIST BROWNIES

For extra chocolate flava, top these brownies with the Chocolate Glaze on pg 260.

1 cup flour	½ cup oil
½ tsp baking soda	½ cup water
½ tsp salt	2 tsp vanilla extract
½ cup unsweetened cocoa powder	½ cup walnuts, chopped
1 cup sugar	½ cup vegan chocolate chips
1 12-oz (300-g) pkg soft *or* silken tofu	

Preheat oven to 350°F (175°C). Lightly oil an 8x8-inch baking pan and set aside. In a medium bowl, stir together the flour, baking soda, salt, cocoa powder, and sugar and set aside. In a food processor, blend together the tofu, oil, water, and vanilla. Add walnuts and tofu mixture to flour and mix together gently until "just mixed." Pour evenly into baking pan and sprinkle top evenly with chocolate chips. Bake for 45-50 minutes or until a toothpick or knife comes out clean. Let cool before cutting into squares. Makes 6-8 brownies.

HAL'S MAPLE CHOCOLATE FLAX BROWNIES

This wonderful dense brownie recipe comes from my friend Hal, who has quite the way with the ladies . . . and man can he make a mean brownie! If you don't dig chocolate, replace the cocoa and chocolate chips with carob.

> ¼ **cup sugar**
> ¼ **cup ground flax seeds (pg 296)**
> ½ **cup maple syrup**
> ¼ **cup oil**
> ¼ **cup "milk"**
> **1 tsp vanilla extract**
> **1½ cups flour**
> ¼ **cup unsweetened cocoa powder**
> ¼ **tsp salt**
> ¼ **cup walnuts, chopped**
> ½ **cup vegan chocolate chips**

Preheat oven to 350°F (175°C). Lightly oil an 8x8-inch baking pan and set aside. In a medium bowl, stir together the sugar, ground flax seeds, maple syrup, oil, "milk," and vanilla. Let stand for 10 minutes. Stir in flour, cocoa, salt, and walnuts until "just mixed." Pour into baking pan, sprinkle top with chocolate chips, and bake for 20-25 minutes or until a toothpick or knife comes out clean. Let cool before cutting into squares. Makes 6-8 brownies.

MAPLE FLAX SQUARES

Don't let anyone tell you that up here in Canada maple syrup doesn't come out of our kitchen taps like water. It really does. And we all live in igloos as well.

Crust:
1 cup flour
¼ cup sugar
¼ tsp salt
½ cup vegan margarine

Filling:
2 tbsp ground flax seeds (pg 296)
6 tbsp water
¼ cup sugar
1 tbsp flour
½ tsp baking powder
¼ tsp salt
¼ tsp vanilla extract
¼ tsp maple extract
1 tbsp oil
1 cup walnuts, chopped

Preheat oven to 350°F (175°C). In a small bowl, stir together the flour, sugar, salt, and margarine until it resembles a coarse meal. Press evenly into the bottom of an 8-inch square cake pan. Bake for 10 minutes. While crust is cooking, in a small bowl, stir together the ground flax seeds and water. Let sit 5 minutes. Stir in the sugar, flour, baking powder, salt, vanilla, maple extract, oil, and walnuts. Spread evenly over baked crust and bake for an additional 25 minutes. Let cool completely before cutting into squares. Makes approx. 9 squares.

WOLFFIE'S B'NANNER BARS

For an extra treat, add ¼ cup of chocolate chips or chopped walnuts to the dough. Ice these bars with "Butter Cream" Frosting (pg 261) and sprinkle some finely chopped walnuts on top. This is Wolffie's recipe, but it was my friend Sarah M who thought they'd be good with walnuts sprinkled on top. Atta girl, now you're thinking!

egg replacer to equal 1 egg (pg 296)
¼ cup vegan margarine
¾ cups sugar
2 bananas
½ tsp vanilla extract
1 cup flour
½ tsp baking soda
¼ tsp salt

Preheat oven to 350°F (175°C). Lightly oil an 8x8-inch baking pan and set aside. In a food processor, blend together the egg replacer, margarine, sugar, bananas, and vanilla extract. Set aside. In a medium bowl, stir together the flour, baking soda, and salt. Add the banana mixture and stir together gently until "just mixed." Pour evenly into pan and bake for 25-30 minutes or until a toothpick or knife comes out clean. Let cool completely before icing and cutting into squares. Makes 6-8 bars.

BERRY OAT SQUARES

This is my favorite recipe. Yippee! – Danielle, Ottawa, ON

¾ cup vegan margarine
1½ cups rolled oat flakes
1¼ cups flour
½ cup sugar
1 cup blueberries
½ cup jam (e.g. raspberry, blueberry)
1 tsp flour

Preheat oven to 350°F (175°C). Lightly oil an 8x8-inch baking pan and set aside. In a small saucepan, melt the margarine until liquefied and set aside. In a medium bowl, stir together the oats, flour, sugar, and melted margarine until well combined. Set aside 1 cup and firmly press the remaining mixture into the baking pan. Bake in oven for 15 minutes. In a medium bowl, stir together the blueberries, jam, and flour. Spread evenly over baked crust and sprinkle remaining oat mixture evenly over top of berries. Bake for an additional 20 minutes. Cool completely before cutting into squares. Makes 6-8 squares.

FRUITY FRUIT SQUARES

Peaches. Blueberries. Strawberries. Blackberries. Raspberries . . . the possibilities are endless.

1½ cups flour
1½ cups rolled oat flakes
½ cup sugar
¾ cup vegan margarine
3 cups frozen fruit (your choice)
2 tbsp sugar
1 tbsp cornstarch
1 tsp lemon juice

Preheat oven 350°F (175°C). Lightly oil an 8x8-inch baking pan and set aside. In a medium bowl, stir together the flour, oats, sugar, and margarine until well mixed. Set aside 1 cup and firmly press the remaining mixture in to baking pan. Bake in oven for 10 minutes. While crust is baking, in a medium bowl, stir together the fruit, sugar, cornstarch, and lemon juice. Spread evenly over baked crust and sprinkle remaining oat mixture evenly over top of fruit. Bake 40-45 minutes. Cool completely before cutting into squares. Makes 6-8 squares.

WOLFFIE'S SNICKERDOODLES

These cookies are delicious – crunchy on the outside and soft on the inside. – Wolffie, Davie, FL

Topping:
3 tbsp sugar
1½ tsp ground cinnamon

Cookies:
1⅓ cup flour
¾ cup sugar
2 tsp baking powder
¼ tsp salt
1 tbsp ground flax seeds (pg 296)
3 tbsp water
½ cup vegan margarine

Preheat oven to 400°F (205°C). In a small bowl, stir together the sugar and cinnamon and set aside. In a medium bowl, stir together the flour, sugar, baking powder, and salt. In a small bowl, stir together the flax seeds and water. Add margarine and flax mixture to flour and stir until well blended. Shape dough into 1¼ inch balls, roll in the cinnamon-sugar mixture, and place on cookie sheet. Bake for 8-10 minutes. Remove from oven and let sit 2-4 minutes before removing to place on cooling rack. Makes 16 cookies.

SIMPLE OATMEAL COOKIES

There is something about the combination of oats, sugar, and margarine that makes me hot. . . ! (File this recipe under "Too much information.")

½ cup vegan margarine (room tempature)
3 tbsp sugar
2 cups rolled oat flakes
½ cup flour
¼ cup raisins
½ tsp baking soda
½ tsp salt
¼ cup "milk"

Preheat oven to 325°F (165°C). In a large bowl, cream together the margarine and sugar. Stir in the oats, flour, raisins, baking soda, salt, and "milk" until well mixed. Drop rounded tbspfuls of dough onto cookie sheet and press down flat with your fingers; repeat process until dough is gone. Bake for 16-18 minutes. Let cool before removing from cookie sheet. Makes 12 cookies.

CHOCOLATE PECAN COOKIES

Gooey, crunchy, chocolately goodness all rolled up into one cookie.

1 cup flour
⅓ cup unsweetened cocoa powder
½ tsp baking powder
¼ tsp baking soda
¾ cup sugar
1 cup soft tofu
½ cup "milk"
2 tsp apple cider vinegar
1 tsp vanilla extract
¾ cup vegan chocolate chips
½ cup walnuts, finely chopped

Preheat oven 375°F (190°C). In a large bowl, stir together the flour, cocoa powder, baking powder, baking soda, and sugar and set aside. In a food processor, blend together the tofu, "milk," vinegar, and vanilla until smooth. Pour tofu mixture into flour mixture and stir together. Add the chocolate chips and walnuts and stir together until well blended. Drop rounded tbspfuls of dough onto cookie sheet and press down flat with your fingers; repeat process until dough is gone. Bake for 10-12 minutes, or until edges are browned. Let sit 10 minutes before removing from cookie sheet. Makes approx. 10-12 cookies.

GINGERBREAD CUT-OUT COOKIES

For this recipe, the baking time will be determined by the size of the cookies. I use 5-inch gingerbread men cookie cutters; they take 8 minutes in my oven, and make 21 gingerbread men. While you're baking a batch, return the unused dough to the fridge; it'll soften too much if you leave it out too long. These are really good! – Wolffie, Davie, FL *(Power to the Ginger People!)*

⅓ **cup vegetable shortening**
¼ **cup sugar**
⅓ **cup molasses**
2¼ **tbsp hot water**
½ **tsp vanilla extract**
1½ **cups flour**
1 **tsp baking powder**
½ **tsp baking soda**
1 **tsp ground cinnamon**
¼ **tsp ground ginger**
¼ **tsp allspice**
¼ **tsp salt**

In a medium bowl, cream together the shortening and sugar. Stir in the molasses, hot water, and vanilla. When mixed, stir in the flour, baking powder, baking soda, cinnamon, ginger, allspice, and salt. Cover dough and chill for 2-4 hours. Preheat oven to 400°F (205°C). On a lightly floured board, roll out dough. Cut out with desired cookie cutters. Use raisins, chocolate chips, etc. to decorate (e.g., eyes, nose). Place on cookie sheet and bake for 8-10 minutes. Let cool before removing from cookie sheet. Makes 18-24 cookies.

COCONUT CHOCOLATE CHIP COOKIES

You HAVE to try these, Sarah. I just took the last batch of these out of the oven. They're scrumptious!
– Wolffie, Davie, FL *(Wolffie. If heaven was a cookie, these chewy gooey cookies would make you an angel.)*

egg replacer to equal 1 egg (pg 296)
½ cup vegan margarine
¾ cup cup sugar
1 tsp vanilla extract
1¼ cup flour
½ tsp baking powder
½ tsp baking soda
¼ tsp salt
½ cup shredded coconut, unsweetened
¾ cup vegan chocolate chips

Preheat oven to 350°F (175°C). In a food processor, blend together the egg replacer, margarine, sugar, and vanilla until smooth and set aside. In a large bowl, stir together the flour, baking powder, soda, salt, coconut, and chocolate chips. Add the margarine mixture and stir together until well incorporated. Roll dough into balls, lay on cookie sheet, and bake for 10-12 minutes. Let cool 5 minutes before removing from cookie sheet. Makes 18-24 cookies.

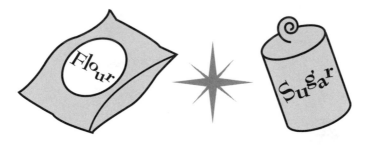

CRANBERRY PUMPKIN COOKIES

Perfect for a holiday treat or for when your boyfriend dumps you for that stupid girl with the gigantic . . . what? Oh. The cookies? They're awesome.

⅓ **cup vegan margarine**
½ **cup unsweetened pumpkin purée**
⅓ **cup sugar**
½ **tsp ground cinnamon**
¼ **tsp ground ginger**
¼ **tsp ground cloves**
¼ **tsp salt**
1 **tsp vanilla extract**
1 **cup flour**
½ **tsp baking powder**
egg replacer to equal 1 egg (pg 296)
½ **cup pecans, roughly chopped**
½ **cup dried cranberries**

Preheat oven to 350°F (175°C). In a medium bowl, cream together the margarine, pumpkin, sugar, cinnamon, ginger, cloves, salt, and vanilla extract until smooth. Add the flour, baking powder, and egg replacer and stir together gently until "just mixed." Add the pecans and cranberries and stir gently until well blended. Drop rounded tbspfuls of dough onto cookie sheet, press down flat with your fingers and repeat process until dough is gone. Bake for 8-10 minutes. Let cool before removing from cookie sheet. Makes 12 large cookies.

DANIYELL'S PEANUT BUTTER COOKIES

Danielle from Ottawa, Ontario sent me this delish cookie recipe. They go purrrfectly with a glass of "milk" and a pair of fuzzy slippers.

½ **cup vegan margarine**
½ **cup peanut butter**
1 **cup sugar**
egg replacer to equal 1 egg (pg 296)
3 **tbsp water**
2 **cups flour**
¾ **tsp baking soda**
¼ **tsp salt**

Preheat oven to 350°F (175°C). In a medium bowl, cream together the margarine, peanut butter, sugar, egg replacer, and water until smooth. Add the flour, baking soda, and salt and stir together well. You may need to add a bit more water at the end if mix is too dry. Roll dough into balls, place on cookie sheet, and flatten with a fork. Bake for 8-10 minutes. Let cool before removing from cookie sheet. Makes approx. 16 cookies.

MAMA MAYHEM'S PERFECTLY EASY NO-BAKE COOKIES

Hi Sarah: First of all, *How It All Vegan* and *The Garden of Vegan* are my very favorite cookbooks in the whole world! I've used *HIAV* so much it's falling apart! Thank you so much for these cookbooks, you've put a lot more than just recipes into them! – Mary, Knoxville, TN *(Just as the recipe name implies, these cookies are perfect and easy and you don't have to bake them!)*

½ **cup sugar**
½ **tsp vanilla**
¼ **cup "milk"**
¼ **cup nut butter (your choice)**
¼ **cup vegan margarine**
2 **tsp unsweetened cocoa powder**
1½ **cups quick oats**
1 **cups walnuts, finely chopped**

Place a sheet of parchment paper or wax paper on cookie sheet and set aside. In a medium saucepan on medium-low heat, melt the sugar, vanilla, "milk," nut butter, margarine, and cocoa powder. Once melted, remove from heat and add the oats and walnuts. Stir until well blended. Drop rounded tbspfuls of dough onto cookie sheet, press down flat with your fingers, and repeat process until dough is gone. Refrigerate for at least 1 hour before serving. Makes 8 large cookies.

NUTTY OATMEAL RAISIN COOKIES

I find the smell of raw oatmeal is an aphrodisiac. Am I weird?

> **1 cup flour**
> **¾ cup rolled oat flakes**
> **½ cup sugar**
> **1 tsp baking powder**
> **½ tsp ground cinnamon**
> **½ tsp nutmeg**
> **¼ tsp ground ginger**
> **⅓ cup vegan margarine**
> **¼ cup nut butter (your choice)**
> **egg replacer to equal 2 eggs (pg 296)**
> **½ tsp vanilla extract**
> **½ cup raisins**
> **¼ cup vegan chocolate chips (optional)**

Preheat oven to 350°F (175°C). In a large bowl, stir together the flour, oats, sugar, baking powder, cinnamon, nutmeg, and ginger. Stir in the margarine, nut butter, egg replacer, vanilla, raisins, and chocolate chips until well blended. Drop rounded tbspfuls of dough onto cookie sheet, press down flat with your fingers, and repeat process until dough is gone. Bake for 10-12 minutes. Let cool before removing from cookie sheet. Makes 12 cookies.

RACHEL'S CHOCOLATE CHIP COOKIES

I thought you might enjoy these cookies that I "veganized" from another recipe. It passed the ultimate test this weekend when I took them to a cookout and left them on a table. This fellow I know, who is the biggest jerk about me being vegetarian, happened along and ate one. Much to my delight, he said, "These are really good, who made them?" With the devil in my heart I said, "Me." He stopped in mid-chew. Then I said, "They're vegan and they've got tofu in them." He narrowed his eyes and with 100% sincerity told me that he did not believe me. When I assured him that I was telling the truth, he hung his head like a 4-year-old. Vengeance is a dish best served at a cookout, mi amiga! – Rachel, Louisville, KY

> **2 cups flour**
> **1 tsp baking soda**
> **¼ tsp salt**
> **1¼ cups sugar**
> **¾ cup vegan margarine (room temperature)**
> **1 tsp vanilla extract**
> **⅓ cup soft** *or* **silken tofu**
> **¾ cup vegan chocolate chips**

Preheat oven to 375°F (190°C). In a large bowl, stir together the flour, baking soda, and salt; set aside. In a food processor, blend together the sugar, margarine, vanilla extract, and tofu until smooth. Add the tofu mixture and chocolate chips to the flour and stir together well. Drop rounded tbspfuls of dough onto cookie sheet, press down with fingers, and repeat process until dough is gone. Bake for 8-10 minutes. Let cool before removing from cookie sheet. Makes 24 cookies.

STEPHANIE'S WHITE DIAMOND COOKIES

Stephanie from Weatherford, Texas sent me this wicked cookie recipe. You can find white chocolate chips at some health food stores and at many online vegan grocers like *FoodFightGrocery.com* and *VeganEssentials.com*, but if you can't find them, dark chocolate chips will do. Then you can rock out to Kiss's "Black Diamond" and pretend that Paul Stanley is your boyfriend.

¾ **cup sugar**
¾ **cup peanut butter**
⅓ **cup "milk"**
egg replacer to equal 2 eggs (pg 296)
½ **tsp vanilla extract**
⅓ **cup unsweetened cocoa powder**
½ **cup flour**
½ **tsp baking soda**
½ **cup vegan white chocolate chips**

Preheat oven to 350°F (175°C). In a food processor, blend the sugar, peanut butter, "milk," egg replacer, and vanilla until smooth. In a large bowl, stir together the cocoa powder, flour, and baking soda. Add the peanut mixture and chocolate chips to the flour and stir together well. Drop rounded tbspfuls of dough onto cookie sheet, press down flat with your fingers, and repeat process until dough is gone. Bake for 8-10 minutes. Let cool before removing from cookie sheet. Makes 8 -10 large sized cookies.

WOLFFIE'S PEANUT BUTTER COOKIES

Serve with a giant glass of "milk" and you're all set.

1¼ **cups flour**
½ **tsp baking soda**
¼ **tsp salt**
egg replacer to equal 1 egg (pg 296)
¼ **cup water**
½ **cup peanut butter (***or* **other nut butter)**
¼ **cup oil**
¾ **cup sugar**
½ **tsp vanilla extract**

Preheat oven to 375°F (290°C). In a medium bowl, stir together flour, baking soda, and salt. Add the egg replacer, water, peanut butter, oil, sugar, and vanilla and stir together until well combined. Roll into 1½-inch balls and place on cookie sheet. Flatten each cookie with a fork, making a criss-cross pattern. Sprinkle each cookie with a pinch of sugar and bake 10-12 minutes. Let cool for 5 minutes before removing from cookie sheet. Makes 20-24 cookies.

PUMPKIN PUFF COOKIES

Sarah, these are fabulous cookies! – Wolffie, Davie, FL *(Puff the pumpkin cookie, lived by the sea. . . .)*

1 cup flour
1 cup sugar
1 tsp baking powder
⅛ tsp baking soda
¼ tsp salt
1 tsp ground cinnamon
½ tsp ground ginger
¼ tsp ground cloves
1 tbsp ground flax seeds (pg 296)
3 tbsp water
½ cup unsweetened pumpkin purée
¼ cup vegan margarine, room temperature
½ tsp vanilla extract
½ tsp maple extract
½ cup raisins
½ cup walnuts, finely chopped

Preheat oven to 350°F (175°C). In a medium bowl, whisk together the flour, sugar, baking powder, baking soda, salt, cinnamon, ginger, and cloves. Set aside. In a food processor, blend together the ground flax seeds, water, pumpkin, margarine, vanilla, and maple extract. Blend until smooth. Add the raisins, walnuts, and pumpkin mixture to the flour mixture and stir together well. Drop rounded tbspfuls of dough onto cookie sheet, press down flat with your fingers, and repeat process until dough is gone. Bake for 12-14 minutes. Let cool before removing from cookie sheet. Makes approx. 12 cookies.

DESSERTS WITH FRUIT
APPLE-WALNUT PUDDING

This is terrific either for breakfast or dessert! – Wolffie, Davie, FL *(I like to serve this with a little almond milk poured over top. I agree with Wolffie: breakfast or dessert, this recipe is a terrific dish. This recipe also appears in the breakfast chapter.)*

Filling:
½ cup flour
⅓ cup sugar
¾ tsp baking powder
¼ tsp salt
¼ tsp ground cinnamon
⅛ tsp ground cloves
¼ cup "milk"
½ tsp vanilla extract
2 medium Granny Smith apples, cubed
¼ cup walnuts, finely chopped

Topping:
⅓ cup water
¼ cup sugar
2 tbsp maple syrup
2 tbsp vegan margarine

Preheat oven to 375°F (190°C). In a medium bowl, whisk together the flour, sugar, baking powder, salt, cinnamon, and cloves. Stir in the "milk," vanilla, apples, and walnuts until well mixed. Spread into an 8x8-inch baking dish. Set aside. In a small saucepan, bring the water, sugar, maple syrup, and margarine to a boil. Reduce heat once margarine has melted. Pour over the batter in the baking dish. DO NOT STIR. Bake for 40-45 minutes. Makes 2 large or 4 small servings.

BEAUTIFUL BLUEBERRY STRUDEL

Phyllo (also spelled fillo) pastry are tissue-paper-thin layers of pastry dough. For some crazy reason, I used to think that phyllo pastry wasn't vegan. Imagine my surprise when I read the ingredients on the side of the box in the freezer section of my local grocery store and realized that it's just flour, water, and oil. Hooray! Let's do some baking! You can use any combination of fruit in this recipe, but blueberry is my favorite.

¼ cup vegan margarine, melted
2 cups blueberries
¼ cup sugar
2 tbsp cornstarch
3 sheets phyllo pastry, thawed
3 tbsp breadcrumbs
1 tbsp sugar

Preheat oven to 375°F (190°C). Lightly oil a cookie sheet and set aside. In a small saucepan, melt the margarine. While margarine is melting, in a small bowl, stir together the blueberries, sugar, and cornstarch until well combined. Set aside. Lay a clean dishtowel down on counter. Unroll phyllo pastry, remove one sheet, and lay on top of dishtowel. Brush evenly with 1 tbsp of melted margarine then evenly spread 1 tbsp of the breadcrumbs over top. Layer another sheet on top of prepared sheet and repeat process with remaining phyllo sheets until done. Spoon blueberry filling along the long edge of the phyllo, leaving a large border around the edge. Carefully turn long edge of phyllo up to cover fruit filling and then fold in the sides. Carefully roll up the pastry and place on cookie sheet folded side down. Brush top lightly with remaining margarine, sprinkle with 1 tbsp of sugar, and bake for 35-40 minutes. Let cool for 4-6 minutes before serving. Makes 2 large or 4 small servings.

BANANA CHOCOLATE PEANUT BUTTER STRUDEL

I "veganized" this recipe I found on the side of the phyllo box, then ate the entire thing in one sitting. Yikes! You can leave the peanut butter out of this recipe, if you're so inclined, but my husband will call you crazy.

¼ cup vegan margarine, melted
2 tbsp peanut butter
2 bananas, peeled
¼ cup vegan chocolate chips, finely chopped
4 sheets phyllo pastry, thawed
1 tbsp sugar

Preheat oven to 425°F (220°C). Lightly oil a cookie sheet and set aside. In a small saucepan, melt the margarine. While margarine is melting, lay a clean dishtowel down on counter. Unroll phyllo pastry and remove one sheet and lay on top of dishtowel. Brush evenly with 1 tbsp of melted margarine. Layer another sheet of phyllo on top of the prepared sheet and repeat process with remaining phyllo sheets until done. Set extra margarine aside. Spread peanut butter evenly over both bananas. Lay one banana along the long edge of the phyllo, leaving a large border around the edge. Lay other banana beside it. Sprinkle bananas evenly with chocolate and then carefully turn long edge of phyllo up to cover filling and then fold in the sides. Carefully roll up the pastry and place on cookie sheet folded side down. Brush top lightly with remaining margarine, sprinkle with 1 tbsp of sugar and bake for 10-12 minutes. Let cool for 4-6 minutes before serving. Makes 2 large or 4 small servings.

ROASTED PEARS IN MAPLE GARAM MASALA SAUCE

I "veganized" this recipe after watching my parents eat a non-vegan version of it at some fancy restaurant that had nothing for little ol' vegan me to eat but salad. Serve with some nice vegan vanilla ice cream and be happy you weren't with me in that crappy restaurant.

2 tsp sugar
½ tsp garam masala (pg 304)
2 tsp sesame seeds, toasted (pg 295)
2 large very ripe pears
3 tbsp water
1 tbsp maple syrup

Preheat oven to 375°F (190°C). Lightly oil an 8x8-inch baking dish and set aside. In a small bowl, stir together the sugar, garam masala, and sesame seeds and set aside. Peel pears and cut in half lengthwise, removing core with small spoon. Set pears, cut side down, onto baking dish. In a small bowl, stir together the water and maple syrup. Pour this mixture over the pears, reserving run-off. Sprinkle pears with sugar mixture and bake for 15-20 minutes, basting pears with juice after 10 minutes. Serve pears warm, drizzled with leftover maple liquid. Makes 2 large or 4 small servings.

BLUEBERRY DILIP

Not quite a crisp, not quite a crumble – this recipe from Dilip in Chapel Hill, North Carolina is simply that . . . a Dilip. A yummy, blueberry Dilip!

¼ cup vegan margarine
1 cup flour
½ cup sugar
2 tsp baking powder
½ tsp ground cinnamon
¼ tsp salt

⅛ tsp ground nutmeg
¾ cup "milk"
¼ cup sugar
½ tsp ground ginger
4 cups blueberries

Preheat oven to 350°F (175°C). Put the margarine into an 8-inch baking dish and place in oven while it's preheating. In a medium bowl, stir together the flour, sugar, baking powder, cinnamon, salt, and nutmeg. Add the "milk," stir well, and set aside. Once the margarine has melted, pour the flour mixture into baking dish *without mixing* into the margarine. In a medium bowl, stir together the ¼ cup sugar, ginger, and blueberries and pour over the batter (do not stir). Bake for 50-55 minutes. Serve warm. Makes 2 large or 4 small servings.

PEACH BLUEBERRY COBBLER

A baked, deep-dish fruit dessert topped with a thick biscuit crust. Life is good!

Filling:
2 large peaches, pitted and roughly chopped
½ cup blueberries
⅓ cup sugar
1 tbsp flour

Topping:
¾ cups flour
¼ tsp salt
1½ tsp baking powder
1 tbsp sugar
2 tbsp oil
½ cup "milk"
1 tbsp sugar

Preheat oven to 375°F (190°C). Lightly oil an 8x8-inch baking dish and set aside. In a medium bowl, stir together the peaches, blueberries, sugar, and 1 tbsp of flour. Spoon evenly into baking dish and set aside. In a medium bowl, stir together ¾ cup flour, salt, baking powder, and 1 tbsp of sugar. Add the oil and "milk" and stir together well. Pour evenly over fruit and sprinkle top with 1 tbsp of sugar. Bake for 35-40 minutes or until topping is browned. Let sit 5 minutes before serving. Makes 2 large or 4 small servings.

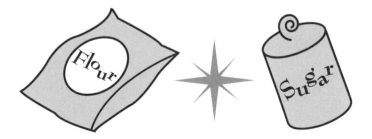

CHERRY COBBLER

Frozen cherries, available in the freezer section of your supermarket, take the hassle out of having to deal with all those pits. Life really is a bowl of cherries – so enjoy every moment life has to offer.

Filling:
3 cups frozen cherries
¼ cup sugar
2 tsp cornstarch
¼ tsp ground cinnamon

Topping:
¾ cup flour
2 tsp sugar
¼ tsp baking soda
¼ tsp baking powder
⅛ tsp salt
2 tbsp oil
⅓ cup "milk"
1 tbsp sugar

Preheat oven to 425°F (220°C). Lightly oil an 8x8-inch baking dish and set aside. In a medium bowl, stir together the cherries, sugar, cornstarch, and cinnamon and spoon evenly into dish and set aside. In a medium bowl, stir together the flour, 2 tsps of sugar, baking soda, baking powder, and salt. Add the oil and milk and stir together gently until "just mixed." Drop 4 even mounds of dough over cherry filling and sprinkle the top with 1 tbsp of sugar. Bake for 30-35 minutes, or until topping is browned. Let sit for 5 minutes before serving. Makes 4 servings.

WOLFFIE'S QUICK PEACH COBBLER

This is a terrific cobbler that's easy to make and is beautiful when it comes out of the oven. – Wolffie, Davie, FL
(You might want to put a cookie sheet underneath the rack that the cobbler sits on to avoid any spillage. There's nothing worse then having to clean up gooey fruit spillage from the bottom of your oven.)

½ cup vegan margarine
1 20-oz (600-g) bag of sliced frozen peaches
¼ cup sugar
¼ cup water
1 cup flour
1 cup sugar
2 tsp baking powder
½ tsp ground cinnamon
¼ tsp salt
1 cup "milk"

Preheat oven to 400°F (205°C). Add margarine to an 8-inch baking dish and place in oven while it's preheating. In a medium saucepan, bring the peaches, sugar, and water to a boil. Reduce heat and let simmer for 5-6 minutes or until peaches become unthawed and hot. In a medium bowl stir together the flour, sugar, baking powder, cinnamon, salt and "milk." Once the margarine has melted, pour the flour mixture into the baking dish *without mixing* into the margarine. Pour the peaches (including liquid) evenly over the batter and bake for 25-30 minutes or until golden brown. Makes 4 servings.

KIM'S PEACH-ZZA

Hey Girly! This is a really good recipe that involves fruit. Keep up the good work, and keep pumping out amazing cookbooks. I live by them! – Kim, Orlando, FL *(What could be better then a Peach Pizza? This recipe uses the All-Purpose Crust [pg 262]. Gotta love this dough, you can use it for just about anything. So get out your pizza slicer and cut me up a slice.)*

Crust:
2 cups flour
1 tsp salt
¾ cup vegan margarine
¼ cup "milk"

Filling:
2½ cups peaches (frozen), finely chopped
2 tbsp flour
¼ cup slivered almonds
¼ cup sugar
1 tbsp sugar

In a food processor, add the flour, salt, and margarine and pulse until mixture resembles a coarse meal. Add "milk" and blend until well combined and dough forms. Roll dough into a ball, wrap in plastic, and refrigerate for at least 1 hour before using. Once dough is chilled, preheat oven to 400°F (205°C). Lightly oil and flour a round pizza sheet and set aside. With lightly floured hands, roll out dough evenly onto pizza sheet and set aside. In a medium bowl, stir together the peaches, flour, almonds, and sugar. Place fruit into center of dough, gently folding up the sides of the dough, folding down over the first 1-2 inches of fruit. Sprinkle top with 1 tbsp of sugar and bake for 35-40 minutes. Makes 4 large or 8 small servings.

CHOCOLATE PEAR-ZZA

Inspired by Kim's Peach-zza (pg 232), I made up this chocolatey sweet recipe when I had some over-ripe pears that were almost past their prime. This recipe uses the All-Purpose Crust (pg 262) and will make your heart beat overtime.

Crust:
2 cups flour
1 tsp salt
¾ cup vegan margarine
¼ cup "milk"

Filling:
2½ cups over-ripe pears, finely chopped
¼ cup walnuts, finely chopped
¼ cup chocolate *or* carob chips
2 tbsp maple syrup
1 tbsp flour
1 tbsp sugar

In a food processor, blend the flour and salt together. Add the margarine and pulse until mixture resembles a coarse meal. Add "milk" and blend until well combined and dough forms. Roll dough into a ball, wrap in plastic, and refrigerate for at least 1 hour before using. Once dough is chilled, preheat oven to 400°F (205°C). Lightly oil and flour a round pizza sheet and set aside. With lightly floured hands, roll out dough evenly onto pizza sheet and set aside. In a medium bowl, stir together the pears, walnuts, chocolate, maple syrup, and flour. Place fruit into center of dough, gently folding up edges and fold down over the first 1-2 inches of fruit. Sprinkle top with 1 tbsp of sugar and bake for 35-40 minutes. Makes 4 large or 8 small servings.

CRANBERRY APPLE CRISP

The purr-fect combination of sweet and sour. Kind of like me.

Filling:
1½ cups frozen cranberries
2 medium apples, cored and chopped
¼ cup sugar
½ tsp ground cinnamon
2 tsp lemon juice
1 tbsp flour

Topping:
1 tbsp flour
3 tbsp sugar
1 cup rolled oat flakes
3 tbsp vegan margarine (room temperature)

Preheat oven to 375°F (190°C). Lightly oil an 8-inch baking dish and set aside. In a medium bowl, combine the cranberries, apples, sugar, cinnamon, lemon juice, and 1 tbsp of flour. Spoon mixture evenly into baking dish. In a medium bowl, stir together the flour, sugar, oats, and margarine until well combined. Sprinkle topping evenly over fruit mixture and bake for 40-45 minutes or until top is browned and apples are tender. Makes 4 servings.

RASPBERRY APPLE CRISP

I think raspberries are the most intensely flavored member of the berry family and are definitely the most delicate. If using fresh, purchase them the day you're going to use them.

Filling:
3 large Granny Smith apples, chopped
1 cup raspberries
1 tbsp sugar
1 tbsp flour
1 tsp ground cinnamon

Crust:
1 cup rolled oat flakes
¼ cup vegan margarine
¼ cup sugar
1 tsp ground cinnamon

Preheat oven to 350°F (175°C). Lightly oil an 8-inch baking dish and set aside. In a medium bowl, combine the apples, raspberries, sugar, flour and cinnamon. Spoon mixture evenly into baking dish. In a medium bowl, stir together the oat flakes, margarine, sugar, and cinnamon until well mixed. Sprinkle evenly over top fruit mixture and bake for 50-55 minutes or until top is browned and apples are tender. Makes 4 servings.

WOLFFIE'S PEACH SHORTCAKE

Good golly-lolly, Wolffie! You are killing me with these desserts! You will need a 3-inch-round cookie cutter or a same sized glass to cut your shortcake. Serve this warm with a nice scoop of vegan vanilla ice cream.

Shortcake:
1 cups flour
2 tsp baking powder
½ tsp salt
2½ tsp sugar
¼ cup vegetable shortening
⅓ cup "milk"
1 tsp lemon juice
½ tsp vanilla extract

Topping:
½ cup sugar
1 tbsp cornstarch
⅛ tsp salt
¼ tsp ground cinnamon
½ cup water
½ tsp lemon juice
1¼ cup (10 oz) frozen sliced peaches
½ tsp vanilla extract

Preheat oven to 400°F (205°C). Line a cookie sheet with parchment paper and set aside. In a medium bowl, stir together flour, baking powder, salt, and sugar. Cut in shortening until mixture resembles coarse crumbs. Stir in the "milk," lemon juice, and vanilla until well blended. On a lightly floured board, knead dough 5-6 times. Roll out dough to a ¾-inch thickness and cut into 3-inch rounds with a cookie cutter or glass. Place on baking sheet and bake for 12-15 minutes. While shortcakes are baking, in a small saucepan, stir together sugar, cornstarch, salt, cinnamon, water, lemon juice, and peaches. Bring to a boil, stirring constantly, then reduce heat. Cover with lid and simmer for 10-15 minutes or until peaches are tender. Turn off heat and stir in vanilla; set aside. To assemble dessert: using serrated knife, cut each shortcake horizontally in half. Place bottom halves on plates and spoon peaches and juice onto each shortcake. Replace top halves of shortcakes and top with a scoop of ice cream. Cover with more peach topping. Makes 2 large or 4 small servings.

MUFFINS

DOUBLE CHOCOLATE MUFFINS

These are great frosted with Chocolate Fudgey Frosting (pg 259) . . . mmm. – Wolffie, Davie, FL

2 cups flour
1 cup unsweetened cocoa powder
1 tbsp baking powder
½ tsp salt
1 cup sugar
1¾ cups "milk"
½ cup oil
1 tsp vanilla extract
1 cup vegan chocolate chips

Preheat oven to 400°F (205°C). Lightly oil 12 muffin tins or line with paper liners and set aside. In a large bowl, stir together the flour, cocoa powder, baking powder, salt, and sugar. Stir in the "milk," oil, vanilla, and chocolate chips. Spoon evenly into muffin cups and bake for 20-25 minutes or until a toothpick or knife comes out clean. Let cool completely before removing from tins. Serve asis or ice with Chocolate Fudge Frosting (pg 259). Makes 12 muffins.

MAPLE STREUSEL MUFFINS

Sarah . . . these are great for breakfast, lunch or snack time. – Wolffie, Davie, FL

Topping:
⅓ cup rolled oat flakes
1 tbsp flour
3 tbsp sugar
½ tsp ground cinnamon
2 tbsp vegan margarine
¼ cup pecans

Muffins:
2 cups flour
2 tsp baking powder
1 tsp baking soda
½ tsp salt
⅔ cup "milk"
2 tsp apple cider vinegar
¼ cup oil
½ cup maple syrup
2 tsp vanilla extract

Preheat oven to 400°F (205°C). Lightly oil 12 muffin tins or line with paper liners and set aside. In a food processor, blend the oat flakes, flour, sugar, cinnamon, and margarine together until crumbly. Add the pecans and pulse until roughly chopped; set aside. In a medium bowl, stir together the flour, baking powder, baking soda and salt. Add the "milk," vinegar, oil, maple syrup, and vanilla and stir together until "just mixed." Spoon evenly into muffin tins. Top each muffin evenly with pecan topping and bake 12-15 minutes or until a toothpick or knife comes out clean. Let cool completely before removing from tins. Makes 12 muffins.

PEACHY PECAN MUFFINS

How do you do that cool dance? Baby, don't split those hot pants!

Topping:
½ cup pecans, chopped
⅓ cup sugar
¼ cup flour
1 tsp ground cinnamon
2 tbsp oil

Muffin:
1½ cups flour
½ cup sugar
2 tsp baking powder
1 tsp ground cinnamon
¼ tsp salt
½ cup oil
¼ cup "milk"
egg replacer to equal 2 eggs (pg 269)
1 cup frozen peaches, finely chopped

Preheat oven to 400°F (205°C). Lightly oil 12 muffin tins or line with paper liners and set aside. In a small bowl, stir together the pecans, sugar, flour, cinnamon, and oil until crumbly. Set aside. In a large bowl, stir together the flour, sugar, baking powder, cinnamon, and salt. Add the oil, "milk," and egg replacer and stir together gently until "just mixed." Fold in peaches and spoon evenly into muffin cups. Sprinkle each muffin with topping and bake for 20-25 minutes or until a toothpick or knife comes out clean. Let cool completely before removing from tins. Makes 12 muffins.

LINDSEY'S PEANUT BUTTER CUPCAKES

These are the best cupcakes EVER! Even my carnivorous father is addicted to them; he'll eat over five of these in one sitting. – Lindsey, Canton, OH *(These cupcakes are like drops of love in paper liners.)*

1 cup flour
¾ cup sugar
1 tsp baking powder
¼ tsp salt
2 tbsp peanut butter (*or* other nut butter)
3 tbsp vegan margarine
½ tsp vanilla extract
1 large banana
⅓ cup "milk"
½ cup vegan chocolate chips

Preheat oven to 375°F (190°C). Lightly oil 12 muffin tins or line with paper liners and set aside. In a medium bowl, stir together the flour, sugar, baking powder, and salt. Set aside. In a food processor, blend together the peanut butter, margarine, vanilla, banana, and "milk" until smooth. Add to the flour and stir together well. Spoon even amounts of dough into paper cups and sprinkle top with chocolate chips. Bake for 18-20 minutes or until a toothpick or knife comes out clean. Let cool completely before removing from tins. Makes 12 cupcakes.

SWEET LOAVES
CHOCOLATE-WALNUT LOAF

This is very chocolatey and delicious! – Wolffie, Davie, FL *(This loaf is best served with a nice hot cup of coffee a generous portion of gossip.)*

1 cup "milk"
1 tbsp apple cider vinegar
2 tbsp ground flax seeds (pg 296)
6 tbsp water
1½ cups flour
1 cup sugar
½ cup unsweetened cocoa powder
1 tsp baking powder
1 tsp baking soda
½ tsp salt
7 tbsp oil
1 tsp vanilla extract
½ cup walnuts, finely chopped

Preheat oven to 350°F (175°C). Lightly oil a 9-inch loaf pan and set aside. In a small bowl, stir together the "milk," vinegar, flax seeds, and water. Set aside. In a medium bowl stir together the flour, sugar, cocoa powder, baking powder, baking soda, and salt. Add the "milk" mixture, oil, vanilla, and walnuts. Stir together gently until "just mixed." Spread into loaf pan and bake 50-55 minutes or until a toothpick or knife comes out clean. Let cool for 10-15 minutes before removing from pan. Makes 1 loaf.

SANTA'S FAVORITE CHRISTMAS BREAD

This loaf makes a great Christmas present for non-vegan friends. – Wolffie, Davie, FL *(If anyone needs a vegan diet, it's Santa. That poor guy is a heart attack waiting to happen. If mandarin oranges aren't in season, then you can use a small tin of canned. Just make sure you drain them well.)*

½ **cup walnuts**
¼ **cup dried cherries**
2 **tbsp ground flax seeds (pg 296)**
3 **tbsp water**
1 **large banana**
¼ **cup vegan margarine**
½ **cup sugar**
½ **tsp vanilla extract**
1 **cups flour**
1 **tsp baking powder**
½ **tsp baking soda**
¼ **tsp salt**
1 **mandarin orange, segments chopped**
¼ **cup vegan chocolate chips**
⅓ **cup shredded coconut, unsweetened**

Preheat oven to 350°F (175°C). Lightly oil a 9-inch loaf pan and set aside. In a food processor, blend the walnuts and cherries until finely chopped. Set aside. In food processor, blend the flax seeds, water, banana, margarine, sugar, and vanilla extract until smooth; set aside. In a medium bowl, stir together the flour, baking powder, baking soda, and salt. Add the banana mixture, walnut/cherry mixture, oranges, chocolate chips, and coconut and stir together gently until "just mixed." Pour evenly into loaf pan and bake for 50-55 minutes or until a toothpick or knife comes out clean. Let cool for 10-15 minutes before removing from pan. Makes 1 loaf.

CAKES

APRICOT "CHEESECAKE"

This is one fabulous cheesecake. I tried it out on my non-vegan friends and they couldn't tell the difference. They loved it. – Wolffie, Davie, FL *(Important: This is a "day before" recipe, meaning you have to make it the day before you want to serve it. You will need a 9-inch spring form pan, which are easy to find and relatively inexpensive; I've had mine for 10 years and it cost me $9.99. If you can't find vegan graham cracker crumbs [watch for honey as an ingredient] then use digestive cookies, or make them yourself [pg 281]. Just grind them up in a food processor and voilà: crumbs. You can also serve this cake as is, with fresh fruit or with the apricot glaze.)*

Crust:

**1½ cups vegan graham cracker crumbs
   (pg 281)**
¼ cup vegan margarine, melted
¼ cup sugar

Filling:

2 12-oz (300-g) pkg soft or silken tofu
2 cups vegan "cream cheese"
¾ cup sugar
1 tbsp vanilla extract
1 tbsp lemon juice
1 tsp lemon rind, finely grated
½ tsp salt
¼ cup flour

Glaze:

1 cup apricot fruit spread (preserves)
1 tbsp corn starch
¼ cup water

Preheat oven to 300°F (150°C). Lightly oil a 9-inch spring form pan and set aside. In a small mixing bowl, stir together graham cracker crumbs, melted margarine, and sugar. Press firmly into the bottom of prepared pan and set aside. In a food processor, process the tofu, cream cheese, sugar, vanilla, lemon juice, lemon rind, salt, and flour until smooth. Pour evenly into prepared pan and bake for 75 minutes. Remove from oven and place on a cooling rack. Allow to cool completely. Cover and refrigerate overnight. To prepare glaze: In a small saucepan, bring the fruit spread, cornstarch, and water to a boil. Reduce heat and simmer for 4-6 minutes, whisking constantly. Remove from heat and cool completely before pouring over cheesecake. Remove the sides of the pan from the cake and spread glaze evenly over the top. Refrigerate for at least 1 hour before serving. Makes 1 cake.

SIUE'S CHOCOLATE CHOCOLATE BROWNIE "CHEESECAKE"

Hey Sarah: Here's something from my upcoming book! (When? Not for a while yet! Only have 35 recipes so far.) You can't go wrong with TWO chocolate orgasms mixed together! – Siue, *DairyFreeDesserts.com*

Brownie:

1½ squares (1.5 oz) unsweetened baking chocolate
2½ tbsp vegan margarine
⅔ cup sugar
2 tbsp flour
½ tsp vanilla extract
egg replacer to equal 1½ eggs (pg 296)

Cheesecake:

2½ squares (2.5 oz) unsweetened baking chocolate
½ cup vegan "cream cheese"
⅓ cup soy "yogurt"
½ cup firm tofu
1 cup sugar
1 tbsp cornstarch
2 tbsp flour
½ tsp vanilla extract
⅛ tsp salt

Preheat oven to 325°F (165°C). Lightly oil an 8-inch round cake pan and set aside. In a small saucepan on medium-low heat, melt the chocolate and margarine. Remove from heat and add the sugar, flour, vanilla, and egg replacer and stir well. Pour evenly into cake pan. Set aside. In a small saucepan on medium-low heat, melt the chocolate. While chocolate is melting, in a food processor, place the "cream cheese," "yogurt," tofu, sugar, cornstarch, flour, vanilla, and salt. Add the melted chocolate and blend together until smooth. Spoon evenly over top of the brownie mixture and bake for 40-45 minutes. Cool completely, refrigerate, and serve chilled. Makes 1 cake.

PUMPKIN TOFU "CHEESECAKE"

Magnificence in a crust! This is another recipe omnivores go crazy for and I figure if I can make something they like, I've done my job. I've noticed that on your website *GoVegan.net*, a lot of kids ask for recipes to make for their omni families and friends. I have the same problem. I live with omnivores, and their tastebuds are different than ours. – Wolffie, Davie, FL *(Gingersnap cookies are generally vegan, so check out the cookie isle at your local grocery store.)*

Crust:
1½ cups gingersnap cookies
¾ cup pecans, finely ground
¼ cup sugar
⅓ cup oil

Filling:
1 14-oz (425-g) pkg firm tofu
1 12-oz (300-g) pkg soft *or* silken tofu
1¼ cups sugar
1 cup unsweetened pumpkin purée
¼ cup flour
1 tsp vanilla extract
½ tsp maple extract
1 tsp ground cinnamon
½ tsp salt
¼ tsp ground ginger
¼ tsp ground cloves
6-10 pecan halves
1 tbsp maple syrup

Preheat oven to 300°F (150°C). Lightly oil a 9-inch spring form pan and set aside. In a food processor, blend the cookies, pecans, sugar, and oil. Press firmly into the bottom of prepared pan and set aside. In a food processor, process the tofu, sugar, pumpkin, flour, vanilla, maple extract, cinnamon, salt, ginger, and cloves until smooth. Pour evenly into pan. Place pecan halves decoratively on top of cake and bake for 75 minutes. Remove from oven and place on a cooling rack; allow to cool completely. Spoon maple syrup over top of cake, cover, and refrigerate overnight. Makes 1 cake.

MINT CHOCOLATE ICE CREAM CAKE

You will need a 9-inch spring form cheesecake pan for this recipe. This recipe is very basic, but you can sass it up by adding different types of ice cream or extracts. Get crazy!

Crust:
20 vegan cream-filled sandwich type cookies
¼ cup vegan margarine, melted

Filling:
4 cups vegan vanilla ice cream, softened
¼ cup vegan chocolate chips
2 tbsp maple syrup
½ tsp mint extract
¼ cup vegan chocolate chips

To prepare the crust: Lightly oil a 9-inch spring form pan and set aside. In a food processor, process the cookies until fine. Add melted margarine and process again until well-combined. Press firmly into the bottom of the pan and refrigerate for 1 hour. With an electric mixer or a food processor, blend together the ice cream, ¼ cup chocolate chips, maple syrup, and mint extract until well blended. Spoon filling evenly into pan and sprinkle top with chocolate chips. Place in freezer for at least 1 hour. Remove from freezer 5 minutes before serving, pop open the pan, and cut cake into slices. Makes 1 cake.

PEANUT BUTTER COOKIE ICE CREAM CAKE

As desserts go, this one is over the edge. Prepare yourself for a total sugar blackout. – Wolffie, Davie, FL *(You will need a 9-inch spring form cheesecake pan for this recipe. They're easy to find and relatively inexpensive.)*

Crust:
20 vegan cream-filled sandwich-type cookies
¼ cup vegan margarine, melted

Filling:
4 cups vegan vanilla ice cream, softened
½ cup peanut butter
2 tbsp maple syrup
¼ cup salted peanuts, finely chopped

To prepare the crust: Lightly oil a 9-inch spring form pan and set aside. In a food processor, process the cookies until fine. Add melted margarine and process again until well-combined. Press firmly into the bottom of the pan and refrigerate for 1 hour. With an electric mixer or a food processor, blend together the ice cream, peanut butter, and maple syrup until well mixed. Spoon filling evenly into pan and sprinkle the top with peanuts. Place in freezer for at least 1 hour. Remove from freezer 5 minutes before serving, pop open the pan, and cut cake into slices. Makes 1 cake.

RENE'S TOMATO SOUP SPICE CAKE

This is a recipe which my mom used to make for the family when I was growing up. It is fast and cheap to make. Don't let the name (or the soup can) scare you; it's delicious! – Rene, Ottawa, ON *(Ice with Rene's Vanilla Frosting [pg 260] when cake has cooled completely.)*

1 10-oz (284-ml) can tomato soup
2 tbsp oil
1 cup sugar
1 tsp baking soda
1 tsp baking powder
1 tsp ground cinnamon
½ tsp ground cloves
1½ cups of flour
½ cup raisins (optional)

Preheat oven to 350°F (175°C). Lightly oil and flour a bunt or 8-inch cake pan and set aside. In a large bowl, stir together the tomato soup, oil, and sugar. Add the baking soda, baking powder, cinnamon, cloves, and flour and mix together well. Stir in raisins and pour batter into bunt or cake pan. Bake for 25-30 minutes or until a toothpick or knife comes out clean. Let cool for 10-15 minutes before removing from pan. Makes 1 cake.

YELLA CAKE

This great recipe can also be used to make great cupcakes – just make sure you cut down the baking time. For a birthday layer cake, double the recipe and bake in two cake tins. This multi-purpose cake takes on many forms depending on what you frost it with. I like the Basic Cake Glaze (pg 260) with a little lemon extract and a sprinkle of poppy seeds.

> ¾ **cup sugar**
> ¼ **cup vegan margarine**
> **egg replacer to equal 1 egg (pg 296)**
> **1 tsp vanilla extract**
> **1½ cups flour**
> **1¼ tsp baking powder**
> ¼ **tsp salt**
> ¾ **cup "milk"**

Preheat oven to 350°F (175°C). Lightly oil a 9-inch round cake pan and set aside. In a large bowl, cream together the sugar, margarine, egg replacer, and vanilla. Add the flour, baking powder, salt, and "milk" and stir together gently until "just mixed." Spread evenly into cake pan and bake for 30-35 minutes, or until a toothpick or knife comes out clean. Let cool for 10-15 minutes before removing from pan. Cool completely before frosting. Makes 1 cake.

ESPRESSO CAKE

If chocolate makes your heart skip a beat, then this cake takes you to the next level of heart-pounding pleasure. You can ice this cake with any of the frostings on pg 259-261.

> **1 cup sugar**
> **1½ cups flour**
> **1 cup unsweetened cocoa powder**
> **1 tsp baking soda**
> ⅛ **tsp salt**
> **1 cup "milk"**
> **1 shot of espresso**
> ⅓ **cup applesauce**
> **1 tsp vanilla extract**

Preheat oven to 350°F (175°C). Lightly oil a 9-inch round cake pan and set aside. In a large bowl, stir together the sugar, flour, cocoa powder, baking soda, and salt; set aside. Add the "milk," espresso, applesauce, and vanilla and stir together gently until "just mixed." Spread evenly into cake pan and bake for 40-45 minutes or until a toothpick or knife comes out clean. Let cool for 10-15 minutes before removing from pan. Cool completely before frosting. Makes 1 cake.

NIKOLE'S BOSS'S MOM'S PEANUT BUTTER CHOCOLATE CAKE

My boss's mom sent me this recipe, so I veganized it and made it my own. – Nikole, Detroit, MI *(So delicious. It looks like a cookie but tastes like a cake. Goes perfectly with a strong cup of tea and Oprah.)*

Topping:

¼ **cup vegan "cream cheese"**
2 **tbsp peanut butter**
3 **tbsp sugar**
egg replacer to equal 1 egg (pg 296)
⅛ **tsp salt**
¼ **cup vegan chocolate chips**

Batter:

1½ **cup flour**
¾ **cup sugar**
3 **tbsp unsweetened cocoa powder**
1 **tsp baking soda**
¼ **tsp salt**
¾ **cup water**
¼ **cup oil**
1 **tsp vanilla extract**
2 **tsp apple cider vinegar**
¼ **cup pecans, chopped**

Preheat oven to 350°F (175°C). Lightly oil an 8-inch cake pan and set aside. In a small bowl, stir together the "cream cheese," peanut butter, sugar, egg replacer, and salt until smooth. Stir in the chocolate chips and set aside. In a medium bowl, mix together the flour, sugar, cocoa, baking powder, and salt. Add the water, oil, vanilla, and vinegar and stir together gently until "just mixed." Pour evenly into cake pan. Spoon peanut butter mixture over cake batter, and cut through batter with a knife to swirl the peanut butter mixture. Sprinkle top with pecans and bake for 35-40 minutes, or until a toothpick or knife comes out clean. Let cool for 10-15 minutes before removing from pan. Cool completely before serving. Makes 1 cake.

SHARON'S BLACK PEPPER COFFEE CAKE

Hi Sarah: Many years ago, when my partner and I were just getting to know each other and impressions were important, I decided to bake him a cake. Never having done much baking or cooking, and knowing he is somewhat of a fussy eater, I asked him what kind of cake he liked. He remembered a coffee cake that he had baked in home economics class in grade eight. He even found his original recipe for me to use. Now the pressure was on! It's a very simple recipe, really. I prepared the topping – so far so good. Then I started the cake. Three quarters of a cup of sugar, one quarter cup of soft shortening, etc ... and ... two teaspoons of B.P.? Of course . . . black pepper! I found out later that B.P. stood for baking powder. – Sharon, Gabriola Island, BC

Topping:
½ **cup sugar**
2 **tbsp oil**
2 **tsp ground cinnamon**
2 **tbsp flour**

Cake:
¾ **cup sugar**
¼ **cup vegan margarine, room temperature**
egg replacer equal to 1 egg (pg 296)
½ **cup "milk"**
1¼ **cups flour**
2 **tsp baking powder (B.P.)**
½ **tsp salt**

Preheat oven to 325°F (165°C). Lightly oil an 8-inch cake pan and set aside. In a small bowl, stir together the sugar, oil, cinnamon, and flour to make your topping; set aside. In a medium bowl, cream together the sugar and margarine. Add the egg replacer, "milk," flour, baking powder, and salt and stir together gently until "just mixed." Spoon into cake pan and sprinkle evenly with reserved topping. Bake for 30-35 minutes or until a toothpick or knife comes out clean. Let cool for 10-15 minutes before serving. Makes 1 cake.

TARA'S CHOCOLATE CAKE

I got this recipe from a friend who got it from a friend and so on and so on. Everyone I've served it to loves it, and is always surprised that it's vegan! Best of all, it take no time to prepare. – Tara, Toronto, ON *(You wouldn't believe how many variations on Auntie Bonnie's Wacky Cake have been submitted over the years. Tara's is a little different, but just as easy and scrumptious as Auntie Bonnie's. Ice with Tara's Chocolate Frosting [pg 261] when cake has cooled completely.)*

1½ cup flour
⅓ cup unsweetened cocoa powder
1 cup sugar
1 tsp baking soda
½ tsp salt

⅓ cup oil
1 tbsp apple cider vinegar
1 tsp vanilla extract
1 cup cold water

Preheat oven to 350°F (175°C). Lightly oil an 8-inch cake pan and set aside. In a medium bowl, stir together the flour, cocoa, sugar, baking soda, and salt. Add the oil, vinegar, vanilla, and cold water and stir together carefully until "just mixed." Spoon evenly into cake pan and bake for 30-35 minutes, or until a toothpick or knife comes out clean. Let cool for 10-15 minutes before removing from pan. Cool completely before frosting. Makes 1 cake.

WOLFFIE'S COCOA CAKE WITH CHOCOLATE FUDGEY FROSTING

This is my roommate's favorite cake, so I make it for her birthday every year. She is an omnivore and can't tell that it's vegan. – Wolffie, Davie, FL *(Frost with Wolffie's Chocolate Fudgey Frosting [pg 259].)*

½ cup unsweetened cocoa powder
2½ cups flour
1¾ cups sugar
1½ tsp baking soda
½ tsp salt
½ cup soft *or* silken tofu

1 cup "milk"
1 tbsp apple cider vinegar
1 tbsp vanilla extract
½ cup oil
½ cup water

Preheat oven to 350°F (175°C). Lightly oil two 8-inch round cake pans and set aside. In a large bowl, whisk together the cocoa powder, flour, sugar, baking soda, and salt. Set aside. In a food processor, blend the tofu, "milk," vinegar, vanilla, and oil until smooth. Pour into bowl along with the water and stir together well. Spread evenly between the two cake pans and bake for 30-35 minutes, or until a toothpick or knife comes out clean. Let cool for 10-15 minutes before removing from pan. Cool completely before frosting. Makes 1 cake.

WOLFFIE'S PINEAPPLE-COCONUT LAYER CAKE

This moist cake is fabulous! I've eaten this cake all by myself before . . . . It's also much better the day after it's made. – Wolffie, Davie, FL *(Frost with Wolffie's "Cream Cheese" Frosting [pg 259].)*

Cake:

2½ cups flour	1 cup sugar
2 tsp baking powder	¾ cup soft or silken tofu
½ tsp baking soda	¼ cup "milk"
½ tsp salt	1 tsp vanilla extract
½ cup vegan margarine	1 19-oz (540-ml) can crushed pineapple

Preheat oven to 350°F (175°C). Lightly oil 2 8-inch cake pans and set aside. In a large bowl, stir together the flour, baking powder, baking soda, and salt. Set aside. In a food processor, blend together the margarine, sugar, tofu, "milk," and vanilla until smooth. Add pineapples and tofu mixture into the flour mixture and stir together gently until "just mixed." Spread evenly between the two cake pans and bake for 30-35 minutes or until a toothpick or knife comes out clean. Let cool 10-15 minutes before removing from pan. Let cool completely before frosting. Makes 1 cake.

CHOCOLATE PUDDIN' CAKE

C'mon, gimme some of that shaky puddin,' cuz it's so doggone good.

Cake:

1 cup flour
½ cup walnuts, chopped
⅔ cup sugar
2 tbsp unsweetened cocoa powder
2 tsp baking powder
⅛ tsp salt
½ cup water
2 tbsp oil
1 tsp vanilla extract

Pudding:

⅔ cup sugar
¼ cup unsweetened cocoa powder
1¾ cup hot water

Preheat oven to 350°F (175°C). Lightly oil an 8-inch cake pan and set aside. In a medium bowl, stir together the flour, walnuts, sugar, cocoa powder, baking powder, and salt. Add the water, oil, and vanilla and stir together gently until "just mixed." Spoon evenly into the pan. In a small bowl, stir together the sugar and cocoa powder until well blended and sprinkle evenly over top of the cake mixture. Carefully pour the hot water over top of the cake. DO NOT MIX TOGETHER. Bake for 40 minutes. Makes 1 cake.

APRICOT-WALNUT COFFEE CAKE

This batter is very thin, and doesn't look like it will make enough, but it really does rise – trust me. This is one fabulous coffee cake. – Wolffie, Davie, FL

1 cup flour
½ tsp baking soda
½ tsp salt
¼ cup vegan margarine
¼ cup soft *or* **silken tofu**
¾ cup sugar
½ cup "milk"
1½ tsp apple cider vinegar
1 tsp vanilla extract
½ cup apricot fruit spread (preserves)
½ cup walnuts, finely chopped

Preheat oven to 350°F (175°C). Lightly oil an 8-inch cake pan and set aside. In a medium bowl, whisk together the flour, baking soda, and salt. Set aside. In a food processor, blend the margarine, tofu, sugar, "milk," vinegar, and vanilla until smooth. Add to the flour mixture, and stir until well combined. Spread half of batter into prepared pan. Spread apricot preserves evenly on top and sprinkle with half of the walnuts. Spread remaining batter on top and sprinkle with remaining walnuts. Bake 35-40 minutes or until a toothpick or knife comes out clean. Let cool 10-15 minutes before serving. Makes 1 cake.

CINNAMON-WALNUT COFFEE CAKE

Hey Sarah – this is really good. I thought you might be able to use it for your "breakfast section." – Wolffie, Davie, FL *(Uhhh. Breakfast? OK. Yum. How about with a cup of tea and some saucy gossip. This recipe is so sweet and tasty I had to include it here in the desserts chapter as well!)*

Topping:
½ cup sugar
1 tsp ground cinnamon
2 tbsp vegan margarine
¾ cup walnuts, chopped

Cake:
1½ cups flour
½ cup sugar
1 tsp baking powder
½ tsp baking soda
½ tsp salt
¾ cup Faux Sour Cream (pg 293)
⅓ cup oil
½ cup "milk"
1 tsp vanilla extract

Preheat oven to 350°F (175°C). Lightly oil an 8x8-inch baking pan and set aside. In a small bowl, stir together topping ingredients, and set aside. In a medium bowl, whisk together flour, sugar, baking powder, baking soda, and salt. Stir in the "sour cream," oil, "milk," and vanilla. Pour evenly into baking pan then sprinkle topping evenly over the top. Bake for 30-35 minutes. Makes 1 cake.

COLLEEN & HOBART'S MELT IN YOUR MOUTH CRUMBCAKE

Hi Sarah: We love your cookbooks! This recipe is a melt-in-your-mouth crumbcake that we adapted from my mom's famous cake recipe. For extra fun, sometimes we use chocolate cake mix and add a layer of raspberry jam in between the cake and crumble. Enjoy! – Colleen and Hobart, Long Island, NY *(This recipe is soooo yum and perfect for serving to your girlfriends at your stitch-n-bitch. But be careful, it lives up to it's name by being crumbly . . . so maybe it's better if you eat it over the kitchen sink while you talk about boys.)*

Cake:
½ of a 230-g box vanilla cake mix
⅔ cup applesauce
⅔ cup water
1 tsp vanilla extract

Crumble:
½ cup vegan margarine
1½ cups flour
½ cup rolled oat flakes
½ cup walnuts, chopped
⅔ cups sugar
1½ tsp ground cinnamon
1½ tsp vanilla extract
⅛ tsp salt

Preheat oven to 350°F (175°C). Lightly oil an 8-inch cake pan and set aside. In a medium bowl, stir together the cake mix, applesauce, water, and vanilla. Spoon evenly into cake pan and bake for 17 minutes. While cake is baking, mix together the margarine, flour, oat flakes, walnuts, sugar, cinnamon, vanilla, and salt. Spread mixture evenly over top of cake and bake for an additional 17 minutes or until a toothpick or knife comes out clean. Let cool for 10-15 minutes before serving. Makes 1 cake.

PEACH CRUMBCAKE

Making cake from scratch is easy, fun, and makes you feel like dancing. You know it, you love it, you got it, you want it!

> **2 cups flour**
> **1½ cups sugar**
> **2 tsp baking powder**
> **1 tsp ground cinnamon**
> **¼ tsp salt**
> **½ cup vegan margarine**
> **¾ cup "milk"**
> **1 tsp vanilla extract**
> **egg replacer to equal 2 eggs (pg 296)**
> **1½ cups peaches, finely chopped**
> **1 tbsp sugar**

Preheat oven to 350°F (175°C). Lightly oil an 8-inch cake pan and set aside. In a medium bowl, stir together the flour, sugar, baking powder, cinnamon, and salt. Stir in the margarine and combine (with your hands) until well mixed and resembles a coarse meal. Set aside 1 cup of mixture for later. Add the "milk," vanilla, egg replacer, and peaches to the remaining dough and stir gently until "just mixed." Spoon evenly into cake pan and spread the reserved mixture evenly over top of cake. Sprinkle top with 1 tbsp of sugar and bake for 40-45 minutes, or until a toothpick or knife comes out clean. Let cool for 10-15 minutes before serving. Makes 1 cake.

PIES

FUDGE PECAN PIE

The pecans rise to the top of this pie while it bakes. It's both pretty and tasty! You might want to place the pie on a cookie sheet as it has a tendency to bubble over. – Wolffie, Davie, FL *(Who are you, Wolffie? And why are all your recipes so freaking good?)*

½ cup water
¼ cup vegan margarine
2 tbsp unsweetened cocoa powder
¾ cup vegan chocolate chips
⅓ cup flour
1 cup sugar

pinch of salt
½ cup "milk"
1 tbsp vanilla extract
1 cup pecan halves
1 unbaked 9-inch pie crust (pg 262)
2 tsp "milk"

Preheat oven to 350°F (175°C). In a medium saucepan, bring water to a boil, and remove from heat. Whisk in margarine, cocoa powder, and chocolate chips until melted. Add flour, sugar, salt, ½ cup "milk," vanilla, and whisk until smooth. Stir in pecan halves and pour into prepared pie crust. Bake 55-60 minutes, or until a toothpick or knife comes out clean. Remove from oven and immediately brush 2 tsp of "milk" evenly over the top of the pie. Let cool to room temperature before serving. Makes 1 pie.

NO-BAKE CHOCOLATE PEANUT BUTTER BANANA CAKE

Just blend, stir, pour, chill, and eat! This is a helluva rich pie, so cut small slices or undo your pants. Whichever is easier.

2 cups vegan chocolate chips
½ cup "milk"
1½ cups nut butter (your choice)
1 12-oz (300-g) pkg soft *or* silken tofu
1 banana, sliced
1 gingersnap *or* graham cracker crust (pg 262-263)
½ tsp lemon juice

In a large double boiler, melt the chocolate chips and "milk" on medium heat, stirring until smooth and creamy. In a food processor, blend the nut butter and tofu together until smooth. Pour into melted chocolate and stir together well until smooth. Gently stir in half of the banana slices and pour evenly into prepared crust. Smooth top with back of spoon and place remaining banana slices on top. Paint banana slices with a drop of lemon juice to prevent browning. Refrigerate for at least 2 hours before serving. Makes 1 cake.

WOLFFIE'S PUMPKIN PIE

I'm thankful for pumpkins, for sugar, and for this pie. Don't worry that it won't look ready when you first take it out of the oven – it sets as it cools.

Topping:
¼ **cup sugar**
¼ **cup flour**
½ **tsp ground cinnamon**
2 tbsp vegan margarine
¼ **cup walnuts** *or* **pecans, finely chopped**

Filling:
1 14-oz (398-ml) can unsweetened pumpkin purée
½ **cup "milk"**
¼ **cup cornstarch**
½ **cup maple syrup**
½ **tsp salt**
¼ **cup sugar**
1 tsp ground cinnamon
1 tsp ground ginger
¼ **tsp allspice**
1 tsp vanilla extract
1 9-inch pie crust (pg 262)

Preheat oven to 375°F (190°C). In a small bowl, stir together the sugar, flour, cinnamon, margarine, and walnuts. Set aside. In a food processor, blend together all of the filling ingredients until smooth. Pour pumpkin mixture into prepared pie crust. Sprinkle topping evenly over top and bake for 40-45 minutes. Remove from oven and let cool. Serve at room temperature. Makes 1 pie.

WOLFFIE'S DERBY PIE

Here's my fabulous Derby Pie recipe. I swear it's better than an orgasm. – Wolffie, Davie, FL *(Better than an orgasm? Hmm.)*

½ cup vegan margarine (room temperature)
1 cup sugar
2 tbsp ground flax seeds (pg 296)
6 tbsp water
½ cup flour
¾ cup "milk"
1 tbsp vanilla extract
1 cup vegan chocolate chips
1 cup walnuts, finely chopped
1 9-inch pie crust (pg 296)

Preheat oven to 350°F (175°C). In a food processor, blend together the margarine, sugar, ground flax seeds, and water until smooth. Add flour, "milk," and vanilla and blend again until smooth. Remove blade and stir in chocolate chips and walnuts and pour evenly into pie crust. Bake for 45-50 minutes. Remove from oven and let cool enough to be transferred to refrigerator. Refrigerate pie for at least 1 hour before serving. Makes 1 pie.

FROSTINGS

CHOCOLATE FUDGEY FROSTING

This makes just enough to frost Wolffie's Cocoa Cake (pg 250), with a little left over for your child (or husband) to lick the bowl.

- 1½ cups water
- ½ cup unsweetened cocoa powder
- 1½ cups sugar
- ¼ tsp salt
- ¼ cup cornstarch
- ¼ cup vegan margarine
- 1½ tsp vanilla extract

In a medium saucepan, whisk together the water, cocoa powder, sugar, salt, and cornstarch. Slowly bring to a boil, whisking constantly for 3-4 minutes to avoid sticking. Once it starts to thicken, remove from heat and stir in margarine and vanilla. Refrigerate far at least an hour before frosting cake, blend frosting in food processor until smooth. Makes approx. 2 cups.

WOLFFIE'S "CREAM CHEESE" FROSTING

Vegan "cream cheese" can be found at most health food stores and is worth the money. It's delish! This recipe goes with Wolffie's Pineapple-Coconut Layer Cake on pg 251 or anywhere you want!

- 1 cup vegan "cream cheese"
- ¼ cup vegan margarine
- 1 tsp vanilla extract
- 2 cups vegan icing sugar
- 6 tbsp shredded coconut, unsweetened (optional)

In a food processor, blend the "cream cheese," margarine, vanilla, and icing sugar until smooth. Sprinkle coconut on top. Makes approx. 3 cups.

BASIC CAKE GLAZE

This glaze can be used on cake, cupcakes, and more. Try rolling the Cinnamon Doughnut Holes (pg 198) in it. The flavor is up to you: lemon, mint, orange, maple extract – get crazy!

> ¼ **cup vegan margarine, melted**
> **2 cups icing sugar**
> **2 tbsp "milk"**
> **extract/flavoring of your choice (to taste)**

In a medium bowl, stir together all of the ingredients until smooth and creamy. Add a little more "milk" if you want a thinner glaze. Drizzle over cooled cake and refrigerate for at least 1 hour before serving. Makes approx. 1½ cups.

CHOCOLATE GLAZE

This chocolate glaze can be poured over a cake or a freshly baked pan of brownies (pg 211-212). Just remember to cool your baking completely before you glaze. Once poured, you can garnish with finely chopped nuts or fancy cake sprinkles.

> **1 cup vegan chocolate chips**
> ⅔ **cup vegan margarine**

In a small double boiler, melt the chocolate chips and margarine on medium heat, stirring until smooth and creamy. Let cool a little before spooning over cake or brownies. Refrigerate to set for at least 1 hour before serving. Makes approx. 1¼ cups.

RENE'S VANILLA FROSTING

Rene from Ottawa, Ontario uses this fabu icing on his Tomato Soup Spice Cake on pg 246.

> ½ **cup vegan margarine**
> **2 cups icing sugar (pg 299)**
> **2 tbsp "milk"**
> **1 tbsp vanilla extract**
> **pinch of salt**

In a food processor or medium bowl, mix together the margarine, sugar, "milk," and vanilla until smooth. Makes approx. 3 cups.

APRICOT FRUIT GLAZE

This glaze is perfect when poured over "cheesecake" (pg 242). If you're not down with apricots, then experiment with different fruit preserves and see what you like best.

> **1 cup apricot fruit spread (preserves)**
> **1 tbsp cornstarch**
> **¼ cup water**

In a small saucepan, bring the fruit spread, cornstarch, and water to a boil. Reduce heat and simmer for 4-6 minutes, stirring constantly. Remove from heat and cool completely before pouring over cheesecake. Makes approx. 1 cup.

TORONTO TARA'S CHOCOLATE FROSTING

This dark and lovely recipe will leave you with heart palpitations. Add a little mint extract for extra yum!

> **2 cup icing sugar (pg 299)**
> **½ cup vegan margarine**
> **¼ cup unsweetened cocoa powder**
>
> **2 tbsp "milk"**
> **1 tsp vanilla extract**
> **pinch of salt**

In a food processor or a medium bowl, mix together all of the ingredients until smooth. Refrigerate for 30 minutes before use. Makes approx. 2 cups.

"BUTTER CREAM" FROSTING

We vegans can never have too many frosting recipes in my opinion! – Wolffie, Davie, FL *(This recipe only seems to work with Earth Balance buttery spread. I don't know why, but consider yourself warned.)*

> **2 tbsp flour**
> **⅔ cup "milk"**
> **½ cup Earth Balance margarine**
> **1 tsp vanilla extract**
> **⅓ cup sugar**

In a small saucepan, whisk together the flour and "milk." Bring to a boil, stirring constantly with whisk, then reduce heat and simmer until it starts to thicken. Remove from heat and set aside to cool. In a food processor, blend together the margarine, vanilla, sugar, and flour mixture until smooth and creamy. Pour into a medium bowl and refrigerate for at least 2 hours before using. Makes approx. 1½ cups.

CRUSTS

ALL-PURPOSE CRUST

This is a wonderful flaky crust that can be used for recipes like Kim's Peach-zza (pg 232) or Veggie Pot Pie (pg 153); it's the crust that keeps on giving. Remember to keep this dough chilled before you using, as it makes it much easier to handle. You can freeze it for later use or it will keep in the refrigerator for up to 3 days. Handle your dough with floured hands in between two pieces of wax paper (or on a lightly floured surface) in order to keep your swearing-to-yelling ratio down to a minimum.

> **2 cups all purpose** *or* **pastry flour**
> **1 tsp salt**
> **¾ cup vegan margarine**
> **¼ cup "milk"**

In a food processor, blend the flour and salt together. Add the margarine and pulse until mixture resembles a coarse meal. Add "milk" and blend until well combined and dough forms. Remove dough, roll into a ball and wrap in plastic and refrigerate for 1 hour before using. Makes 1 crust.

CRUST TO LOVE BASIC PIE CRUST

Crust to love . . . was the last thing I was dreaming of. Another easy pie crust to add to your collection.

> **1¼ cups all purpose** *or* **pastry flour**
> **½ tsp salt**
>
> **½ cup vegetable shortening**
> **3 tbsp cold water**

In a food processor, blend the flour and salt together. Add the shortening and pulse until mixture resembles a coarse meal. Add cold water and blend until well combined and a dough forms. Remove dough, roll into a ball, and wrap in plastic and refrigerate for 1 hour before using. Makes 1 crust.

GINGER SNAP CRUST

This crust is from the Pumpkin Tofu "Cheesecake" (pg 244), but is also great for other "cheesecake"-type recipes. Gingersnap cookies are generally vegan. Check out the cookie aisle at your local grocery store.

> **1¼ cups gingersnap cookies, crumbled**
> **¾ cup finely ground pecans**
> **¼ cup sugar**
> **5 tbsp oil**

Lightly oil a 9-inch spring form pan and set aside. In a food processor, blend the cookies and pecans until finely ground. Stir in the sugar and oil until well mixed. Press firmly into the bottom of pan and set aside. Makes 1 crust.

GRAHAM CRACKER CRUST

This recipe is for the amazing Apricot "Cheesecake" (pg 242), but can also be used for other cheesecake-type recipes. If you can't find vegan graham cracker crumbs (watch for honey as an ingredient) then use digestive cookies or make your own graham crackers (pg 281). Just grind them up in a food processor and voilà: crumbs.

> **1¼ cups vegan graham cracker crumbs**
> **¼ cup vegan margarine (melted)**
> **¼ cup sugar**

Lightly oil a 9-inch spring form pan and set aside. In a small mixing bowl, stir together graham cracker crumbs, melted margarine, and sugar. Press firmly into the bottom of pan and set aside. Makes 1 crust.

SANDWICH COOKIE CRUST

Use this recipe for the base of your Ice Cream Cake (pg 245-246).

> **20 vegan cream-filled sandwich-type cookies**
> **¼ cup vegan margarine, melted**

Lightly oil a 9-inch spring form pan and set aside. In a food processor, blend the cookies until fine. Add melted margarine and blend again until well mixed. Press firmly into the bottom of pan. Refrigerate for 1 hour. Makes 1 crust.

WOLFFIE'S QUICH WHOLE WHEAT PIE CRUST

This pie crust is quick to prepare and comes out very flaky. This crust never fails.– Wolffie, Davie, FL *(You heard the woman. NEVER FAILS! This crust is really simple, and if you're using it for dessert, you may want to add a little sugar to help with the sweetness. Or not. Either way, it's a kick-ass crust.)*

> **1½ cups whole-wheat flour**
> **½ tsp salt**
> **½ cup oil**
> **1 tsp cider vinegar**
> **3 tbsp ice water**

In a medium bowl, whisk together the flour and salt. Add the oil, vinegar, and water and stir until well blended. Press into a 9-inch pie plate. Makes 1 crust.

Baked
Goods

Vegan baking is just like conventional baking. You must follow the recipes exactly – this is chemistry, people! One false move can result in a mess, so measure your ingredients with care.

All of the recipes in this chapter are made with all-purpose flour unless otherwise stated. Don't forget to always use fresh ingredients. Purchase small amounts of baking soda, baking powder, and yeast because these items have a short shelf life and using stale ingredients can result in baking mishaps.

For recipes that call for baking soda and baking powder, don't forget to preheat your oven before you mix the liquid and dry ingredients together. The baking soda and baking powder start activating as soon as the liquid ingredients hit them – so have your oven ready! Once the recipe is prepared, make sure to put your dough in the oven immediately. Don't forget that when you're making a quick bread that does not contain yeast, you must handle with care. Stir gently until the ingredients are "just mixed." If you overmix the dough, your bread may not rise the way you want it to.

My oven's internal thermometer is off by about 25°F (4°C) and that's a huge difference. Use a stand-alone oven thermometer to ensure you're baking at the correct temperature. They're inexpensive and you can purchase them in any kitchen or housewares store.

Check for readiness by inserting a toothpick or knife into the center of your baked goods before you remove them from the oven. If it comes out clean, then you are good to go. If it comes out gooey, then bake another 2-4 minutes and test again.

Check out pg 29 for other cooking tips. Now preheat your oven and let's get baking!

KALAMATA & SUN-DRIED TOMATO SODA BREAD

Olives rule!

3 cups flour
1 tbsp baking powder
1 tsp ground thyme
½ tsp salt
2½ cups water
1 tbsp oil
¾ cup Kalamata olives, chopped
¼ cup sun-dried tomatoes, finely chopped
¼ cup sunflower seeds (optional)

Preheat the oven to 400°F (205°C). Lightly oil a 9-inch loaf pan. Set aside. In a large bowl, stir together the flour, baking powder, thyme, and salt. Add the water, oil, olives, sun-dried tomatoes, and sunflower seeds and gently stir dough until "just mixed." Pour evenly into loaf pan and bake for 45-50 minutes or until a toothpick or knife comes out clean. Let cool on a rack for 10-15 minutes before removing from pan. Makes 1 loaf.

SARAH'S SANDWICH SPELT BREAD

Spelt is one of my favorite grains to use instead of wheat flour. It's a distant cousin of wheat, but some people with wheat intolerances find they can eat spelt just fine. This bread is perfect for sandwiches, but my favorite way to eat it is fresh out of the oven, with a thin layer of vegan margarine. This is a seriously heavy delicious loaf.

> **4 cups spelt flour**
> **½ cup sunflower seeds**
> **1 tsp salt**
> **2 tsp baking soda**
> **2 cups "milk"**
> **1 tbsp apple cider vinegar**
> **1 tbsp maple syrup**

Preheat oven to 350°F (175°C). Lightly oil a 9-inch loaf pan and set aside.In a large bowl, stir together the flour, sunflower seeds, salt, and baking soda. Add the "milk," vinegar, and maple syrup and gently stir dough until "just mixed." Pour evenly into loaf pan and bake for 55-60 minutes or until a toothpick or knife comes out clean. Let cool on a rack for 10-15 minutes before removing from pan. Makes 1 loaf.

KISSING COUSINS OAT BREAD

Oats are a distant cousin of the wheat family, but that doesn't stop them from marrying each other in this easy-to-make oat bread.

> **2 cups rolled oat flakes**
> **2 cups flour**
> **1 tbsp baking powder**
> **1 tsp salt**
> **3 tbsp maple syrup**
> **2 tbsp oil**
> **2 cups "milk"**

Preheat oven to 450°F (230°C). Lightly oil a 9-inch loaf pan and set aside. In a food processor, grind the oat flakes until smooth and set aside. In a medium bowl, stir together the oat flakes, flour, baking powder, and salt. Add the maple syrup, oil, and "milk" and gently stir dough until "just mixed." Pour evenly into loaf pan and bake for 25-30 minutes or until a toothpick or knife comes out clean. Makes 1 loaf.

CUMIN-SPICED QUICK BREAD

Cumin is one of my all-time favorite spices because of its rich, distinctive scent and warm, earthy flavor.

3 cups flour
¼ cup sugar
2 tbsp baking powder
3 tsp ground cumin
1 tsp cumin seeds
2 tsp salt
egg replacer to equal 2 eggs (pg 296)
1½ cups "milk"
⅓ cup oil

Preheat the oven to 350°F (175°C). Lightly oil a 9-inch loaf pan and set aside. In a large bowl, stir together the flour, sugar, baking powder, ground cumin, cumin seeds, and salt. Add the egg replacer, "milk," and oil and gently stir dough until "just mixed." Pour evenly into loaf pan and bake for 50-55 minutes or until a toothpick or knife comes out clean. Let cool on a rack for 10-15 minutes before removing from pan. Makes 1 loaf.

CHAPATI FLAT BREAD

Chapatis are great because they can be made in only a few minutes and can be used to scoop up your food instead of a fork or spoon!

1 cup flour
½ tsp salt
⅓ cup water
2 tsp oil
vegan margarine

In a medium bowl, stir together the flour and salt. Add the water and oil and stir together until it becomes a stiff dough (add a drop or two more of water if the dough is too stiff). Knead until dough is very smooth. Cover with cloth and set aside in a warm, non-drafty spot for 30 minutes. Place a dry frying pan on medium-high heat. Divide dough into 4 balls. Roll out each ball on a lightly floured surface into thin 6-inch discs. Place a disc in the hot frying pan and let cook until bubbles star to appear and the chapati starts to brown and puff up. Turn chapati over and cook other side. Remove immediately from frying pan and spread a thin amount of margarine on one side of the chapati after cooking. Repeat with remaining dough. Keep chapatis wrapped in a clean dish towel so they will stay warm and won't dry out. Makes 4 chapatis.

WOLFFIE'S "BUTTERMILK" CORNBREAD

Serve this light and tasty cornbread topped with a nice heaping spoonful of gravy (pg 181) or with a big bowl of soup.

1½ cups flour
1½ cups stone ground cornmeal
3 tbsp sugar
1 tbsp baking powder
¾ tsp baking soda

1½ tsp salt
2 cups "milk"
2 tbsp apple cider vinegar
3 tbsp oil

Preheat the oven to 425°F (220°C). Lightly oil an 8x8-inch baking pan and set aside. In a large bowl, stir together the flour, cornmeal, sugar, baking powder, baking soda, and salt. Stir in the "milk," vinegar, and oil until "just mixed." Pour evenly into baking pan and bake for 25-30 minutes or until a toothpick or knife comes out clean. Let cool on a rack for 10-15 minutes before removing from pan. Makes 1 square loaf.

JEN'S RAISIN SODA BREAD

It really doesn't get easier than this! This Irish bread tastes even better the second day and is particularly good for breakfast. Feel free to add 1 teaspoon of grated orange rind and use dried cranberries instead of raisins. – Jen, Kingston, ON *(Make sure the oven is preheated before you add the vinegar and "milk" mixture to the flour. The dough starts processing as soon as the liquid hits the flour, so the sooner you can get it into your hot oven, the better.)*

2¼ cups flour
2 tsp baking powder
¼ tsp baking soda
2 tbsp sugar
½ tsp salt
½ tbsp caraway seeds
½ cup raisins
1 cup "milk"
1 tbsp apple cider vinegar

Preheat the oven to 350°F (175°C). Lightly oil a 9-inch loaf pan and set aside. In a large bowl, stir together the flour, baking powder, baking soda, sugar, salt, caraway seeds, and raisins. Add the "milk" and vinegar and gently stir dough until "just mixed." Pour evenly into loaf pan and bake for 40-45 minutes or until a toothpick or knife comes out clean. Let cool on a rack for 10-15 minutes before removing from pan. Makes 1 loaf.

SIMPLE SASSY SODA BREAD

This is a moist, chewy soda bread that makes great sandwiches, but is best when dipped in a thick stew (pg 116).

3 cups flour
1 tbsp baking powder
½ tsp salt
2½ cups water
1 tbsp oil
½ cup sesame seeds (optional)

Preheat the oven to 400°F (205°C). Lightly oil a 9-inch loaf pan and set aside. In a large bowl, stir together the flour, baking powder, and salt. Add the water, oil, and sesame seeds and gently stir dough until "just mixed." Pour evenly into loaf pan and bake for 45-50 minutes or until a toothpick or knife comes out clean. Let cool on a rack for 10-15 minutes before removing from pan. Makes 1 loaf.

EASY FRENCH BREAD

Baking yeasted breads is one of my favorite hobbies. I love to do it on days when I'm puttering around the house doing things like folding laundry, sorting through my junk drawer or laying around reading a magazine. Making bread is easy, and takes just a little time, patience, and practice. Try misting the loaf with water during the last 10 minutes of baking – it will give the bread a hard shiny crust.

2½ tsp or one packet active dry yeast
¼ cup warm water
1 tbsp sugar
1¼ cup water
2½ tsp salt
3½ - 4 cups flour
¼ cup poppy seeds or toasted sesame seeds (pg 295)

In a large bowl, stir together the yeast with ¼ cup of the warm water and sugar. Let sit for 10 minutes. Stir in the 1¼ cup of water, salt, and 1 cup of flour. Slowly stir in the remaining flour, 1 cup at a time. On a lightly floured surface, knead dough until smooth and elastic; add a little extra flour if it's too sticky. Transfer dough to a large, lightly oiled bowl, turning dough until covered with oil. Cover with cloth and set aside in a warm, non-drafty spot and let dough rise for 1½ hours. Preheat oven to 400°F (205°C). Punch down dough and knead out air bubbles. On a lightly floured surface, shape dough into large loaf or two small baguettes and place on a baking sheet. Make 4-5 slashes diagonally across the top. Sprinkle top evenly with seeds and let rise for 15 minutes. Bake for 20 minutes or until a toothpick or knife comes out clean. Let cool on a rack for 10-15 minutes before serving. Makes 1 large loaf or 2 small baguettes.

HEATHER'S SWEDISH RYE BREAD

I come from a very traditional Swedish family, and during the winter holidays we make traditional dishes. I veganized our family recipe for rye bread. My great grandmother can't tell the difference between the vegan version and the original. Everyone who has tried it wanted the recipe, so I thought I would share it with the author of my favorite cookbook. Thanks for all the hard work and good food. – Heather Ebba, Pullman, WA

2¼ tsp *or* **1 packet active dry yeast**
¾ cup warm water
1 tsp sugar
1¾ cups rye flour
½ cup "milk"
1 tbsp margarine
1 tbsp molasses
1 tsp salt
1 tsp anise seeds
½ tsp fennel seeds

In a large bowl, stir together the yeast with the warm water and sugar. Let sit for 10 minutes. Add the rye flour, "milk," margarine, molasses, salt, anise seeds, and fennel seeds and stir until smooth; this will be a sticky dough. Cover with cloth and set aside in a warm, non-drafty spot and let dough rise for 1 hour. Preheat oven to 375°F (190°C). Lightly oil a 9-inch loaf pan and set aside. Punch down dough then knead out air bubbles and place into loaf pan. Cover and let rise again for 15 minutes. Bake for 30 minutes or until a toothpick or knife comes out clean. Let cool on a rack for 10-15 minutes removing from pan. Makes 1 loaf.

SASSY SANDWICH BREAD

This bread is wicked for sandwiches, toast, or with a big bowl of soup.

> **2¼ tsp** *or* **1 packet dry active yeast**
> **¼ cup warm water**
> **2 tbsp sugar**
> **1 cup water**
> **3 cups flour**
> **1½ tsp salt**
> **2½ tbsp oil**

In a large bowl, stir together the yeast with the ¼ cup of warm water and sugar. Let sit for 10 minutes. Stir in the 1 cup of water, 1 cup of flour, salt, and oil. Slowly stir in remaining flour, 1 cup at a time. On a lightly floured surface, knead dough until smooth and elastic; add a little extra flour if it's too sticky. Transfer dough to a large, lightly oiled bowl, turning dough until covered with oil. Cover with cloth and set aside in a warm, non-drafty spot and let dough rise for 1 hour. Preheat oven to 375°F (190°C). Lightly oil a 9-inch loaf pan and set aside. Punch down dough then knead out air bubbles and place in loaf pan. Lightly brush top of loaf with oil or cut a slit down the middle and spread some vegan margarine in the slit. Cover and let rise again for 15 minutes. Bake for 25 minutes or until a toothpick or knife comes out clean. Let cool on a rack for 10-15 minutes before removing from pan. Makes 1 large loaf.

BASIC BAKING POWDER BISCUITS

There is nothing I like better with a bowl of soup than a baking powder biscuit. Super easy to make and full of starchy comfort. For a fancier biscuit, separate each of your six biscuit balls into three. Roll in poppy seeds and place 3 of the balls into each muffin tin. You biscuits will puff up to be a pretty cloverleaf shape.

> **2 cups flour**
> **3 tsp baking powder**
> **1 tsp dried oregano**
> **¾ tsp salt**
> **¼ cup vegan margarine**
> **¾ cup "milk"**
> **1 tsp apple cider vinegar**

Preheat oven to 450°F (230°C). In a large bowl, stir together the flour, baking powder, oregano, and salt. Stir in the margarine, "milk," and vinegar until well blended. Cut dough into 6 even amounts and place into lightly oiled muffin tins; or roll dough out on a lightly floured surface and cut with large cookie cutters and place on baking sheet. Bake for 12-15 minutes or until a toothpick or knife comes out clean. Makes 6 large biscuits.

BANANA CURRANT RICE FLOUR MUFFINS

A sweet treat for those who don't eat wheat.

- ½ cup "milk"
- 1 banana
- ¾ cup rice flour
- ¼ cup sugar
- ¼ tsp ground nutmeg
- ½ tsp baking powder
- ¼ tsp baking soda
- ½ cup currants (*or* other dried fruit)

Preheat oven to 350°F (175°C). Lightly oil 6 muffin tins or line with paper liners and set aside. In a food processor, blend together the "milk" and banana until smooth. Set aside. In a medium bowl, stir together the flour, sugar, nutmeg, baking powder, and baking soda. Stir in the banana mixture and currants until "just mixed" and spoon evenly into muffin cups. Bake for 20-25 minutes or until a toothpick or knife comes out clean. Let cool completely before removing from tins. Makes 6 muffins.

BRAN MUFFINS

What way to start your day!

- 1⅓ cup flour
- 1 cup wheat bran
- ½ cup sugar
- 1 tsp baking soda
- ⅛ tsp salt
- 1¼ cups "milk"
- ¼ cup apple sauce
- 2 tbsp ground flax seeds (pg 296)
- 2 tbsp oil
- 1 tsp vanilla extract
- ¼ cup raisins (*or* other dried fruit)
- ¼ cup sunflower seeds

Preheat oven to 350°F (175°C). Lightly oil 12 muffin tins or line with paper liners and set aside. In a large bowl, stir together the flour, wheat bran, sugar, baking soda, and salt. Stir in the "milk," apple sauce, flax seeds, oil, vanilla, raisins, and sunflower seeds and stir together gently until "just mixed." Spoon evenly into muffin cups and bake for 25-30 minutes or until a toothpick or knife comes out clean. Let cool completely before removing from tins. Makes 12 muffins.

WOLFFIE'S EGGNOG MUFFINS

These can be made when vegan eggnog is in season, or you can make your own "eggnog" with that great recipe you have in *How It All Vegan!*. They are vunderbar. – Wolffie, Davie, FL *(There are two times a year that make me jump up and down like a crazy person. One is when the new phone book arrives [insert goofy Steve Martin dance] and the other is when the X-mas Soynog hits the grocery shelves.)*

> 2 cups flour
> 1 tbsp baking powder
> 1 tsp salt
> ⅓ cup sugar
> 1 tsp ground nutmeg
> ½ tsp ground ginger
> 1¼ cups vegan "eggnog"
> 3 tbsp oil
> 1 tsp vanilla extract

Preheat oven to 400°F (205°C). Lightly oil 12 muffin tins or line with paper liners and set aside. In a large bowl, stir together the flour, baking powder, salt, sugar, nutmeg, and ginger. Stir in the "eggnog," oil, and vanilla. Spoon evenly into muffin cups and bake for 15-20 minutes or until a toothpick or knife comes out clean. Let cool completely before removing from tins. Makes 12 muffins.

WOLFFIE'S BANANA BLUEBERRY MUFFINS

I know you're thinking this is just another muffin recipe, but these are really good – light and moist. Non-vegans wouldn't be able to tell the difference.

2 cups flour	⅔ cup "milk"
1 tbsp baking powder	1 large banana
1 tsp ground cinnamon	¼ cup oil
1 tsp ground ginger	2 tbsp molasses
¾ tsp salt	1 tsp vanilla extract
¾ cup sugar	1 cup blueberries, fresh or frozen

Preheat oven to 375°F (190°C). Lightly oil 12 muffin tins or line with paper liners. In a medium bowl, stir together the flour, baking powder, cinnamon, ginger, salt, and sugar. Set aside. In a food processor, blend together the "milk," banana, oil, molasses, and vanilla until smooth. Stir banana mixture and blueberries into flour mixture until "just mixed" and spoon evenly into muffin cups. Bake for 20-25 minutes or until a toothpick or knife comes out clean. Let cool completely before removing from tins. Makes 12 muffins.

HAYLEY'S LEMON CRANBERRY MUFFINS

Hayley! These are for you, my little soul-sista!

¾ cup sugar
¼ cup vegan margarine
egg replacer to equal 1 egg (pg 296)
1½ - 2 tsp lemon extract
1½ cups flour
¼ cup dried cranberries
1 tbsp poppy seeds
1¼ tsp baking powder
¼ tsp salt
¾ cup "milk"

Preheat oven to 350°F (175°C). Lightly oil 12 muffin tins or line with paper liners and set aside. In a large bowl, cream together the sugar, margarine, egg replacer, and vanilla. Add the flour, cranberries, poppy seeds, baking powder, salt, and "milk" and stir together gently until "just mixed." Spoon evenly into muffin cups and bake for 20-25 minutes or until a toothpick or knife comes out clean. Let cool completely before removing from tins. Makes 12 muffins.

CINNAMON APPLE MUFFINS

These are scrumtrulescent!

Topping:

¼ cup sugar
¼ cup walnuts *or* **pecans, finely chopped**
½ tsp ground cinnamon
2 tsp oil

Muffin:

1½ cups flour
½ cup sugar
2 tsp baking powder
1½ tsp ground cinnamon
½ tsp salt
¼ cup vegan margarine
egg replacer to equal 1 egg (pg 296)
½ cup "milk"
1 small Granny Smith apple, finely diced

Preheat oven to 350°F (175°C). Lightly oil 12 muffin tins or line with paper liners and set aside. In a small bowl, stir together the sugar, walnuts, cinnamon, and oil until crumbly. Set aside. In a large bowl, stir together the flour, sugar, baking powder, cinnamon, and salt. Add the margarine, egg replacer, "milk," and stir together gently until "just mixed." Fold in apples and spoon evenly into muffin cups. Sprinkle each muffin with topping and bake for 20-25 minutes or until a toothpick or knife comes out clean. Let cool completely before removing from tins. Makes 12 muffins.

STEPHANIE'S SUGARLESS POWER MUFFINS

These sugar free muffins from Stephanie in Weatherford, Texas are sweetened with stevia, which you can find in most health food stores and some grocery stores. Don't be fooled by the small measurement amount; stevia is strong and too much will leave an odd flavor.

2 cups oat bran
2 tsp baking powder
2 packets stevia *or* **½ tsp stevia powder**
1 tsp ground cinnamon
¼ tsp ground ginger
¼ tsp salt
2 cup "milk"
egg replacer to equal 1 egg (pg 296)
¼ cup tahini
1 cup assorted dried fruit (e.g. cranberries, raisins, pineapple)
½ cup sunflower seeds

Preheat oven to 425°F (220°C). Lightly oil 12 muffin tins or line with paper liners and set aside. In a medium bowl, stir together the oat bran, baking powder, stevia, cinnamon, ginger, and salt. Add the "milk," egg replacer, tahini, fruit, and sunflower seeds and stir together gently until "just mixed." Spoon evenly into muffin cups and bake for 15-20 minutes or until a toothpick or knife comes out clean. Let cool completely before removing from tins. Makes 12 muffins.

CUMIN RICE FLOUR DINNER MUFFINS

A wonderful, cumin-spiced, WHEAT-FREE dinner muffin.

1½ cups water
¼ cup ground flax seeds (pg 296)
2 tbsp oil
1½ cups brown rice flour
1 tbsp baking powder
1 tbsp sugar
1 tsp cumin seeds
¼ tsp ground cumin
½ tsp salt

Preheat oven to 375°F (190°C). Line 12 muffin tins with paper liners and set aside. In a small bowl, stir together the water, flax seeds, and oil. Set aside. In a large bowl, stir together the flour, baking powder, sugar, cumin seeds, cumin, and salt. Add the water-flax mixture and stir together gently until "just mixed." Spoon evenly into muffin cups and bake for 10-12 minutes or until a toothpick or knife comes out clean. Makes 12 muffins.

FRAGRANT ONION DINNER ROLLS

These wonderful muffins are best when served warm, slathered in vegan margarine, and served with a hot bowl of soup.

1 large onion
1 tbsp olive oil
1 cup rolled oat flakes
1 cup flour
1 cup rye flour
3 tsp baking powder
½ tsp baking soda

2 tsp caraway seeds
½ tsp salt
¼ cup oil
¾ cup water
1 tbsp vinegar
egg replacer to equal 2 eggs (pg 296)

Preheat oven to 350°F (175°C). In a medium frying pan on medium heat, sauté the onions in oil until translucent. Set aside. In a food processor, grind the oat flakes until smooth. In a large bowl, stir together the ground oat flakes, flour, rye flour, baking powder, baking soda, caraway seeds, and salt. Add the oil, water, vinegar, egg replacer, and cooked onions. Stir together gently until "just mixed." Spoon dough into lightly oiled muffin tins and bake for 15-17 minutes or until a toothpick or knife comes out clean. Makes 6 muffins.

SESAME BREAD STICKS

The nutritional yeast adds a little "cheesy" flava. Serve with some whipped vegan margarine and tell your family that you're not ashamed to eat carbs!

¼ **cup poppy seeds** *or* **toasted sesame seeds (pg 295)**
2 tbsp coarse sea salt
2½ tsp *or* **1 packet dry active yeast**
¼ **cup warm water**
1 tsp sugar
¼ **cup oil**
¼ **cup water**
1½ cups flour
1 tbsp nutritional yeast
1 tsp salt
½ **tsp garlic powder**
½ **tsp onion powder**

On a large, shallow plate, stir together the poppy seeds and coarse salt. Set aside. In a large bowl, stir together the yeast with the ¼ cup of warm water and sugar. Let sit for 10 minutes. Stir in the oil, ¼ cup of water, ½ cup flour, nutritional yeast, salt, garlic powder, and onion powder. Slowly stir in the remaining cup of flour. On a lightly floured surface, knead dough until smooth and elastic; add a little extra flour if it's too sticky. Roll out dough and cut into 10 equal pieces. Roll out each piece to desired shape and then coat in poppy seed-salt mixture. Place on baking sheet then repeat with remaining dough. Cover with cloth and set aside in a warm, non-drafty spot and let rise for 20 minutes. Preheat oven to 400°F (205°C). Place baking sheet in oven and bake for 15 minutes. For a crispier breadstick, turn off the oven and let breadsticks sit in oven for another 10 minutes. Makes approx. 10 – 6-inch bread sticks.

BROWN RICE FLOUR BANANA BREAD

A wonderful flour-less banana bread. Banana bread doo doo da doo doo!

1 banana
¼ cup oil
⅓ cup maple syrup
egg replacer to equal 1 egg (pg 296)
2 tbsp "milk"
½ tsp vanilla extract
1 cups brown rice flour
¼ cup walnuts, finely chopped
1½ tsp cornstarch
½ tsp baking powder
¼ tsp baking soda
¼ tsp salt

Preheat oven to 350°F (175°C). Lightly oil a 9-inch loaf pan and set aside. In a food processor, blend the banana, oil, maple syrup, egg replacer, "milk," and vanilla extract until smooth. Set aside. In a medium bowl, stir together the flour, walnuts, cornstarch, baking powder, baking soda, and salt. Add the banana mixture and stir gently until "just mixed." Pour evenly into loaf pan and bake for 40-45 minutes or until a toothpick or knife comes out clean. Let cool on a rack for 10-15 minutes before removing from pan. Makes 1 loaf.

MIKI'S PUMPKIN BREAD

I recently played around with some traditional recipes and came up with a very nice vegan pumpkin bread. The recipe makes 2 loaves, so you can use up a whole can of pumpkin and not have any waste, but you can also easily cut the recipe in half. – Miki, *RandomHag.com*

2 cups sugar
½ cup oil
½ cup applesauce
egg replacer to equal 3 eggs (pg 296)
1 14-oz (397-ml) can unsweetened pumpkin purée
3 cups flour
1 tsp ground cloves
1 tsp ground cinnamon
1 tsp ground nutmeg
1 tsp baking soda
½ tsp baking powder
½ tsp salt
1 cup walnuts, coarsely chopped
1 cup vegan chocolate chips (optional)

Preheat oven to 350°F (175°C). Lightly oil 2 9-inch loaf pans and set aside. In a large bowl, stir together the sugar, oil, applesauce, egg replacer, and pumpkin. In a medium bowl, stir together the flour, cloves, cinnamon, nutmeg, baking soda, baking powder, and salt. Stir gently into pumpkin until it's "just mixed." Stir in the walnuts and chocolate chips and spoon dough equally into 2 loaf pans. Bake for 55-60 minutes or until a toothpick or knife comes out clean. Let cool for 10-15 minutes before removing from pan. Makes 2 loaves.

SCRUMPTIOUS BANANA-NUT BREAD

This is a wonderful bread. – Wolffie, Davie, FL

1 large banana
6 tbsp "milk"
⅔ cup sugar
½ cup silken *or* **soft tofu**
⅓ cup oil
1 tsp vanilla extract
1¾ cup flour
1 tsp baking powder
1 tsp baking soda
¾ tsp salt
½ tsp nutmeg
½ cup walnuts, chopped

Preheat oven to 350°F (175°C). Lightly oil a 9-inch loaf pan and set aside. In a food processor, process the banana, "milk," sugar, tofu, and oil until smooth. Set aside. In a medium bowl, whisk together the flour, baking powder, baking soda, salt, and nutmeg. Add the walnuts and banana mixture and stir together gently until "just mixed." Spread evenly into loaf pan and bake 40-45 minutes or until a toothpick or knife comes out clean. Let cool for 10-15 minutes before removing from pan. Makes 1 loaf.

HOMEMADE GRAHAM CRACKERS

Most graham crackers contain honey, but can easily be made with maple syrup instead. Check it!

½ cup graham *or* **whole wheat flour**
½ cup all purpose flour
½ tsp salt
½ tsp baking powder
2 tbsp vegan margarine
2 tbsp maple syrup
1 tsp molasses
1 tsp vanilla extract
2 tbsp "milk"

Preheat oven to 400°F (205°C). In a food processor, blend the flours, salt, baking powder, and margarine; pulse until mixture resembles a coarse meal. Add the maple syrup, molasses, vanilla, and "milk" and blend until well combined and a dough forms. Remove dough and roll out on a floured surface to ¼-inch thickness. Cut into 2x2-inch squares. Place on a baking sheet and prick cookie evenly with fork. Bake for 10-12 minutes depending on thickness. Makes 12 crackers.

Faux Fare

As vegans, we sacrifice many things for the love of animals, and sometimes we miss recipes that contain animal ingredients. Here are a few recipes to help you realize that as a vegan, you don't need to compromise taste. These recipes may take a bit more time than others – but they're worth the effort!

PRAISE SEITAN!

Store-bought mock meat products are expensive, but they are quite easy to make yourself using instant vital wheat gluten flour, which can be found in most health food stores or in the baking aisle of your local supermarket.

Gluten flour is a high-protein, hard-wheat flour treated to remove most of the starch and is similar to tofu in that it has no strong flavor, but works like a sponge; gluten and tofu will soak up whatever flavors you surround them with. Seitan is what wheat gluten becomes once it is cooked in a broth. Gluten can be made from scratch (pg 284) using regular flour and water, but it is quite time-consuming and can get a little messy. I prefer to use the instant vital wheat gluten flour as it takes almost no time to prepare, so I can get on with making the rest of my meal. But making your own gluten is just fine for those times when you're stuck at home with nothing but a bag of flour, or if you can't find the instant stuff.

I usually make these mock meat products ahead of time and store them in the freezer (up to 6 months) or refrigerator (up to 6 days) for use at a later date. Once your gluten is made, you can use it with any of the broth recipes below. For a chewier, "meatier" texture, once I've boiled the gluten in its flavored broth, I will pop it in a lightly oiled baking dish and bake it at 350°F (175°C) for 30 minutes.

WHAT ABOUT TOFU?

All of these mock meat recipes can also be made with firm or extra firm tofu. It is not quite the same as wheat gluten, as tofu doesn't take on the same chewy, "meaty" quality that gluten has but it picks up flavors just the same. Tofu is a great alternative for those who can't eat wheat. The trick is to change the consistency of the tofu by freezing it. Drain a block of tofu and squeeze out any excess water. Place in an airtight container and store in the freezer overnight. Once frozen and thawed, you'll notice that the tofu has a different "meatier" consistency. To add "mock flavors," slice the thawed tofu into chunks, and then boil in the "mock" gluten recipe of your choice.

BASIC INSTANT GLUTEN

Cook this dough in any of the mock meat flavors or in a broth of your own invention. Either way, it's quick and easy . . . just the way I like it!

> ½ **cup instant vital wheat gluten flour**
> ½ **cup water**

In a medium bowl, stir together the wheat gluten and water until it becomes elastic. Knead for 5 minutes and set aside. Choose a mock meat flavoring (pg 285-289) to use with your prepared dough. Makes 2 large or 4 small servings.

BASIC GLUTEN FROM SCRATCH

This recipe might seem a bit complicated. But if you can't find or don't have instant vital wheat gluten flour, what are you going to do? You work with what you have, so let's get our hands gooey. Let's go!

> **2 cups whole wheat flour**
> **2 cups all purpose flour**
> **1¾ cup water**

In a large bowl, stir together the flours. Add the water and mix, then knead together until well combined. Cover bowl with cloth and let sit for 30 minutes. Wet hands and knead dough for 1 minute, then return to bowl. Place bowl in sink and add cold water until bowl is filled. Squeeze dough with your hands until water turns cloudy (don't worry if it falls apart . . . just keep kneading). Carefully pour off water (holding back dough with your hands) and fill bowl again with cold water. Repeat process of squeezing dough in fresh cold water 4-6 times until dough starts to solidify and water is no longer cloudy. Repeat process 2 more times, alternating between warm and cold water. Start stretching and pulling the dough as you rinse it. Once it becomes a cohesive elastic mass (similar to bubble gum), rinse one final time in cold water. Squeeze any remaining water from the dough and set aside. Choose a faux meat flavoring (pg 285-289) to use with your prepared dough. Makes 2 large or 4 small servings.

MOCK MEATS
FAUX SAUSAGE

Earthy, peppery, smoky. Try some on the Mushroom "Sausage" Pizza on pg 167.

Basic Instant Gluten (pg 284) or Basic Gluten from Scratch (pg 284)

Broth:
2 cups water
2 tbsp tamari
1 tbsp nutritional yeast
1½ tsp sugar
1 tsp vegan Worcestershire sauce
1 tsp dried sage
1 tsp onion powder
1 tsp salt
½ tsp garlic powder
½ tsp ground black pepper
¼ tsp dried oregano
⅛ tsp red pepper flakes
⅛ tsp ground cloves
1 tsp liquid smoke

In a large saucepan, bring all of the broth ingredients to a boil. Slice gluten into steaks, chunks or strips and drop carefully into broth. Reduce heat and cover with lid. Let simmer for 50-60 minutes, stirring every 10 minutes, until broth has reduced completely. Use "sausage" immediately in your dish of choice or store in the refrigerator (for up to 6 days) or the freezer (for up to 6 months). For a chewier texture, once you've boiled the "sausage," bake it at 350°F (175°C) in a lightly oiled baking dish for 30 minutes. Makes 2 large or 4 small servings.

FAUX FISH

Roll your "fish" in Shook 'N' Cook Breading (pg 56), and make some Sweet Potato Fries (pg 186). Wrap them in newspaper and sing "God save the Queen" . . . the Sex Pistols, version of course!

Basic Instant Gluten (pg 284) or Basic Gluten from Scratch (pg 284)

Broth:
2 cups water
2 tbsp tamari
½ tsp kelp powder
¼ tsp salt
¼ tsp cayenne pepper

In a large saucepan, bring all of the broth ingredients to a boil. Slice gluten into steaks, chunks or strips and drop carefully into broth. Reduce heat and cover with lid. Let simmer for 50-60 minutes, stirring every 10 minutes, until broth has reduced completely. Use "fish" immediately in your dish of choice or store in the refrigerator (for up to 6 days) or the freezer (for up to 6 months). For a chewier texture, once you've boiled the "fish," bake it at 350°F (175°C) in a lightly oiled baking dish for 30 minutes. Makes 2 large or 4 small servings.

FAUX HAM

The only squeal you'll hear is one of delight when you try this recipe . . . oink!

Basic Instant Gluten (pg 284) or Basic Gluten from Scratch (pg 284)

Broth:
2 cups water
¼ cup tamari
2 tsp vegan Worcestershire sauce
1 tsp liquid smoke
2 tbsp nutritional yeast
1 tsp onion powder
1 tsp garlic powder
1 tsp salt
½ tsp ground black pepper
½ tsp dried oregano
¼ tsp dried sage

In a large saucepan, bring all of the broth ingredients to a boil. Slice gluten into steaks, chunks or strips and drop carefully into broth. Reduce heat and cover with lid. Let simmer for 50-60 minutes, stirring every 10 minutes, until broth has reduced completely. Use "ham" immediately in your dish of choice or store in the refrigerator (for up to 6 days) or the freezer (for up to 6 months). For a chewier texture, once you've boiled the "ham," bake it at 350°F (175°C) in a lightly oiled baking dish for 30 minutes. Makes 2 large or 4 small servings.

FAUX CHICKEN

Your cookbooks have been so inspiring and your personality really shines through. This recipe originally comes from the book, *Simply Heavenly*, but I tweaked it to make it more to my liking. I hope you enjoy it. – Cori, Missoula, MT *(Try making Jay's Fried "Chicken" [pg 289] with this recipe!)*

Basic Instant Gluten (pg 284) or Basic Gluten from Scratch (pg 284)

Broth:
2 cups water
¼ cup nutritional yeast
2 tbsp tamari
1 tsp onion powder
1 tsp dried sage
½ tsp dried thyme
½ tsp salt
¼ tsp celery seed

In a large saucepan, bring all of the broth ingredients to a boil. Slice gluten into steaks, chunks or strips and drop carefully into broth. Reduce heat and cover with lid. Let simmer for 50-60 minutes, stirring every 10 minutes, until broth has reduced completely. Use "chicken" immediately in your dish of choice or store in the refrigerator (for up to 6 days) or the freezer (for up to 6 months). For a chewier texture, once you've boiled the "chicken," bake it at 350°F (175°C) in a lightly oiled baking dish for 30 minutes. Makes 2 large or 4 small servings.

FAUX BEEF

Cut the Seitan into thin strips for the Mock Beef and Rice Noodle Toss on pg 135.

Basic Instant Gluten (pg 284) or Basic Gluten from Scratch (pg 284)

Broth:
2 cups water
¼ cup tamari
2 tsp vegan Worcestershire sauce
2 tbsp nutritional yeast
1 tsp onion powder
½ tsp cayenne pepper
¼ tsp dried sage

In a large saucepan, bring all of the broth ingredients to a boil. Slice gluten into steaks, chunks or strips and drop carefully into broth. Reduce heat and cover with lid. Let simmer for 50-60 minutes, stirring every 10 minutes, until broth has reduced completely. Use "beef" immediately in your dish of choice or store in the refrigerator (for up to 6 days) or the freezer (for up to 6 months). For a chewier texture, once you've boiled the "beef," bake it at 350°F (175°C) in a lightly oiled baking dish for 30 minutes. Makes 2 large or 4 small servings.

FAUX TURKEY

Turkeys are too neat to eat.

> **Basic Instant Gluten (pg 284) or Basic Gluten from Scratch (pg 284)**
>
> *Broth:*
> **2 cups water**
> **3 tbsp nutritional yeast**
> **2 tbsp tamari**
> **1 tsp vegan Worcestershire sauce**
> **1 tsp onion powder**
> **½ tsp salt**
> **½ tsp dried sage**
> **½ tsp dried thyme**

In a large saucepan, bring all of the broth ingredients to a boil. Slice gluten into steaks, chunks or strips and drop carefully into broth. Reduce heat and cover with lid. Let simmer for 50-60 minutes, stirring every 10 minutes, until broth has reduced completely. Use "turkey" immediately in your dish of choice or store in the refrigerator (for up to 6 days) or the freezer (for up to 6 months). For a chewier texture, once you've boiled the "turkey," bake it at 350°F (175°C) in a lightly oiled pan for 30 minutes. Makes 2 large or 4 small servings.

JAY-LO'S FRIED "CHICKEN"

When you prepare your "chicken" (pg 287), shape and cut them so they resemble a nice breast. Tee hee. I said breast. This is my good friend Jason's fried chicken recipe that he makes for BBQs at his house. It's delish and quite a dish . . . just like Jay. (This recipe also appears in entrées.)

> **¼ cup flour**
> **½ tsp paprika**
> **½ tsp salt**
> **½ tsp ground black pepper**
> **½ cup "milk"**
> **Faux Chicken (pg 287)**
> **3 - 4 tbsp olive oil**

In a shallow dish, stir together the flour, paprika, salt, and pepper. Set aside. In a small bowl, pour "milk" and set aside. Dip "chicken" into flour, then dip in "milk," and then into the flour again. In a large frying pan on medium-high heat, fry "chicken" in oil until well browned on both sides. Makes 2 large or 4 small servings.

MARSHALLOWS

Marshmallows are easy to make, but require steely focus; so turn off your phone, don't answer the door, and make sure the kids are NOT in the kitchen and that you're prepared to commit because the next 40 minutes or so are dedicated to "Marshmallow Making Time."

IMPORTANT: You will need a candy thermometer and an electric mixer with a large bowl attachment. Read the instructions through before you start, so you understand what you're doing before you get into it. Please remember to follow the instructions EXACTLY. Making marshmallows is like chemistry. One false move and you're in deep sticky trouble. If they don't turn out, just spoon the goop into a jar and voilà! Marshmallow fluff.

Vegan gelatin is available at stores that carry kosher products or online at websites like *FoodFightGrocery.com* or *VeganEssentials.com*. Once you've mastered the art of making marshmallows, start getting crazy. Add some mint extract instead of vanilla. How about a dash or two of food coloring? Use your imagination!

HOMEMADE VEGAN MARSHMALLOWS

½ cup icing sugar (for dusting)
3 envelopes (3 tbsp) vegan gelatin
½ cup cold water
1½ cups sugar
1 cup light corn syrup
¼ tsp salt
½ cup water
2 tsp vanilla extract

Lightly oil an 8x8-inch baking dish with margarine. Dust the baking dish with ¼ cup of icing sugar and set aside. In the mixer bowl, pour the envelopes of gelatin and ½ cup of cold water. Whisk together and set aside. In a large saucepan on medium-low heat, stir together the sugar, corn syrup, salt, and ½ cup of water. Simmer for 4-6 minutes, stirring constantly, until sugar has dissolved completely and the liquid is clear-ish. Attach candy thermometer to side of saucepan (careful – make sure that the tip is submerged in the liquid, but NOT touching the bottom of the pan) and increase heat onto high. DO NOT STIR SYRUP. Allow it to boil and reach 235°-240°F (112°-115°C) (firm ball stage). Immediately remove from heat and carefully pour into mixer bowl. Slowly turn on mixer and increase speed to high. Add the vanilla extract and continue beating for 8-10 minutes. The mixture will triple in volume and will be very thick. Pour evenly into prepared baking dish. Dust top with remaining ¼ cup of icing sugar and let stand for 6-8 hours. Do not refrigerate. To cut marshmallows, remove carefully from dish and place on cutting board. Cut with a dry, sharp knife. Dust the gooey edges with icing sugar. Makes approx. 25-50 marshmallows (depending on size).

VEGAN FRUIT JUICE FLAVORED JELL-O-TIN

J-e-l-l-o-t-i-n! Vegan gelatin is available at stores that carry kosher products or online at stores like *FoodFightGrocery.com* or *VeganEssentials.com*. You can also use an equal amount of agar agar instead of vegan gelatin, but it's not quite the same. For fun, stir in goodies like sliced fruit or sliced marshmallows (pg 290) once the liquid has cooled down a little. This recipe also appears in the desserts chapter.

2 cups fruit juice (your choice)
1 envelope (1 tbsp) vegan gelatin
¼ cup sugar
pinch of salt

In a medium saucepan, whisk together all of the ingredients. Bring to a boil, reduce heat, and simmer for 1 minute. Pour into shallow glass bowl or individual serving bowls and refrigerate for 4-6 hours before serving. Makes approx. 2 cups.

WOLFFIE'S TOFU WHIPPED "CREAM"

Whip it! Whip it good! Agar agar can be found in most health food stores or Asian markets. Remember that 1 tsp of powdered equals 1 tbsp of flakes.

½ tbsp powdered agar agar *or* **½ envelope (½ tbsp) vegan gelatin**
2 tbsp hot water
¾ cup soft *or* **silken tofu**
¼ cup sugar
3 tbsp oil
2 tbsp soy milk powder
½ tbsp vanilla extract
1 tsp lemon juice
pinch of salt

In a food processor, combine the agar agar and hot water. Pulse briefly to mix and let sit 2-3 minutes. Add the remaining ingredients and blend until very smooth. Spoon into bowl and refrigerate 2-3 hours before serving. Makes approx. 1½ cups.

FAUX FETA CHEESE

This old stand-by is used to perfection in Tyler & Phoebe's Perfect Pesto Pizza on pg 152.

½ lb firm tofu, cubed *or* crumbled
2 tbsp olive oil
2 tbsp water
¼ cup red wine vinegar
1 tsp salt
½ tbsp dried basil
¼ tsp dried oregano
¼ tsp dried dill
¼ tsp ground black pepper

In a medium bowl, mix together all the ingredients. Marinade tofu for at least an hour before using. Makes approx. ¾ cup.

CHERYL'S FAUX CHEESE

Sarah! I know there are a ton of faux cheese recipes out there, but this one is mine. I hope you like it. – Cheryl, Salt Lake City, UT *(Grate it, shred it, any way you slice it – it's yum!)*

¾ cup cashews
¼ small orange bell pepper, roughly chopped
1 tsp salt
1 tsp onion powder
½ tsp oil
2 tbsp lemon juice
1 cup water
4 tsp powdered agar agar (*or* ¼ cup flakes)

In a food processor, combine the cashews, bell peppers, salt, onion powder, oil, and lemon juice and blend until smooth. In a small saucepan, bring the water to a boil. Reduce heat and whisk in agar agar, stirring often until it starts to thicken. Spoon into food processor and blend with cashew mixture until smooth. Spread evenly in square or rectangle container and refrigerate for at least 1 hour before using. Makes approx. 16-oz.

FAUX SOUR CREAM

And you thought you'd never have sour cream again . . .

1 12-oz (300-g) pkg soft *or* **silken tofu**
1 tbsp oil
1 tbsp lemon juice
2 tsp apple cider vinegar
1 tsp sugar
½ tsp salt
1 tbsp tamari

In a blender or food processor, blend all ingredients until smooth and creamy. Makes approx. 1 cup.

QUICK & EASY FAUX MAYONNAISE

Faux Mayo can be used in a number of different ways such as Tu-No Sandwiches (pg 159) or Mama Mayhem's Tofu Extravaganza (pg 160).

1 12-oz (300-g) pkg soft *or* **silken tofu**
1 tsp dry mustard
½ tsp onion powder
½ tsp salt
1 tbsp sugar
2 tbsp lemon juice *or* **apple cider vinegar**
1 tbsp cashews

In a blender or food processor, blend all ingredients until smooth and creamy. Makes approx. 1¼ cups.

Odds & Sods

When I was a kid, "Odds & Sods" was the section in my mother's recipe box that I loved to look at the most: a rag-tag collection of recipes that couldn't be easily categorized. I could totally relate!

TOASTED NUTS AND SEEDS

Toasting nuts and/or seeds is a simple and delicious way of bringing out the natural flavors of your favorite nuts. There are two easy methods you can follow: pan toasting or oven toasting.

Remember that the natural oils in the nuts will keep "cooking" after you remove them from the hot baking sheet or skillet, so be careful to avoid overcooking.

OVEN-TOASTED NUTS

Oven toasting is great, because you can pop your tray in the oven, set the timer, and walk away . . . but remember that using your oven wastes a lot of energy.

Preheat oven to 350°F (175°C). Spread nuts out on a small baking tray and roast them for 5-10 minutes. Remove from oven immediately and let cool before chopping or serving.

PAN-TOASTED NUTS

Pan toasting takes less time and you're saving energy by not turning on your oven.

Place nuts in a dry skillet and cook over medium heat for 3-4 minutes. Remember to stir or shake the pan frequently to prevent burning. Once nuts begin to brown, remove from heat and let cool before chopping or serving.

EGG REPLACERS

Which came first – The vegan or the egg? Replacing eggs in vegan baking is as easy as 1, 2 . . . wait . . . I have 5 different alternatives for you. Check it out.

FLAX SEED EGG REPLACER

Purchase an inexpensive coffee grinder to use for grinding flax seeds or spices. Don't use your regular coffee grinder unless you want everything to taste like coffee. This recipe makes enough flax powder for 4 "eggs."

½ cup flax seeds

In a coffee grinder, process the flax seeds until powdered. Keep powder stored in refrigerator in a container with a tight fitting lid.

2 tbsp flax powder + 3 tbsp water = 1 egg

In a small bowl, combine all ingredients and allow to sit for 2-3 minutes before adding to baking.

TOFU EGG REPLACER

Remember to use soft or silken tofu as egg replacer.

¼ cup blended soft tofu = 1 egg

ENER-G EGG REPLACER

You can purchase Ener-G Powdered Egg Replacer in most health food stores.

1½ tsp + 2 tbsp water mixed well = 1 egg

BANANA EGG REPLACER

Not to be used in every recipe, bananas are a terrific egg substitute when you don't mind adding a little tropical flavor to your baking.

½ banana, blended or well mashed = 1 egg

APPLE SAUCE EGG REPLACER

Like bananas, apple sauce is a great egg replacer when you don't mind having a little extra fruit flavor added.

3 tbsp apple sauce = 1 egg

SPAGHETTI TOFU BALLS

It's all about timing, people! This recipe can be made earlier to save time, and they freeze well for future use. Or if you get into multi-tasking like I do, prepare your tofu balls while your sauce (pg 129) is simmering on one burner and your spaghetti noodles are doing their thing on another, then throw your tofu balls into the tomato sauce and voilà! You're ready to rumble.

½ lb of firm or extra firm tofu, mashed *or* crumbled
½ cup flour
1 tbsp tahini (*or* nut butter)
2 tbsp tamari
⅛ cup fresh parsley
½ small onion, finely chopped
½ tsp dry mustard
¼ tsp ground black pepper
¼ cup flour for coating
2 tbsp olive oil

In a large bowl, stir together the tofu, ½ cup flour, tahini, tamari, parsley, onions, mustard, and pepper. Place ¼ cup of flour onto a small plate and roll ½ tbsp of tofu mixture into a ball and coat with flour. In a frying pan on medium heat, fry tofu balls in oil until browned all over. Makes approx. 10-14 balls.

AVOCADO TOMATO SALSA

This lightning fast salsa is best served over Black Bean Tortilla Chip Soup (pg 123) or can be used as an appie when accompanied by some tortilla chips.

1 medium tomato, chopped
1 avocado, cubed
¼ cup fresh cilantro, minced
1 stalk green onion, minced
1 tbsp oil (e.g. flax, hemp, olive)
2 tsp lime juice
tortilla chips

In a medium bowl, stir together the tomatoes, avocados, cilantro, green onions, oil, and lime juice. Serve with tortilla chips. Makes approx. 2 cups.

CRISPY GARLIC CROUTONS

Crouton, noun (usually plural): a small square piece of bread that is fried or toasted (heated until it is crisp and brown) and which is added to soup or a salad just before you eat it. (*I love the dictionary.*)

4 cups stale *or* **lightly toasted bread, cubed**
4 garlic cloves, minced
1 tsp ground thyme
½ tsp fresh rosemary, finely chopped
3 tbsp olive oil
¼ tsp coarse salt
¼ tsp ground black pepper

Preheat oven to 325°F (165°C). In a large bowl, toss together all ingredients until well coated. Spread evenly onto baking sheet and bake for 15 minutes, stirring occasionally to avoid burning. Makes 4 cups.

FRYING PAN CROUTONS

A quick and easy way to make croutons. Best served with Caesar salad or a nice hot soup.

3 cups stale *or* **lightly toasted bread, cubed**
2 garlic cloves, minced
2 tsp No-Salt Shaker (pg 303)
½ tsp ground black pepper
3 tbsp olive oil

In a medium bowl, toss together the bread, garlic, no-salt, pepper, and olive oil until well coated. In a medium frying pan on medium-high heat, toss the croutons until well browned. Let cool before serving. Makes approx. 3 cups.

ICING SUGAR

Hey. My birthday is June 27th . . . who is going to bake me a cake?

> **4 cups sugar**
> **1 cup cornstarch**

In a food processor, blend ingredients together for 2 minutes. Makes approx. 4½ cups.

CRANBERRY SAUCE

This recipe goes beautifully with the Tofu Roast on pg 170.

> **1½ cups frozen cranberries**
> **½ cup maple syrup**
> **½ cup cranberry juice**
> **¼ cup golden raisins**
> **¼ cup walnuts, roughly chopped**
> **2 tbsp apple cider vinegar**
> **¼ tsp ground cinnamon**
> **¼ tsp ground cloves**
> **¼ tsp ground ginger**

In a medium saucepan, bring all of the ingredients to a boil. Reduce heat and simmer for 15-20 minutes. Stir occasionally, while mashing the cooked cranberries with the back of a spoon. Serve chilled or hot. Makes approx. 1½ cups.

TERIYAKI MARINADE

This recipe is for the Mock Beef and Rice Noodle Toss (pg 135) but can also be used as a marinade for tofu or anything else that soaks up flavor. Mmm.

¼ **cup tamari**
¼ **cup water**
2 tbsp maple syrup
2 tbsp sugar
2 tbsp lemon juice
1 inch fresh ginger, finely grated
1 garlic clove, minced

In a jar or dressing bottle, combine all ingredients. Cap and shake well before using. Makes approx. ¾ of a cup.

YEAST-FREE PIZZA CRUST

A quick and easy thin crusty crust that you don't have to wait for an hour to rise. Booo-ya!

1½ cups flour
1 tsp baking powder
½ **tsp dried oregano**
½ **tsp dried basil**
½ **tsp salt**
⅛ **tsp ground black pepper**
egg replacer to equal 1 egg (pg 296)
¼ **cup oil**
½ **cup "milk"**

Preheat oven to 425°F (220°C). Lightly oil a pizza-baking sheet. Set aside. In a large bowl, stir together the flour, baking powder, oregano, basil, salt, and pepper. Stir in the egg replacer, oil, and "milk" until well mixed. Place dough on baking sheet and with floured hands press dough down to fit pizza pan. Bake for 10 minutes BEFORE adding pizza toppings. Then bake for another 10-15 minutes. Makes 1 pizza crust.

PIZZA CRUST

Store your active dry yeast in the fridge. To check if your yeast is still active, add warm water and sugar to it; if it doesn't foam and bubble right away, it's dead. You can't resuscitate it, so let it go and buy another jar.

2 tsp active dry yeast
¼ cup warm water
1 tsp sugar
3 cups flour
1 tsp salt
1 tsp dried oregano
1 tsp dried basil
½ tsp ground black pepper
1¼ cup warm water

In a small bowl, stir together the yeast, ¼ cup warm water, and sugar. Let stand for 10 minutes. In a large bowl, stir together the flour, salt, oregano, basil, and pepper. Add the yeast mixture and 1¼ cups warm water to the flour mixture and stir together until well combined. With floured hands, knead the dough until smooth and elastic. Cover bowl with plastic wrap or clean dishtowel and let stand in a draft-free place for 60 minutes. Knead again, roll dough onto pizza pan, and prick dough all over with a fork before adding your goodies. See pg xx for pizza topping ideas. Makes 1 pizza crust.

BEAR'S NOODLES

Hi, Sarah! The greeting cards at *GoVegan.net* are soooo cool! Here's a recipe that I concocted. I made it gluten-free for myself but you could use other flours and it would turn out just as good. This recipe is named after my daughter, who can eat gluten but prefers my noodles over any others. Thanks! – Mary, Hollywood, CA *(Holy cow, Mary. Who knew making homemade noodles could be so easy. Thank you for this recipe!)*

> ½ **cup crumbled extra-firm tofu, drained and crumbled**
> ½ **cup brown rice flour (***or* **other flour of your choice)**
> ¼ **cup soy flour (***or* **other flour of your choice)**
> ¼ **tsp salt**
> **1 tbsp olive oil**
> ½ **- 1 tbsp water**

In food processor, blend together the tofu, flours, salt, and olive oil. Slowly add water until it reaches dough-like consistency. Remove and shape into a ball. Place in a container or plastic wrap and refrigerate for at least 1 hour. On a lightly floured cutting board, roll out dough with rolling pin. Using a pizza wheel, knife or pasta cutter, cut long noodles, circles, raviolis, or whatever shape you desire. Bring a large pot of salted water to a boil. Carefully scoop pasta from cutting board and drop into boiling water and cook for 3-5 minutes (for thin noodles; thicker noodles may need a bit longer). Drain well and top with your favorite sauce. Makes 2 servings.

NO-SALT SHAKER

Looking for an alternative to the great white powder? No need for rehab. Just try this no-salt seasoning. Come on. Try it. Everyone else is.

- **3 tsp garlic powder**
- **2 tsp onion powder**
- **2 tsp dried thyme**
- **2 tsp paprika**
- **2 tsp ground black pepper**
- **2 tsp dry mustard**
- **1 tsp celery seed**

In a medium bowl, combine all ingredients. Store in an airtight container. Makes approx. ¼ cup.

VEGANICA.COM'S CAJUN SPICE

This is spicy. Oooooh doggie. It's the reason why Veganica's Cajun Sweet Potato Fries (pg 186) taste so good. Spicy. Hot. Mmm. Good. Check out Derek's website; it's full of wonderful art made by vegetarian/vegan artists. What are you waiting for?

- **2 tbsp paprika**
- **1 tbsp dried thyme**
- **1 tbsp dried oregano**
- **1 tsp garlic powder**
- **1 tsp salt**
- **¼ tsp ground black pepper**
- **⅛ tsp cayenne pepper**

In a small jar, combine all ingredients. Cap and shake well before using. Makes approx. ¼ cup.

GRINDER GARAM MASALA

Garam is the Indian word for warm or hot. This blend or spices makes me hot. I wish I had perfume that smelled this good.

1 tbsp cumin seeds
1 tbsp coriander seeds
1 tbsp black peppercorns
1 tsp ground cardamom
¼ tsp ground cinnamon
⅛ tsp ground cloves
⅛ tsp ground nutmeg

In a dry frying pan over medium-high heat, stir/shake the cumin and coriander seeds continually for 3-5 minutes, until seeds start to pop and brown. Remove from heat and let cool completely. Place in a coffee grinder or food processor with peppercorns, cardamom, cinnamon, cloves, and nutmeg, and grind until smooth. Store in an airtight container. Makes approx. ¼ cup.

KITCHEN CUPBOARD GARAM MASALA

Just raid your pantry. I'm sure you'll have most of these ingredients on hand.

2 tbsp cumin
2 tbsp coriander
2 tsp ground black pepper
1 tsp ground cardamom
1 tsp ground ginger
¼ tsp allspice

In a small jar, combine all ingredients. Cap and shake well before using. Makes approx. ⅓ cup.

GOMASHIO

Gomashio can be used to season soups, salads, pasta . . . I sometimes eat it with a spoon. Ack!

1 cup raw sesame seeds
1 tsp sea salt
1 tsp kelp powder
½ sheet nori (seaweed), cut *or* torn into small pieces

In a dry frying pan over medium-high heat, stir/shake the sesame seeds continually for 3-5 minutes, until seeds start to pop and brown. Remove from heat and let cool completely. In a food processor, combine dried seeds with salt, kelp, and nori and grind for 5-10 seconds (you don't want the seeds to become powder, just lightly ground). Store in an airtight container. Makes approx. 1 cup.

"NEEDS A LITTLE EXTRA" SPICE

Do you ever find yourself saying, "This recipe needs a little extra oomph"? Add a little shake or two of this recipe and pack your bags, cuz we're going on a trip down Flavor Lane.

2 tbsp chili powder
2 tsp onion powder
2 tsp garlic powder
2 tsp ground cumin
1 tsp dried basil
2 tsp dried oregano
1 tsp paprika
½ tsp cayenne pepper
½ tsp salt

In a medium bowl, combine all ingredients. Store in an airtight container. Makes approx. ¼ cup.

HERBIVORE
A VEGETARIAN CULT
premier

COMMUNITY
ANIMALS!

SARAH
KRAMER
The World's Coolest Vegan?

DIY

Ever since I was a child I've loved trash – anything dirty, dingy, or dusty; everything ragged, rotten, or rusty. I've kept rocks, beach glass, buttons, stamps, toys, coins, playing cards I've found on the street. I admit it – I'm a packrat. A well-organized packrat, but a packrat nonetheless. It runs in the family; my dad keeps string, extension chords, paperclips – "just in case," and my Auntie Bonnie has the largest towel collection I've ever seen, not to mention the fact that she hoards cans of chickpeas like they're going out of style.

Everyday objects that we throw out without a second thought can almost always be recycled; you just have to use your imagination. I enjoy turning found treasures into objets d'art: a fridge magnet, an earring, a broach, a barrette, a planter. All it takes is a little ingenuity and a lot of glue. I highly recommend Weldbond Glue (weldbond.com); it attaches almost everything and is animal-friendly (it says so right on the bottle). You can purchase it at most hardware stores.

All of the ideas I have in this chapter are basic. It's important for you to put your own unique touch to these projects to make them special. (I can't do everything for you, now can I?) As with all projects, you will need items that I haven't bothered to list, such as a multi-head screwdriver, glue, nails, screws, drill, needlenose pliers. . . . Everyone needs a fully equiped toolbox. And don't forget to wear safety goggles. You may look like a geek in them, but you'll look like even more of a geek with an eye patch.

HOUSEHOLD FUN
DIY KITCHEN MAGNETS

I have a gigantic jar full of 1-inch punk rock buttons. Why? Cuz I'm crazy. So I decided to take a few of my coolest ones and turn them into kitchen magnets. Basic magnets can be found in most hobby or arts and craft stores. (If using pin-back buttons, remove copper pin with needle nose pliers. You may need to double up the magnets to reach the fridge surface.)

> **6 small magnets**
> **6 objects of your choice (e.g. buttons, coins, bottle caps)**

Lay objects on paper or crafting cutting board back side up. Spread a thin layer of glue on both magnet and object. Let sit 2-3 minutes to become tacky. Squeeze both surfaces together with slight turning motion. The longer this is left to cure the stronger the bond.

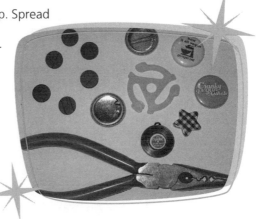

DIY PUSH PINS

Push, push in the bush. Wait a second . . . I think that disco song is dirty.

> **6 flat-ended pushpins *or* tacks**
> **6 objects, your choice (e.g. game tiles, buttons, coins)**

Lay objects on paper or crafting cutting board back side up. Spread a thin layer of glue on both pushpin end and object. Let sit 2-3 minutes to become tacky. Squeeze both surfaces together with slight turning motion. The longer this is left to cure, the stronger the bond.

FOUND OBJECT CLOCK

Do you have a Pee Wee Herman paper plate that you love, but don't know what to do with? What about that Chinese takeout box that you can't throw out? Or that cool LP cover that you have shoved in the back of your closet? Have you thought about making it into a clock? Head down to your local craft store where you will find clock guts all packaged and waiting for you to do something creative with. These clock guts come with different lengthy attachments depending on the surface you're attaching it to. For these objects below, I used ¼-inch because the surface of my objects are thin. What time is it, Mr. Wolf?

> **clock guts (includes all your necessary parts)**
> **object of your choice (for clock face)**

Figure out where on your object you want to place your clock, making sure that the watch hands can rotate completely without interference. Carefully punch hole where you want your clock to be centered. Secure clock in place (see instructions on clock gut package) and then hang on the wall.

GAME BOARD SERVING TRAY

I found a wooden Ouiji game board but I was too scared to hold a séance, so I decided to do the next best thing and turn it into something practical. I found some wooden doweling, a couple of handles, mac-tacked the top (to make it spill-proof) and voilà – serving tray. Not only can I conjure up the devil, I can do it at the same time as I serve tea and cookies. You can also use a cardboard game board, but you must secure it to a thin piece of wood. Get it cut to size at your local hardware store.

> **4 wooden dowels (cut to size)**
> **1 wooden game board (*or* cardboard game board)**
> **2 handles**

Lay clear mac-tac (tie-tac) on top of game board and cut to size. Measure and cut doweling to size. Secure doweling and handles to game board with screws.

GARDEN PLANTER

Mary, Mary, quite contrary. Why you buggin'?

Spruce up your garden or patio with planters made from objects like old shoes and empty olive oil containers. I was walking my dog the other night and someone had dumped all their junk onto the street (tsk tsk). I spotted an old 1940s tin picnic basket that had seen better days, so I punched a few holes into the bottom for drainage and ta da! – instant planter.

AND THE DISH RAN AWAY WITH THE SPOON WIND CHIME

I have a thing about collecting forks. I know, I know – what don't I collect? For this, you will need a drill with a small drill bit. (Don't hurt yourself, okay?) You can make this as simple or ornate as you want by adding beads or bells or rhinestones. Just remember to make it beautiful.

> **base (e.g. soup pot, soup pot lid)**
> **6-10 utensils (e.g. spoons, forks, knifes)**
> **piece of fishing line**

Your base can be anything. Because it's the center of your chime, you want it to be round-ish. Drill a small hole in the end of each utensil. String utensils to your base using fishing line, attaching at varying lengths. Hang outside.

TOOTHBRUSH BRACELET

Every since I was a child, I've always hated to throw out my toothbrushes. Mr. Toothbrush must be so sad to leave the bathroom to go to unknown landfills. It wasn't until I had to use a mouth guard while I slept that I had an epiphany: I realized that you could morph just about any plastic item into something useful. I've found that clear plastic toothbrushes are the easiest to manipulate. (Don't be stupid: you're dealing with hot stuff here, so please take the necessary precautions.)

> **1 toothbrush**
> **a pair of oven mitts**
> **1 set of tongs**
> **1 large mug**

Remove all the bristles from the toothbrush with pliers. In a large pot, boil water and place toothbrush in pot for 4-5 minutes. While wearing oven mitts, remove toothbrush with tongs, and start to bend toothbrush to desired shape. If it doesn't bend enough, submerge again in boiling water until it's more pliable. Remove brush and bend as much as possible into desired shape. If you want, place bent toothbrush in bottom of large coffee cup to hold its shape while it cools. Pour cold water in mug and remove your new bracelet. If you don't like its shape, re-boil and re-shape.

PUNK ROCK STUDDED BRACELET

Oi, oi, oi – you can make a punk rock cuff out of just about anything. Check out your local hardware store for rubber or vinyl and purchase studs, grommets, and snaps at any craft store.

> **1 piece rubber** *or* **vinyl**
> **a variety of snaps, studs, grommets, etc.**

Cut your rubber/vinyl to the correct size (I use an existing bracelet as my guide). Attach snaps at the end of bracelet. Adorn your new bracelet with studs, grommets, and fancy bits and bobs.

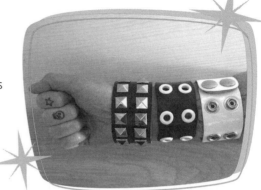

FOUND OBJECT EARRINGS

You can make just about anything into an earring. Purchase earring hooks or blank earring posts at any craft store.

> **2 earring hooks (** *or* **blank posts)**
> **objects**

Punch a small hole into your object to attach the hook or glue your object to your earring post.

FOUND OBJECT NECKLACE

Personalize your necklace with anything you can think of – a lock, an old key, a wooden domino, or Scrabble piece. Then purchase links, chains, and anything else you might need at any craft or bead store.

> **1 object**
> **1 piece of chain/string/necklace**

Punch a small hole into your object to attach ring through the hole and thread chain through your object.

GLASS BEAD RINGS AND PENDANTS

Ring blanks, glass beads, and glass pendants can be found in any craft or bead store.

> **1 image**
> **1 glass bead**
> **1 blank ring** *or* **glass pendant**

Cut your image to size so it fits behind the glass bead or pendant. Glue to back of bead (image side down) and let dry. Glue bead to blank ring.

BARRETTES & HAIR ELASTICS

Barrette blanks, combs, and hair elastics are found in craft stores and you can use any sort of bobbly bit to dress up your hair.

> **1 object**
> **1 barrette** *or* **blank hair accessory**

Glue, wire or sew object to blank barrette.

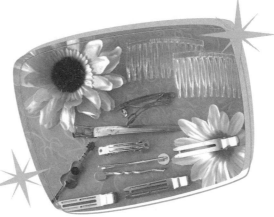

BROACH PIN

Broach blank pins are found in craft stores, and you can glue, wire or sew just about anything you want to a blank pin.

> **1 broach blank pin**
> **1 object**

Glue object to blank pin.

SEWING PROJECTS
DUCT TAPE DUMMY

Who you calling a dummy? Anyone who sews knows how handy a sewing dummy, with your body measurements, can be for checking your progress, hemming or fixing up your clothes. But sewing dummies are expensive, so go down to the local hardware store, grab some duct tape and start wrapping yourself up in tape for the fraction of the cost. *You will need a friend to help you with this project*, preferably someone you don't mind getting naked in front of.

> **1 knee-length T-shirt (that you don't mind cutting up)**
> **1-2 rolls of duct tape**
> **pair of scissors**
> **stuffing (e.g. rags, newspaper)**

Put on your best push up bra and an old T-shirt that you don't mind cutting up.

Start duct taping under and around your chest to create a cross-your-heart bra. Remember that you want the tape to be tight, but not so tight that you can't breathe.

Once you have established your chest area, start filling in the chest and back areas with tape.

Duct tape around your waist and rib cage area all the way down to the top of your hips.

If you feel dizzy, faint or are unable to breathe – don't panic. Just take a moment to relax.

Cut a straight line down the back of your new dummy, being careful not to cut your bra.

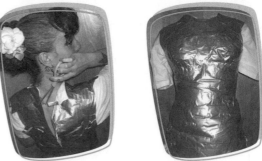

Remove dummy from your body and tape the back of your dummy together. Stuff dummy with crumpled newspaper, rags, old towels, etc. Check yourself out, you look hot all in silver.

HOW TO MAKE A FAUX FUR MUFF BY CLAIRE

If you are on a creative kick, you can make all kinds of modifications to this muff, like lining the inside with a pretty satin or cozy fleece, or adding in an inside pocket to make your muff a purse. The possibilities are only limited by your imagination. Too lazy to sew? You can always visit *CoquetteFauxFurriers.com* for ready-made, vegan-friendly muffs in a variety of colors and fabrics. Good luck, and get crafty! – Claire, *CoquetteFauxFurriers.com*

▍ **Faux fur fabric (approx. 12" x 16")**

Fold fabric in half (right side in) so the two shortest edges meet and sew a seam along the edge to create a tube. Hem each end of the tube so you have nice finished edges, then turn the tube inside out. Ta-da! You now have a lovely muff to keep your hands warm. For extra sass, sew a little loop of cord to one end to make a handle, so you don't drop your muff when you need to use your hands for something more important, like shopping.

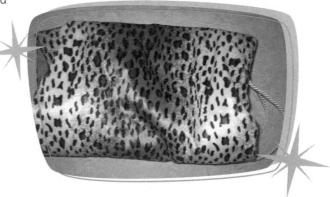

EVERYTHING OLD CAN BE NEW AGAIN

Don't have the moola to buy a new wardrobe? Who does? So jazz up your old clothes and make them new again.

> **Spice up an old skirt by adding appliqués, ribbons, skull patches, etc.**
> **Add ruffles to a skirt or shirt, made from an old T-shirt, lace etc.**
> **Sew buttons down the edges of your pants for a sailor look.**
> **Sew buttons in a pattern on an old cardigan and end up with a fancy-looking sweater.**
> **Add a ribbon to the collar of your sweater for a new look.**

PUNK ROCK T-SHIRTS

I have a bazillion punk rock T-shirts that I never wear anymore, and how many "night shirts" can one girl have? There are a million different things you can do to recycle a T-shirt. Here's a few suggestions.

> **Cut the prints into squares, sew them together, and turn them into a quilt.**
> **Cut T-shirt print into a large square, sew to another equal-sized square, and stuff with stuffing. Voilà – instant graphic pillow.**
> **Cut out the graphic and sew it on to something else – get crazy!**
> **Cut up, sew, and customize your boyfriend's XXL T-shirt into a form-fitting tank top.**
> **Cut the top off your T-shirt. Add elastic and now you have a tube top!**

PILLOW CASE SKIRT

Have you ever seen a pretty pillowcase and thought, "I wish I could wear that." Now you can!

Cut the top off of your pillowcase and sew on a waistband. Depending on your body shape, you may need to sew in some darts or cut in a slit in the back, so you can walk up the stairs and not look like you have a stick up your butt. Then you can girly up your pillow case by sewing ruffles to the hem for added sass. Imagination is key!

RAG DOLL

Making a doll out of rags is fun. My mum used to make me stuffed animals out of scrap pieces of fabric and buttons for eyes. If you have a digital camera and a printer, you can give your doll a face . . . . YOUR FACE! Go to your local computer store and check out the transfer paper (that you can iron onto clothing). Take a photo of your face, print it up, and make it into a doll.

> **transfer paper (for inkjet printer)**
> **fabric (for making doll body)**
> **stuffing**

Cut out fabric to desired doll shape. Sew pieces together leaving a space for stuffing. Stuff, sew seam together, and cuddle.

VINYL PURSE

There is a fantastic vegan purse company called Matt & Nat (*ViaVegan.com*) out of Montreal. I *heart* every single one of their purses. But as wicked as they are, it's also fun to sew/create your own stuff. Vinyl is easy to sew and you can make anything! A purse, change purse, wallet, cell phone holder – get crazy! Check out this vinyl bag and change purse my friend Hayley made me for my birthday; she's so talented. You can get vinyl at any fabric store.

This bag is as simple as cutting a piece of vinyl into a long rectangle and sewing up the sides. Turn it inside out, add a handle, and you have a purse that will make everyone jealous. The flowers on the front were also made from vinyl! What a cute purse. Thank you, Hayley!

VINYL CUFF

Vinyl cuffs are very easy to make; you just need some snaps, scissors, and some imagination! I like to sew two contrasting colors together, to get extra va-va-voom as well as a sturdier cuff.

> **1 piece of vinyl**
> **a variety of snaps, studs, grommets, etc.**

Cut your vinyl to the correct size (I use an existing bracelet as my guide). Attach snaps at the end of bracelet.

VINYL BELT

There are a thousand different ways you can make a belt. It all depends on what you can find: an old seat belt buckle, a broken strap from a purse. Let your imagination run wild! Add a few grommets, studs, and a belt buckle and then you'll have something snazzy to keep your pants up.

> **1 piece of vinyl**
> **grommets**
> **snaps**
> **1 buckle**

I like to use a belt I already have as a guide for length/width, etc. For a 1½-inch wide belt, cut a piece of vinyl 4½ inches wide and as long as you need it for your waist size. Fold the vinyl over into thirds and sew around the edges to create a strong thick belt. Punch holes and attach grommets to one end of the belt (for your belt buckle to attach to) and attach snaps and grommets and your belt buckle to the other.

INDEX

INDEX

INDEX

INDEX

INDEX

INDEX

MEASUREMENT EQUIVALENTS

Being a Canadian who switched from Imperial to Metric in grade school, I am in a constant struggle between the two of them. This chart keeps me from going mad.

A few grains/pinch/dash, etc. (dry): Less than ⅛ tsp

3 teaspoons: 1 tablespoon
½ tablespoon: 1½ teaspoons
1 tablespoon: 3 teaspoons
2 tablespoons: 1 fluid ounce
4 tablespoons: ¼ cup
5⅓ tablespoons: ⅓ cup
8 tablespoons: ½ cup
8 tablespoons: 4 fluid ounces
10⅔ tablespoons: ⅔ cup
12 tablespoons: ¾ cup
16 tablespoons: 1 cup
16 tablespoons: 8 fluid ounces

⅛ cup: 2 tablespoons
¼ cup: 4 tablespoons
¼ cup: 2 fluid ounces
⅓ cup: 5 tablespoons plus 1 teaspoon
½ cup: 8 tablespoons
1 cup: 16 tablespoons
1 cup: 8 fluid ounces
1 cup: ½ pint
2 cups: 1 pint

2 pints: 1 quart
4 quarts (liquid): 1 gallon
1 kilogram; approximately 2 pounds